Mystical MOODS OF IRELAND
Magical Irish Countryside

Volume III
Second Edition

Praise for James A. Truett's work...

"Over the water and far away, I only need turn the pages of James A. Truett's masterpiece to feel the magical, mystical mood of Ireland. Through exceptional imagery and narrative, I inhabit the landscape, lore, lyrics, literature... indeed, the very love of Truett's homeland. This gorgeous tome is a treasure for those living upon, or longing for, the Emerald Isle." ~ **Vivienne Nichols**

"James Truett's photos, words and descriptions have brought to life what's been in my heart most of my life. From my grandmother's stories to my first visit to Ireland, he makes it real for those who cannot be there." ~ **Linda Metcalf**

"James has a way of capturing the true magic of Ireland. His pictures are glorious and make you feel like you're right there with him when he takes them." ~ **Allison Elliott**

"James Truett's beautiful pictures speak to my soul."
~ **Jennifer Dudley Nelson**

"These photos bring Ireland to your eyes and soul. It is the closest to Heaven you will get without being in Ireland." ~ **Kit Joslyn**

"James' photos show the mystical beauty of Ireland, long learned through poetry and stories, now seen through the lens of a true artist! His photos make you 'feel' more than you can imagine!"
~ **Pamela Jo Hugaert**

"James A. Truett's gorgeous pictures take me back to Ireland, and show me parts of Ireland I didn't get to see when I was there. His pictures are honest and real as well as mystical and peaceful."
~ **Sue Ann Stannert Rivera**

Mystical
MOODS OF IRELAND
Magical Irish Countryside

Volume III
Second Edition

James A. Truett

www.JamesTruettBooks.Com

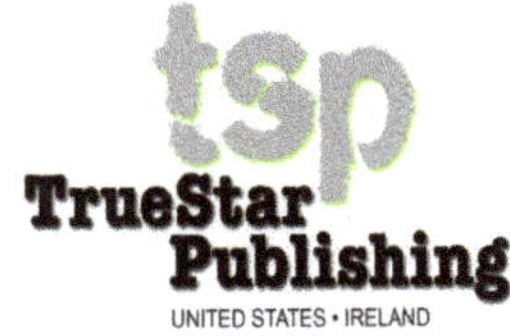

TrueStar Publishing

UNITED STATES · IRELAND

Published by TrueStar Publishing
United States • Ireland
www.TrueStarPublishing.Com

Ordering Information:
All products in the Moods of Ireland series including books, calendars, posters, cards and prints are available at special quantity discounts for bulk purchases for sales promotions, premiums, fund raising, educational, corporate or institutional use. Specially customized books, calendars, posters, cards and prints can also be created to fit specific needs. For details, please e-mail the publisher at:
specialsales@truestarpublishing.com

ISBN: 978-1-948522-02-1

First Edition: April 2015
Second Edition: June 2016

10 9 8 7 6 5 4 3 2

COVER: *A horse grazes in a meadow in the County Clare townland of Decomade, near Lissycasey.*

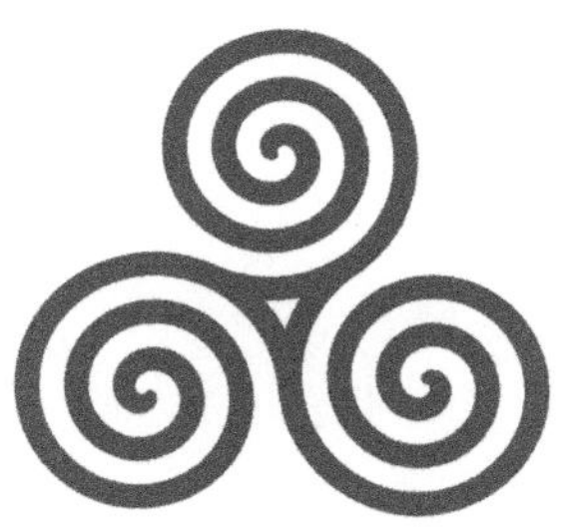

Dedication

For my ancestors who led me home...
My Grandmother, Johanna Agnes Cullinan of County Clare, and my
Great Grandfather, Patrick Henry Murphy of County Kilkenny.

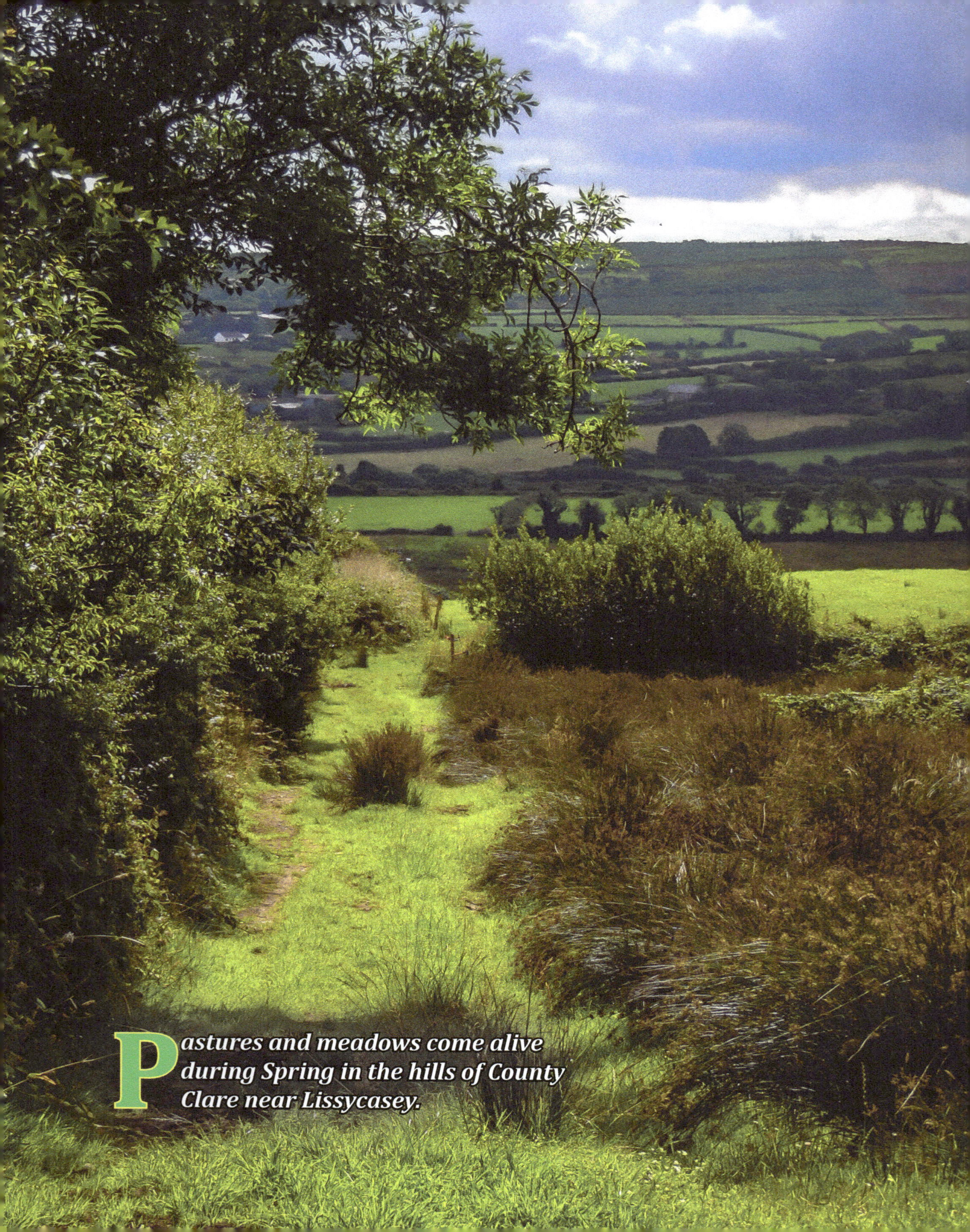
Pastures and meadows come alive
during Spring in the hills of County
Clare near Lissycasey.

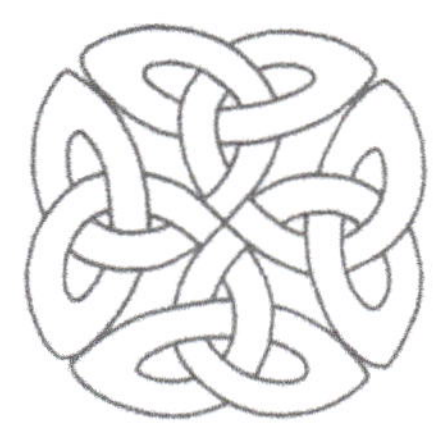

Introduction
Magical Irish Countryside

It's no wonder poets and artists for centuries have been inspired by the sheer natural beauty of Ireland. Despite its rocky human history with wars, religious persecution and famine, the Irish countryside continues its divine annual cycle of rebirth, death and rebirth again through the seasons.

Each Spring and Summer, the rolling hills of the Emerald Isle burst into a symphony of colors — the ubiquitous "40 shades of green" with accents of yellows, reds, purples, oranges and blues, and every combination under the rainbow. Choruses of birds gather to serenade the rising sun, and murmurations of Starlings dance into the sunsets.

Each Autumn, flowers fade and deciduous trees take on a copper glow as once fluorescent green leaves transition to opulent shades of yellow, red and orange before cascading to the ground. The countryside goes into Winter hibernation for rest and rejuvenation before Spring resurrection.

No where is this cycle of life so elegantly orchestrated.

The Irish countryside truly is magical. All cliches apply — awe-inspiring, stunning, spectacular, soul-enhancing...

Not all of this magic is visible to the eyes. A magnetism gently pulls at the souls of Irish and non-Irish alike. I receive hundreds of messages from people around the world reporting this attraction, this compulsion, to experience this beauty first-hand.

Whether you've visited Ireland or not — or even if you live here — I hope this book and my images touch you with this deep and profound connection to the spirit and soul of the Magical Irish Countryside.

Go Raibh Mile Maith Agat!
A Thousand Thanks!

James A. Truett
County Clare, Ireland

The legendary Irish Mist rises from the rolling hills and pastures near Lissycasey in County Clare, as the sun rises over Ireland's Galtee Mountains. The mist forms as warm air from Gulf Stream currents of the Atlantic Ocean clash with the colder Arctic air as it moves in over Ireland.

In the background are the Galtee Mountains, Ireland's highest inland mountain range, topping out at 3,009 ft. and crossing counties Limerick and Tipperary.

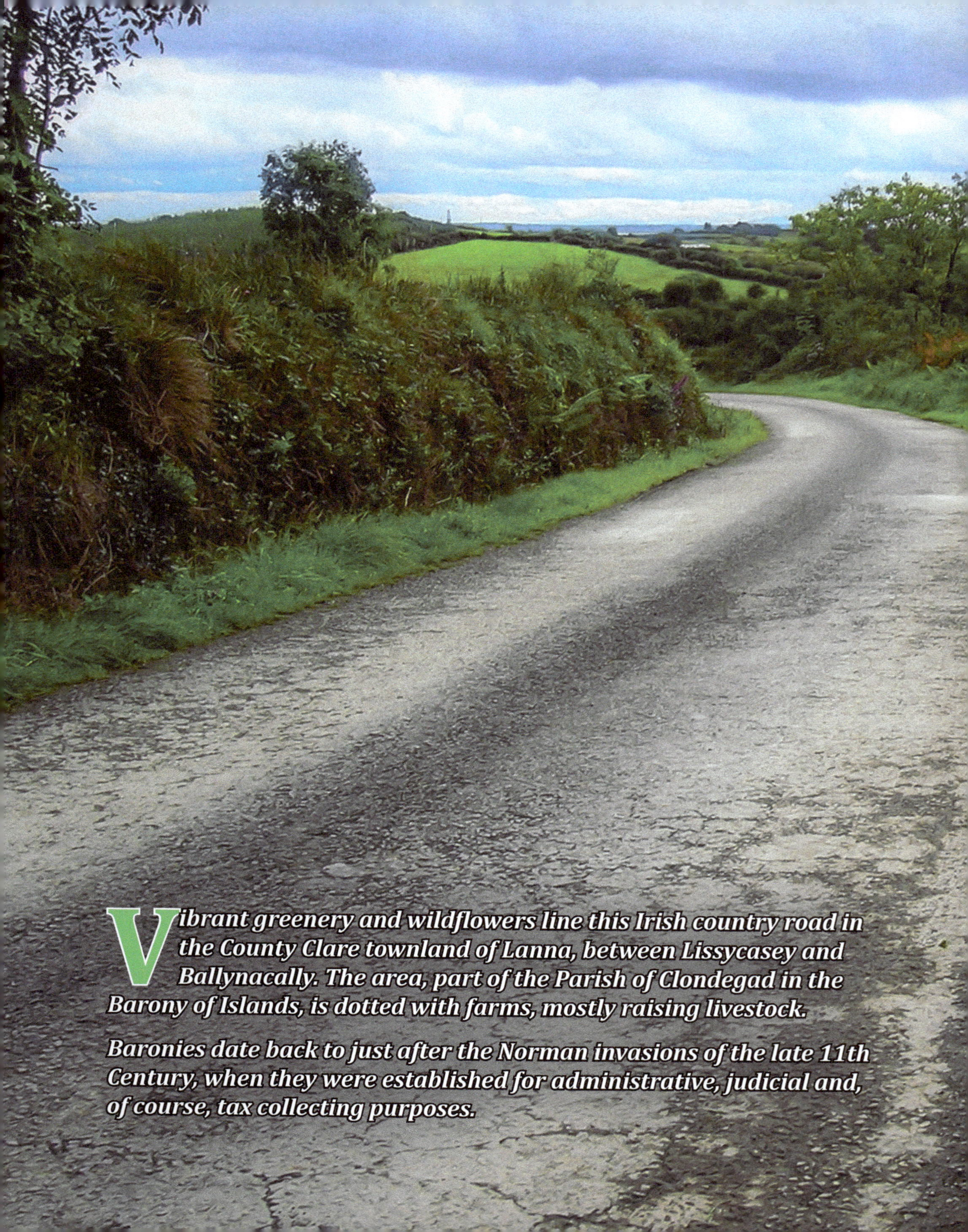

Vibrant greenery and wildflowers line this Irish country road in the County Clare townland of Lanna, between Lissycasey and Ballynacally. The area, part of the Parish of Clondegad in the Barony of Islands, is dotted with farms, mostly raising livestock.

Baronies date back to just after the Norman invasions of the late 11th Century, when they were established for administrative, judicial and, of course, tax collecting purposes.

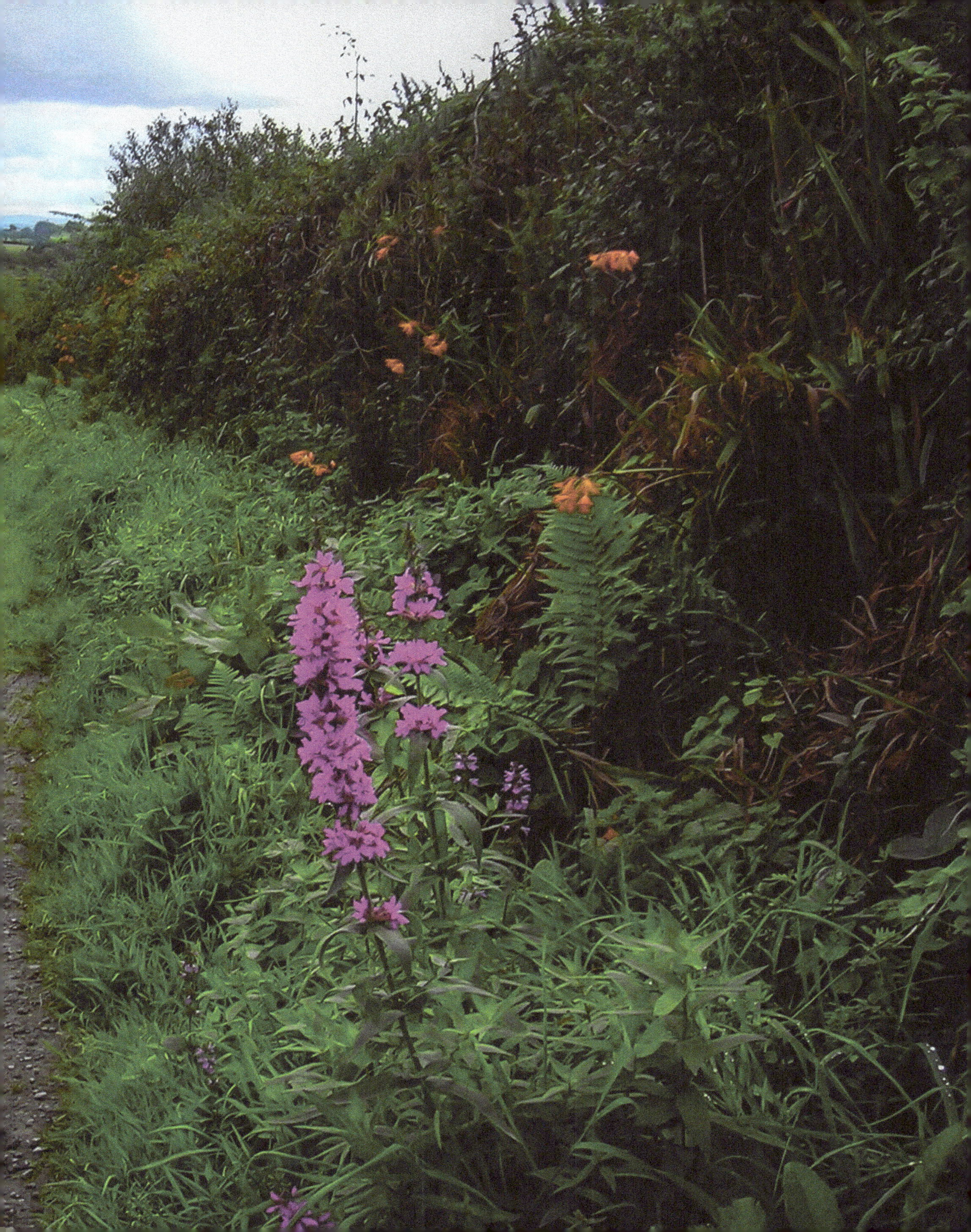

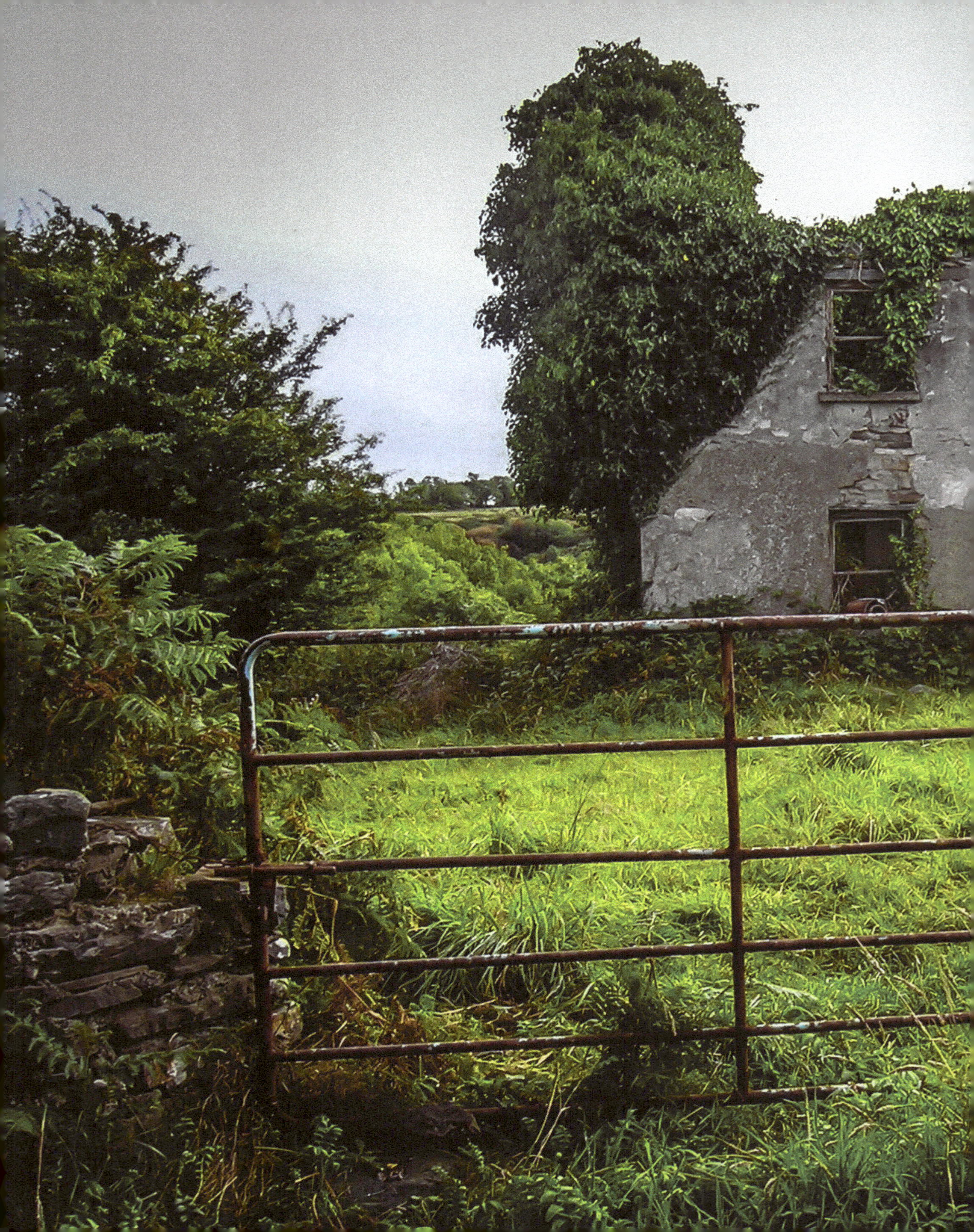

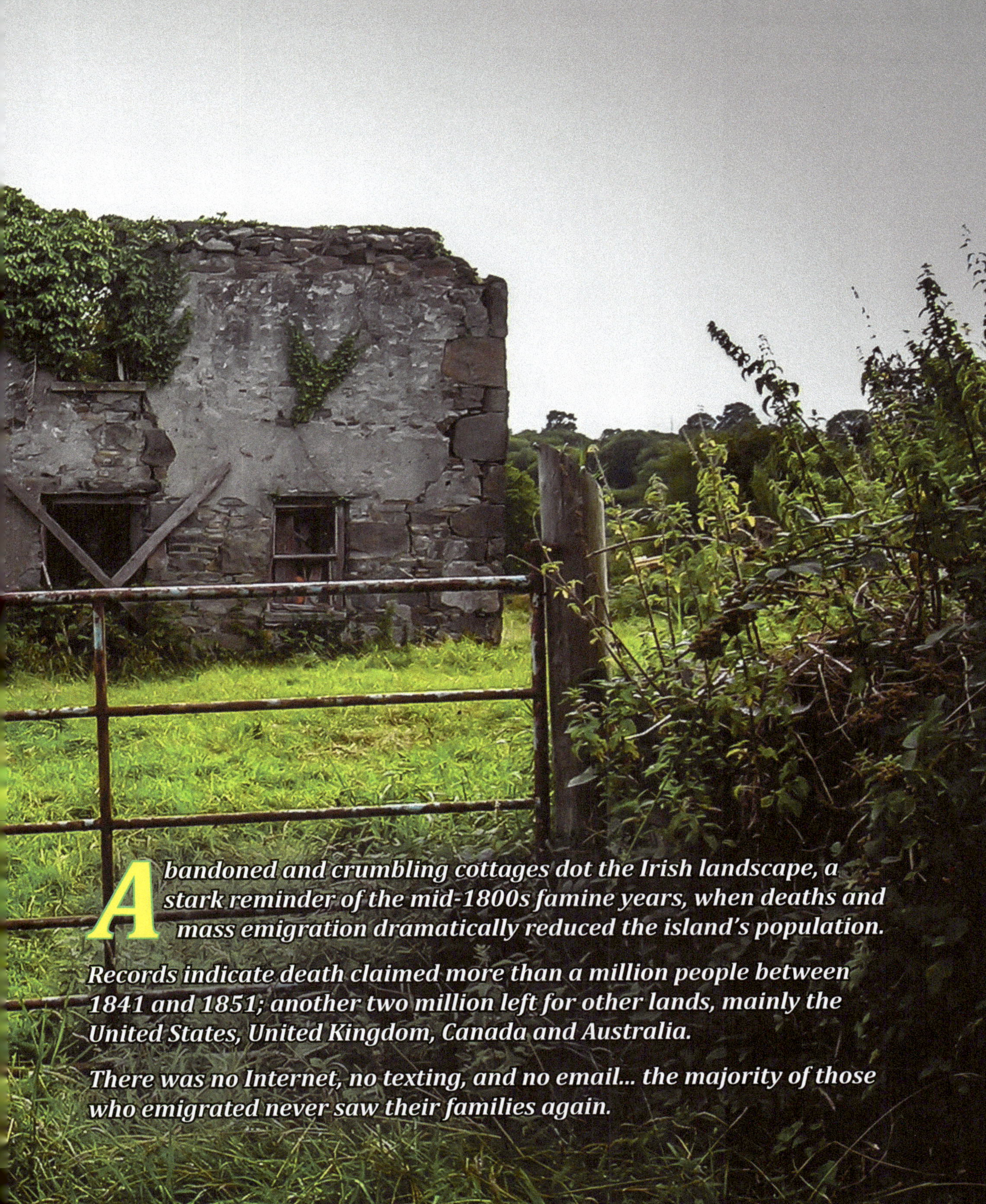

Abandoned and crumbling cottages dot the Irish landscape, a stark reminder of the mid-1800s famine years, when deaths and mass emigration dramatically reduced the island's population.

Records indicate death claimed more than a million people between 1841 and 1851; another two million left for other lands, mainly the United States, United Kingdom, Canada and Australia.

There was no Internet, no texting, and no email... the majority of those who emigrated never saw their families again.

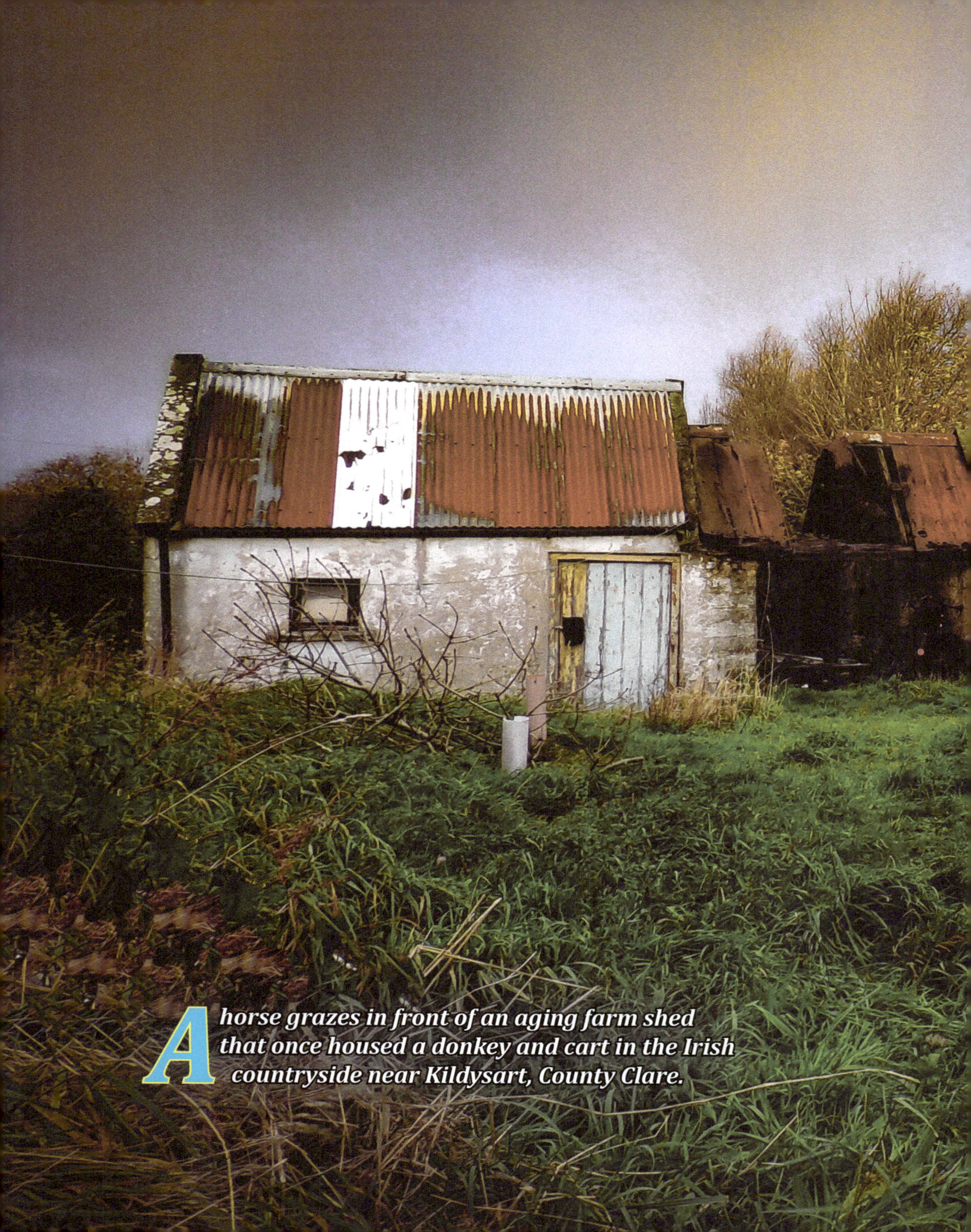

A horse grazes in front of an aging farm shed that once housed a donkey and cart in the Irish countryside near Kildysart, County Clare.

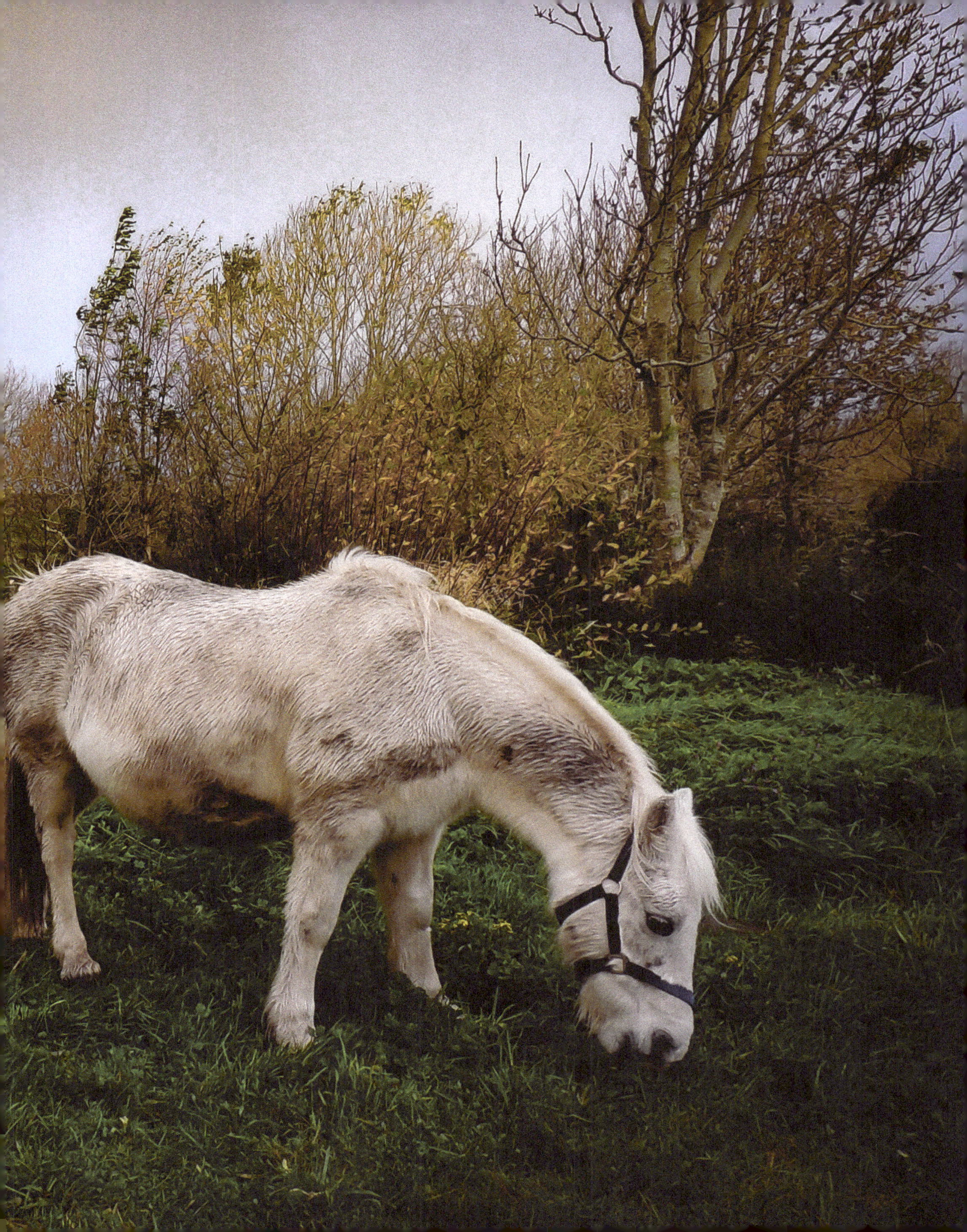

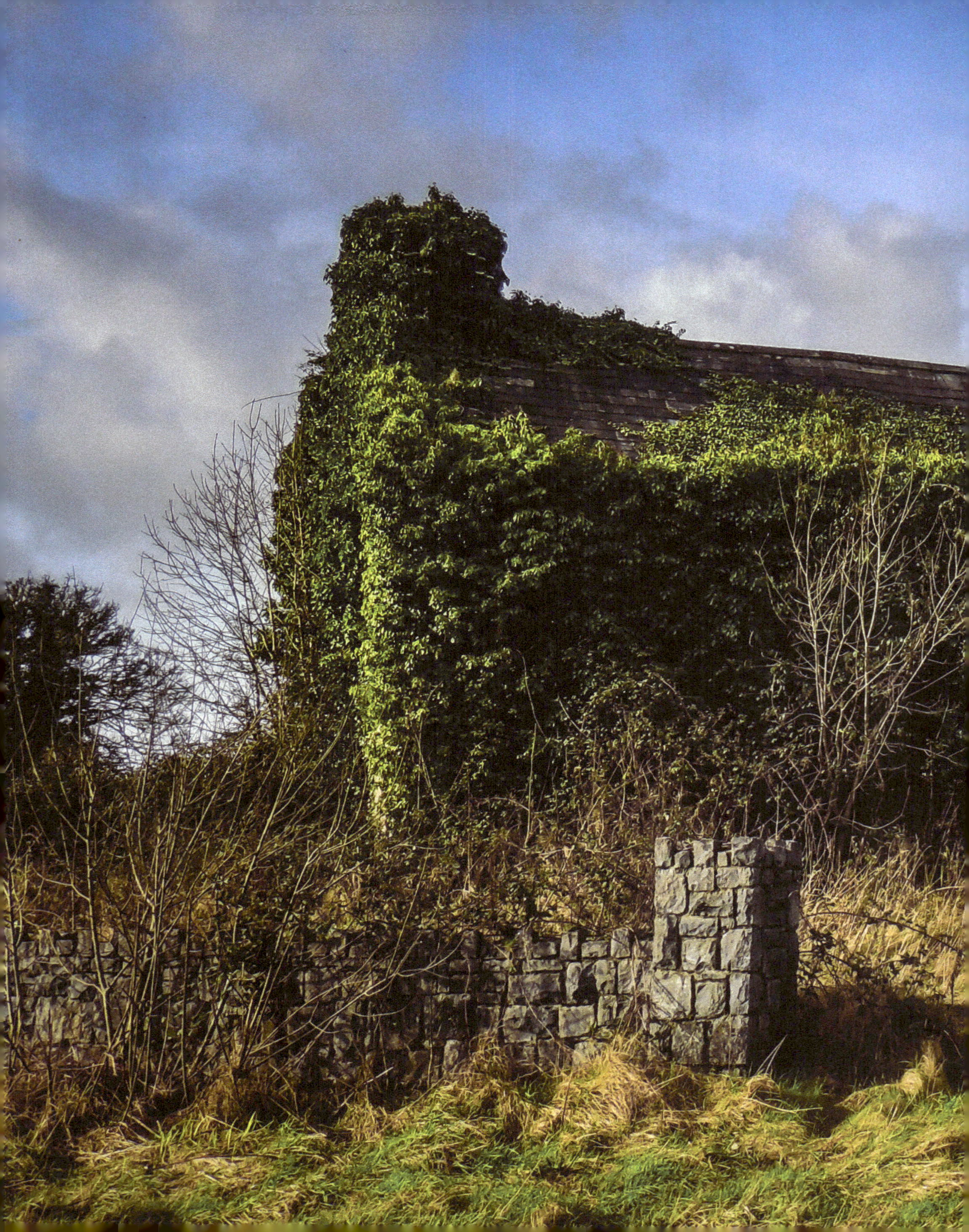

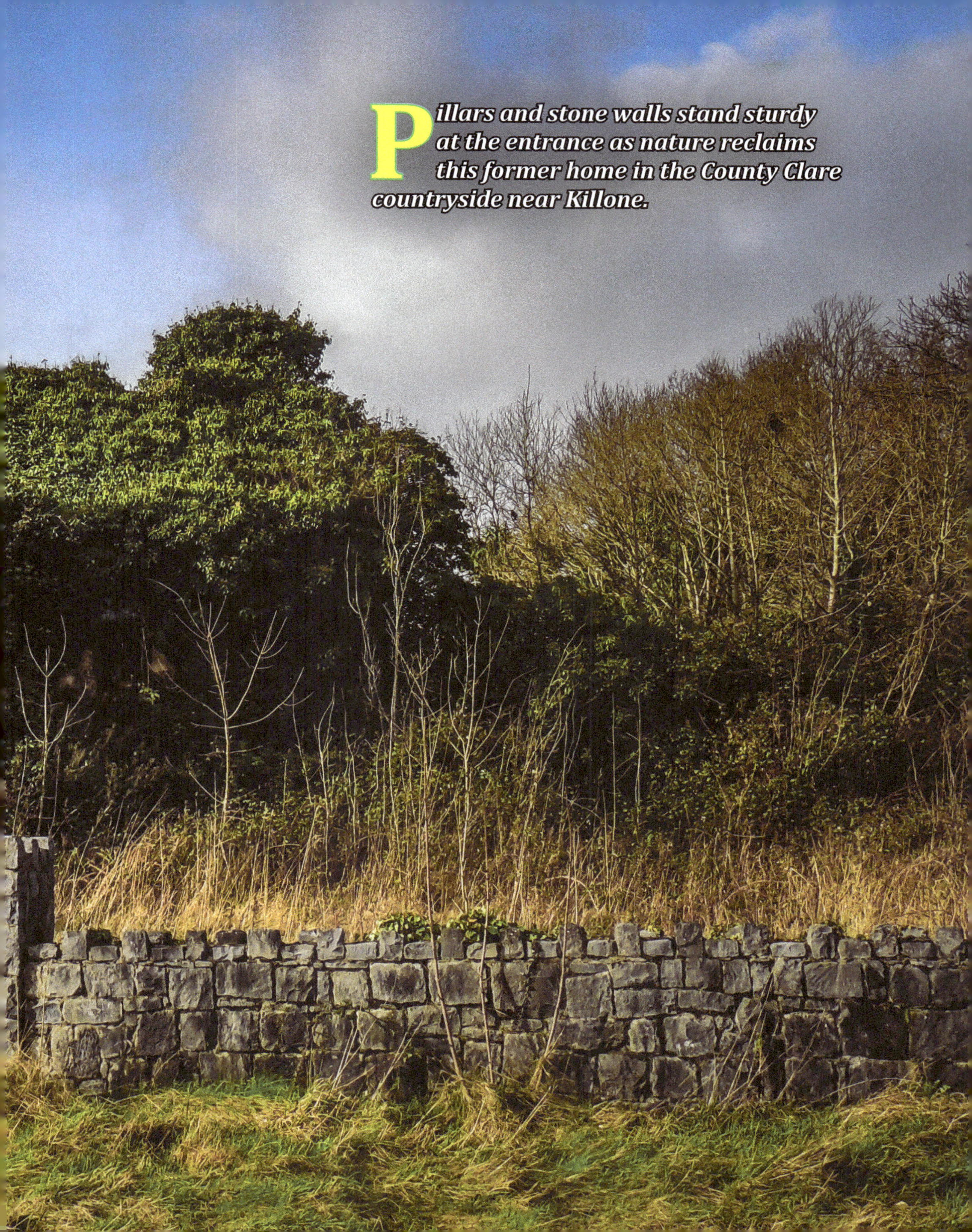

Pillars and stone walls stand sturdy at the entrance as nature reclaims this former home in the County Clare countryside near Killone.

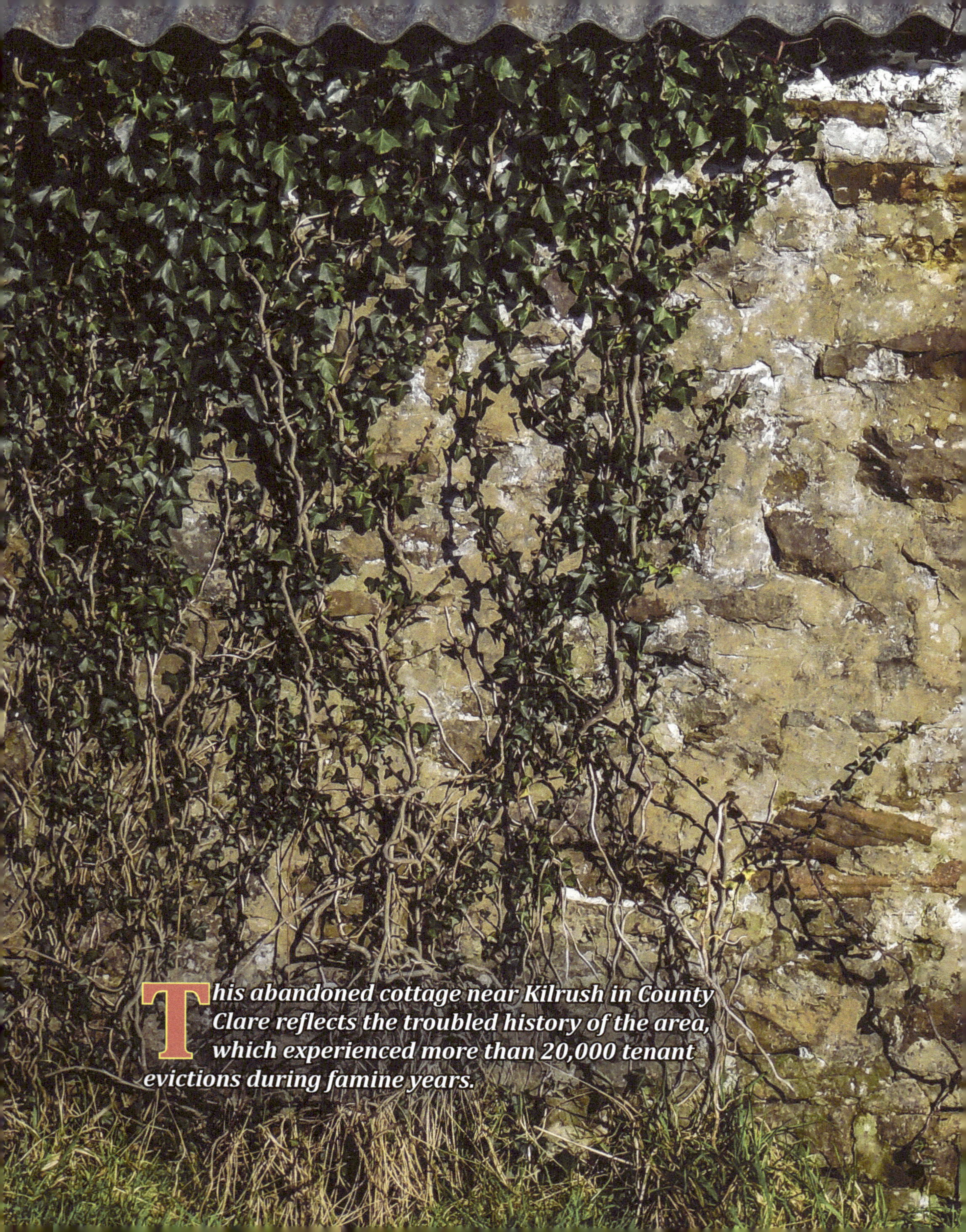

This abandoned cottage near Kilrush in County Clare reflects the troubled history of the area, which experienced more than 20,000 tenant evictions during famine years.

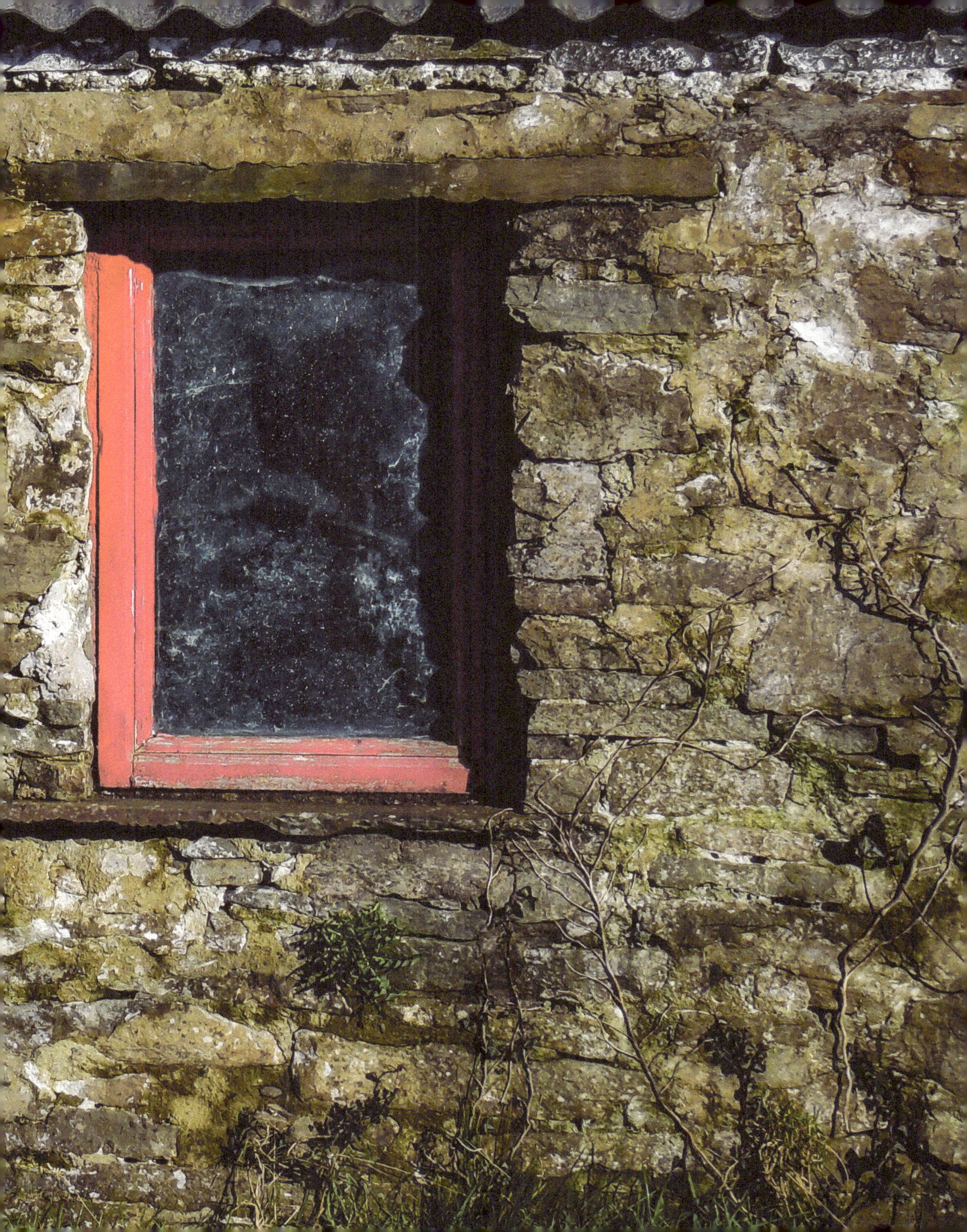

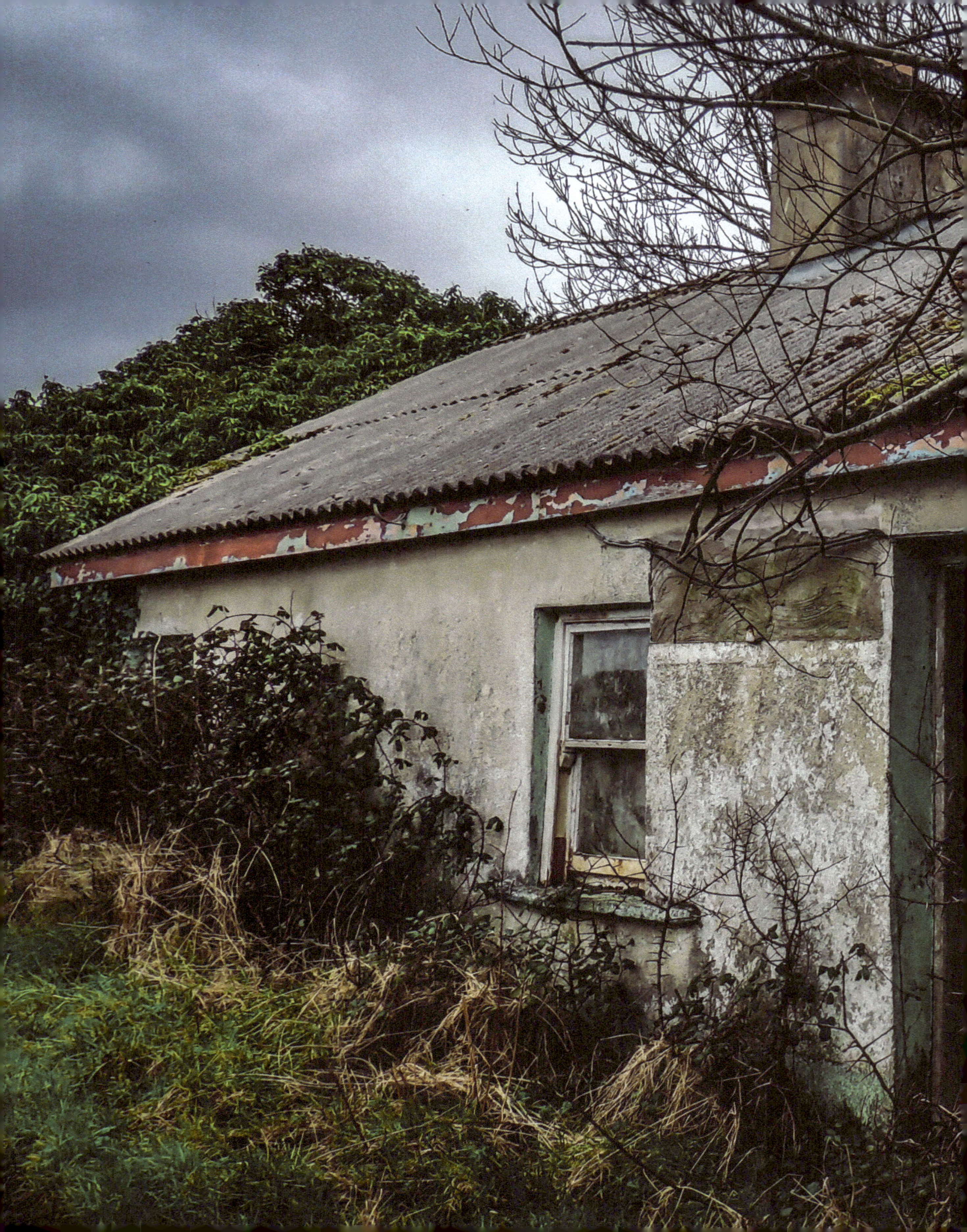

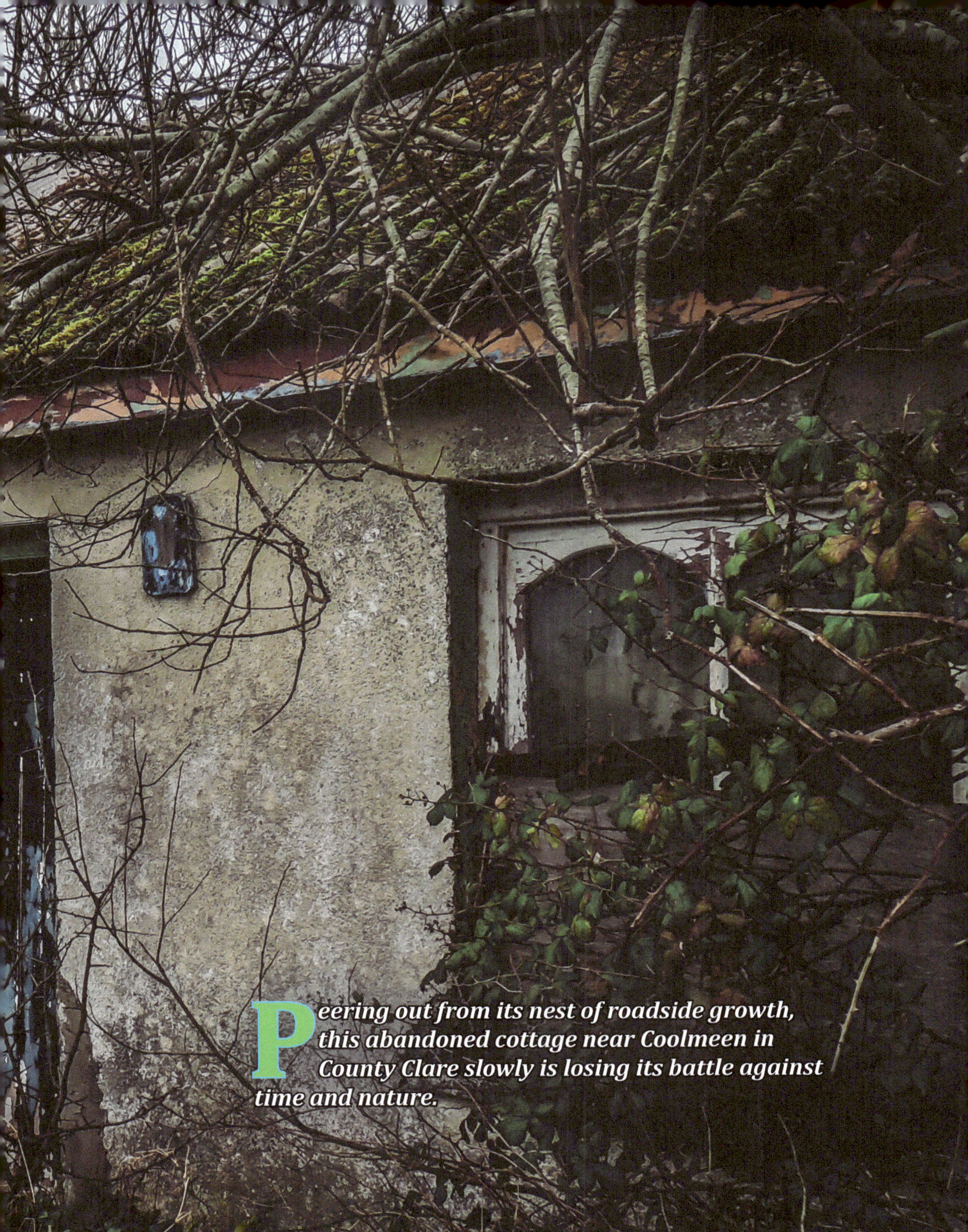

Peering out from its nest of roadside growth, this abandoned cottage near Coolmeen in County Clare slowly is losing its battle against time and nature.

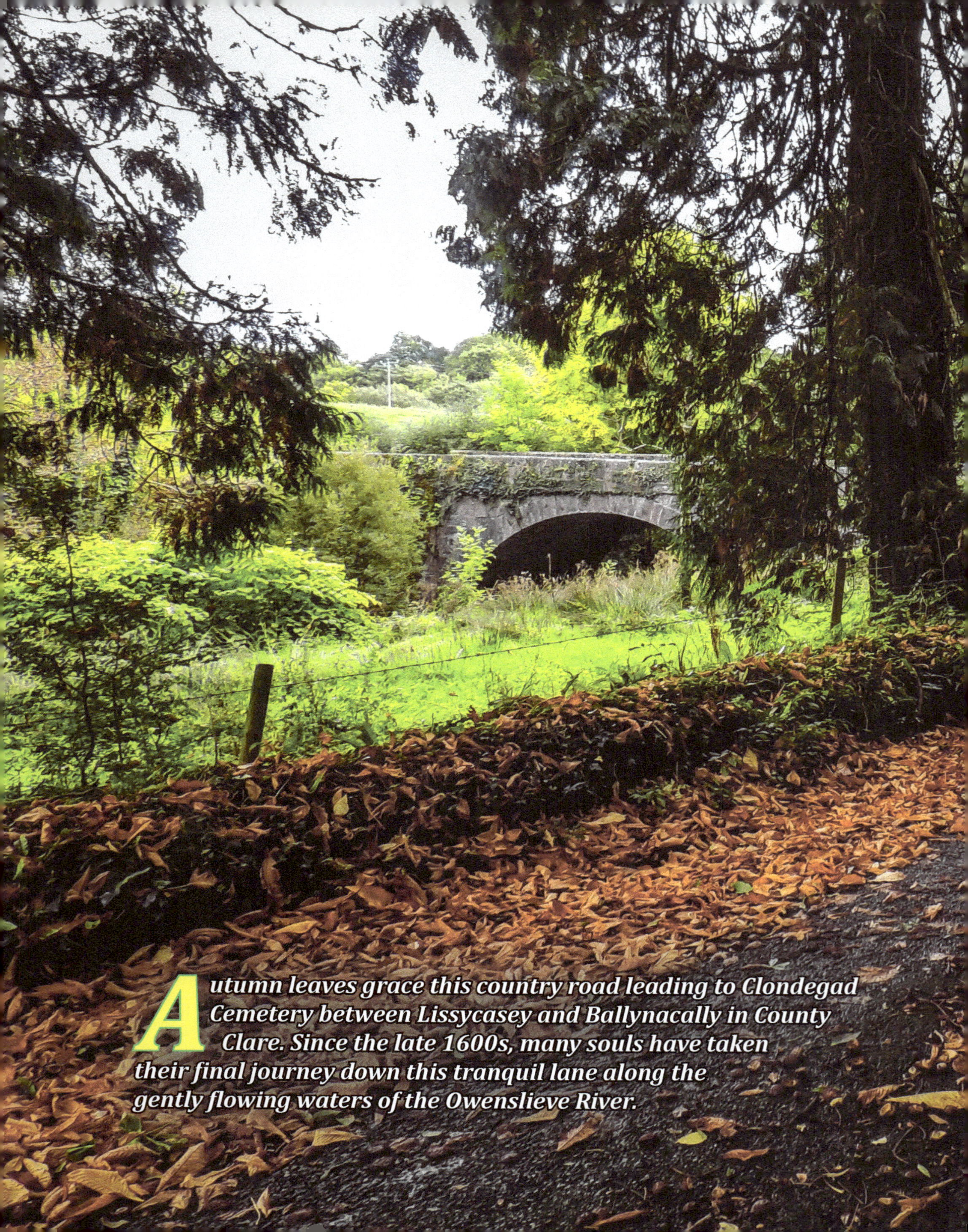

Autumn leaves grace this country road leading to Clondegad Cemetery between Lissycasey and Ballynacally in County Clare. Since the late 1600s, many souls have taken their final journey down this tranquil lane along the gently flowing waters of the Owenslieve River.

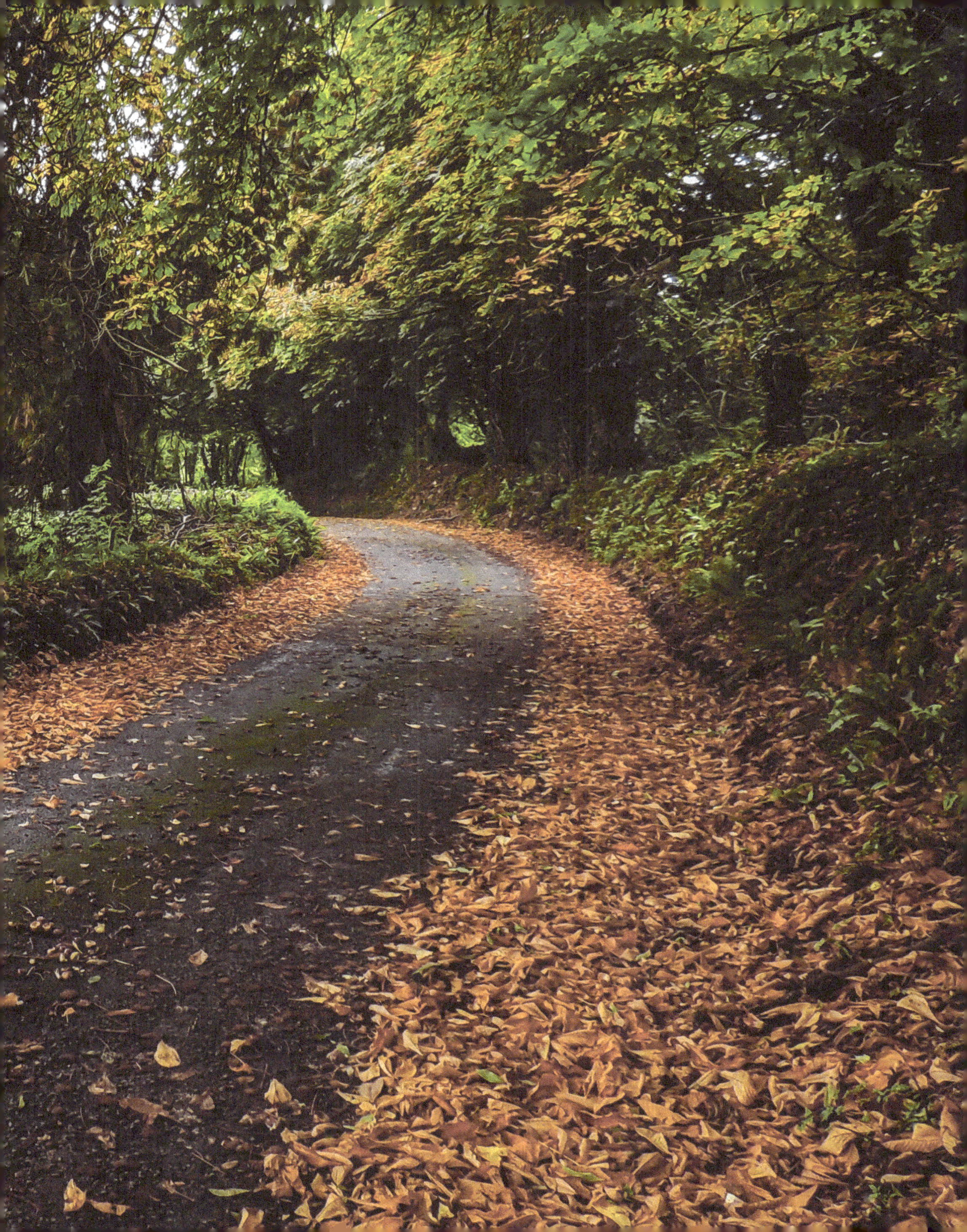

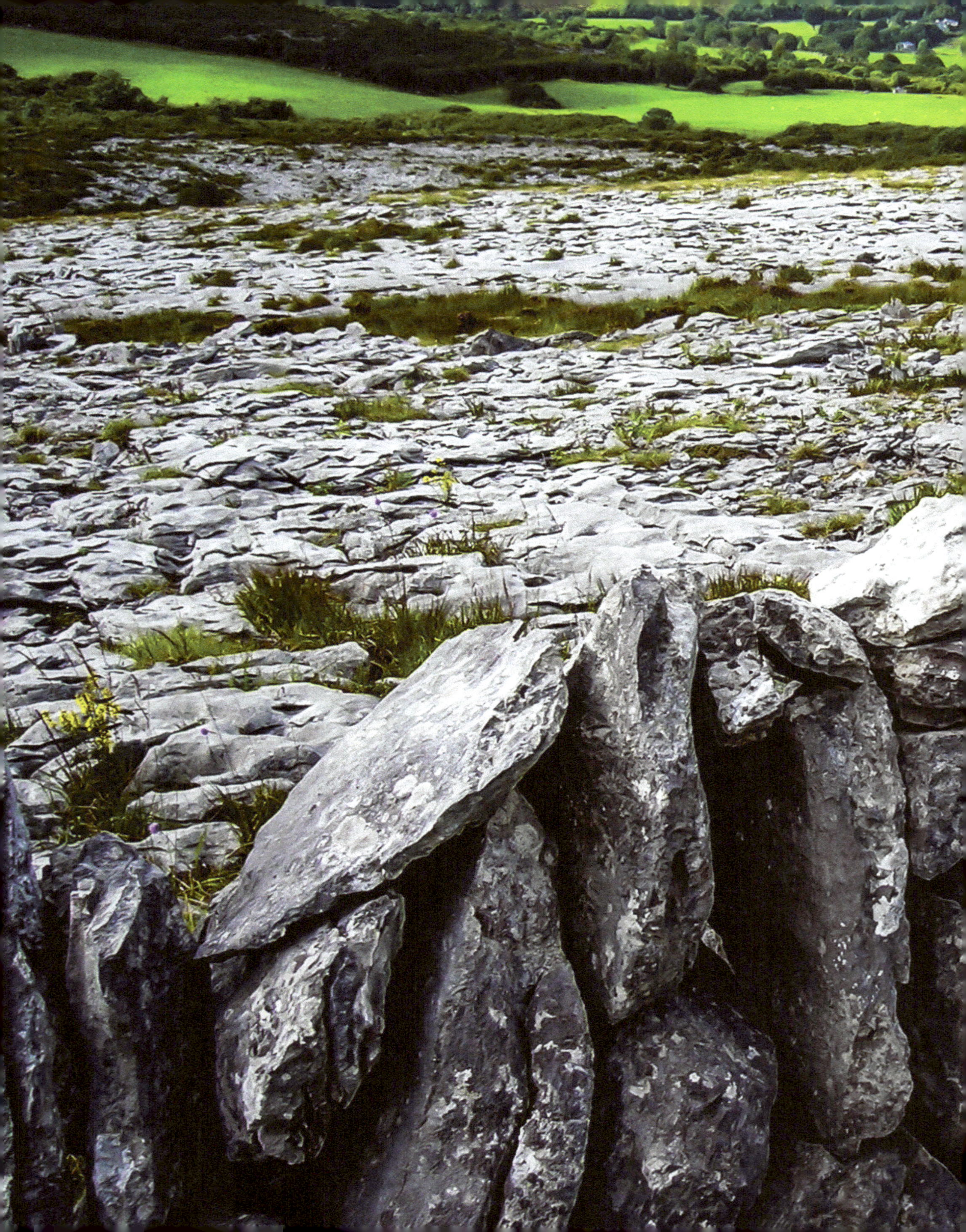

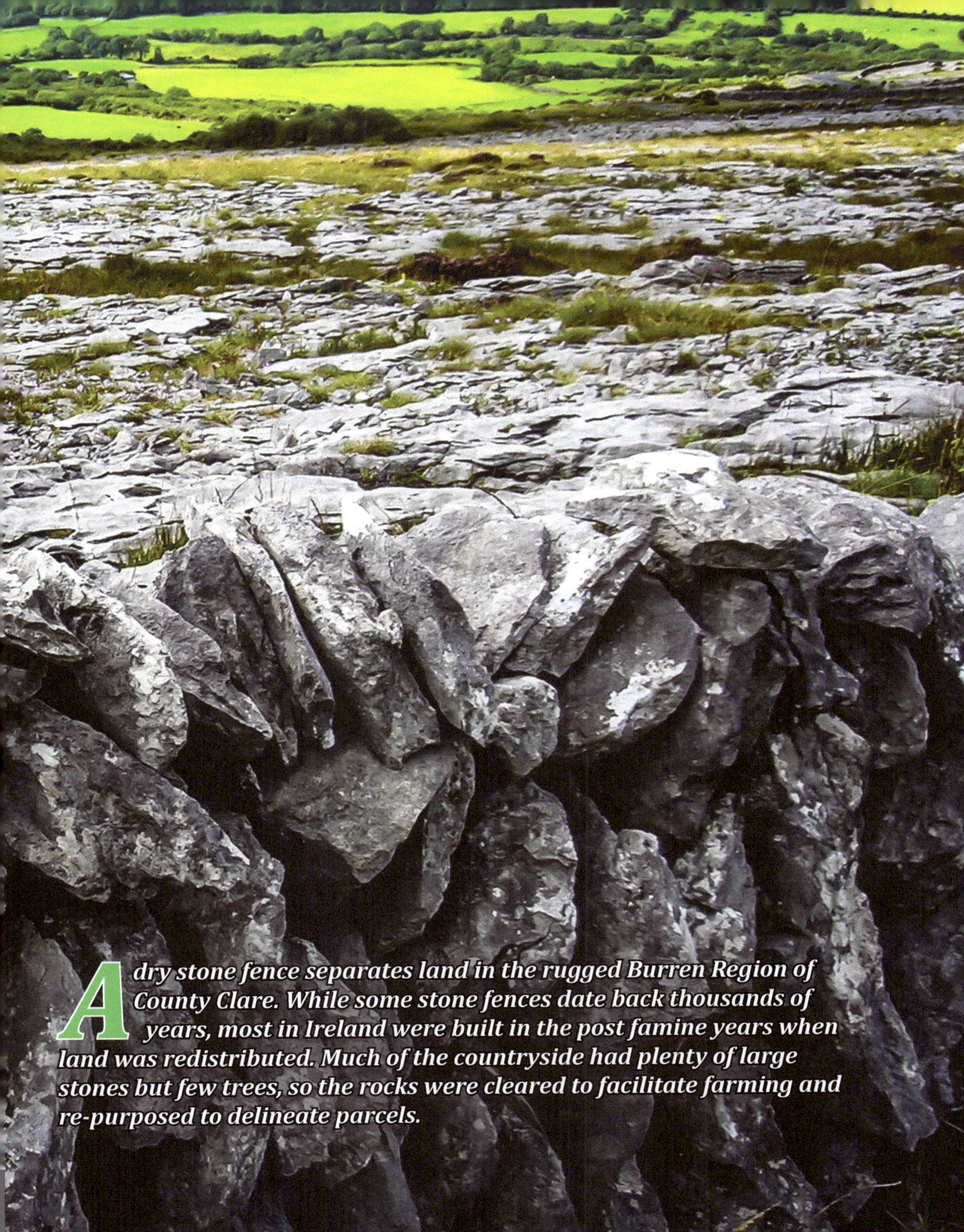

A dry stone fence separates land in the rugged Burren Region of County Clare. While some stone fences date back thousands of years, most in Ireland were built in the post famine years when land was redistributed. Much of the countryside had plenty of large stones but few trees, so the rocks were cleared to facilitate farming and re-purposed to delineate parcels.

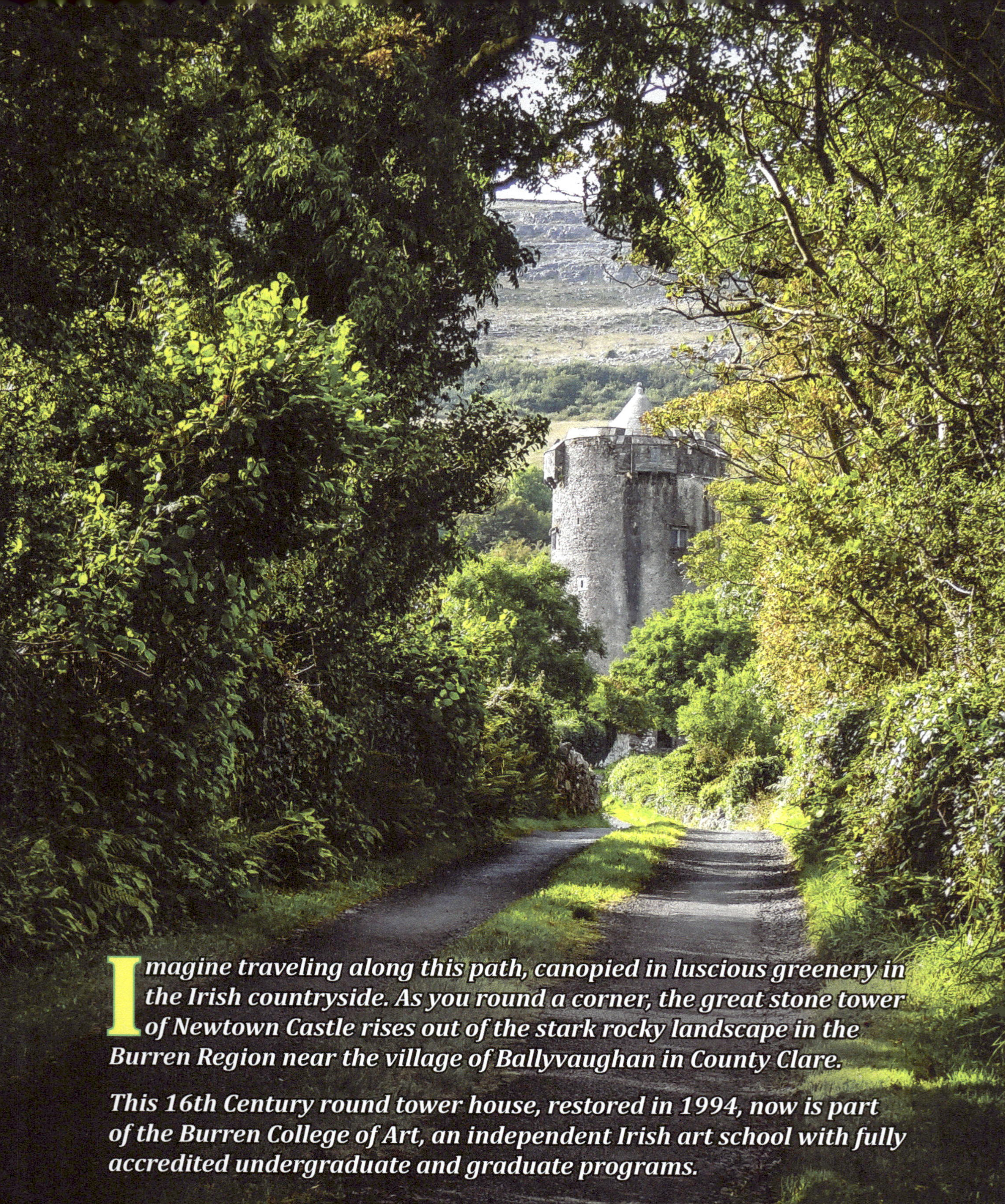

I magine traveling along this path, canopied in luscious greenery in the Irish countryside. As you round a corner, the great stone tower of Newtown Castle rises out of the stark rocky landscape in the Burren Region near the village of Ballyvaughan in County Clare.

This 16th Century round tower house, restored in 1994, now is part of the Burren College of Art, an independent Irish art school with fully accredited undergraduate and graduate programs.

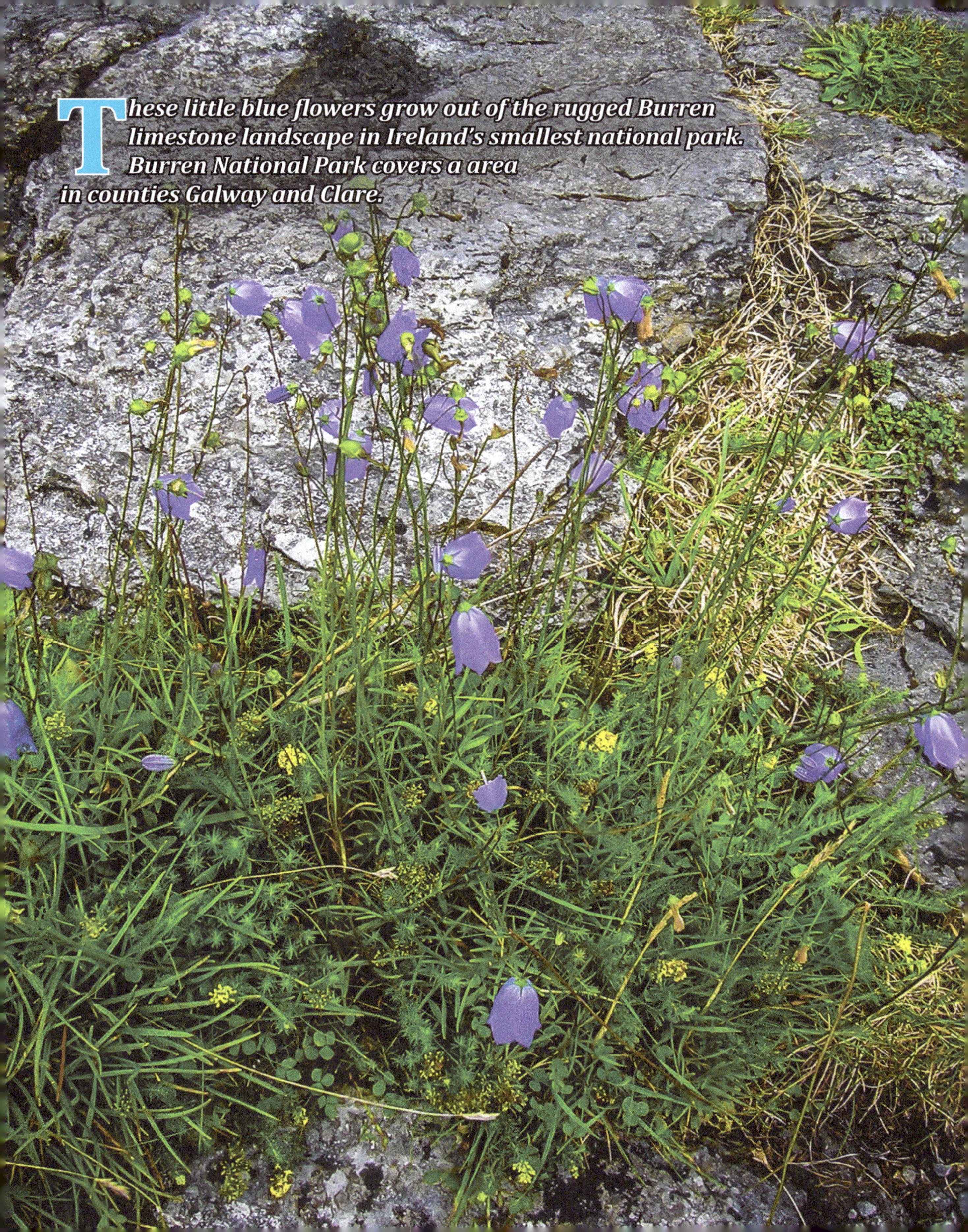
These little blue flowers grow out of the rugged Burren limestone landscape in Ireland's smallest national park. Burren National Park covers a area in counties Galway and Clare.

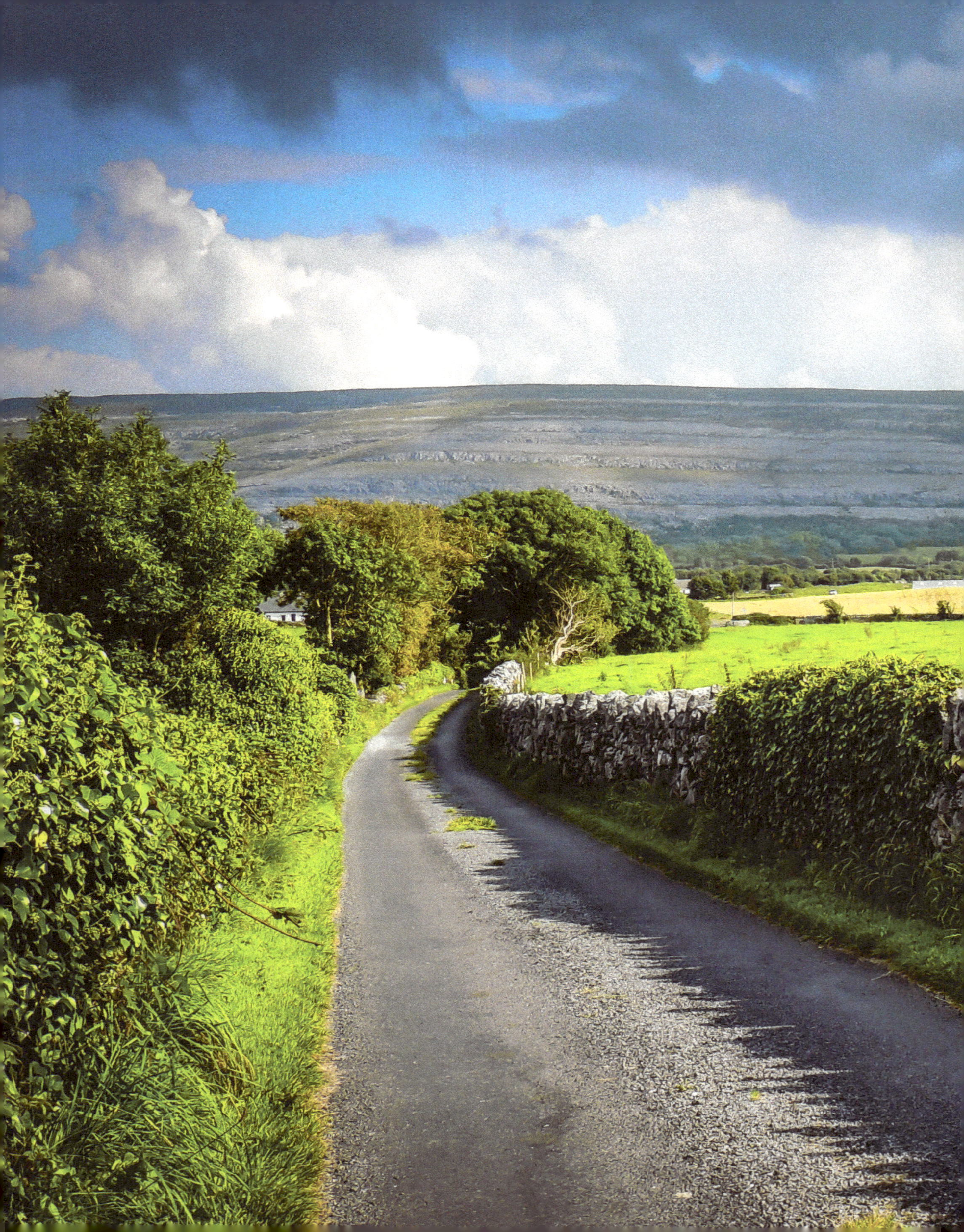

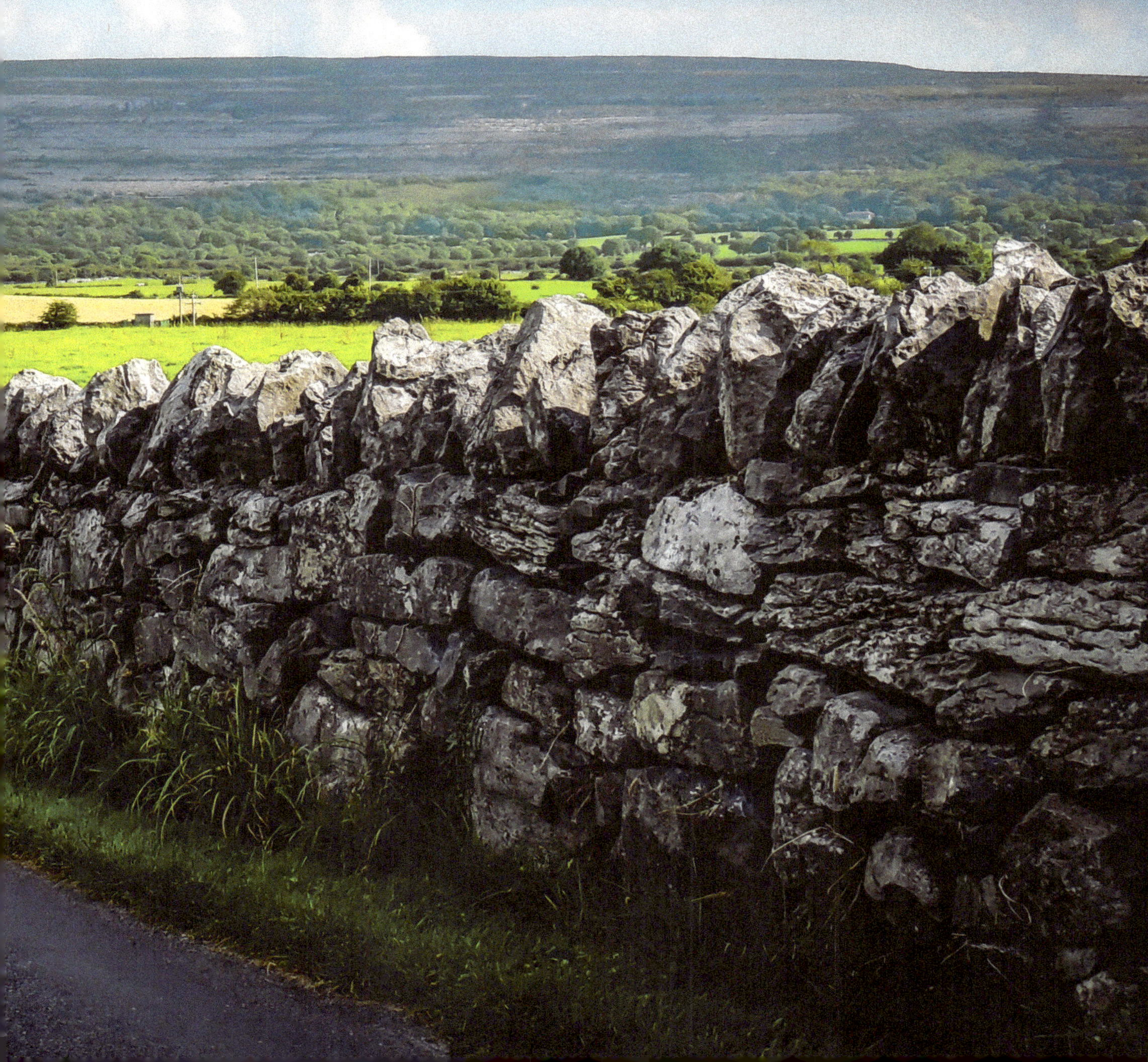

Ireland's unique and magnificent Burren landscape presides over this country road in County Clare. This is the rock-fenced path to the 16th Century Newtown Castle, which now is home to the Burren College of Art.

From this view, the castle would be behind you, with more glacier-sculpted limestone outcroppings offering a formidable backdrop.

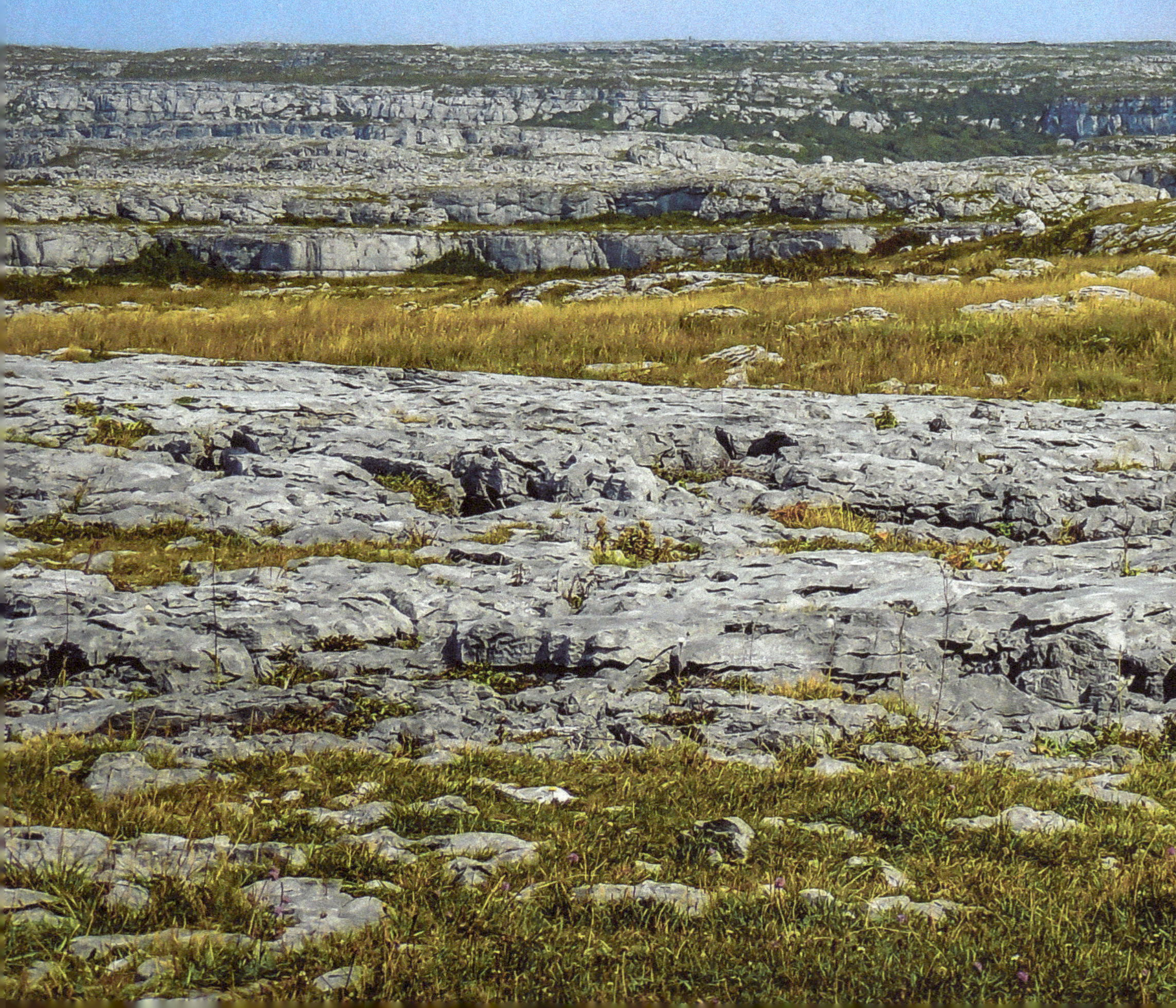

Ice, rain and the oceans joined forces millions of years ago to sculpt Ireland's rugged limestone Burren landscape. As recently as 15,000 years ago, this region was covered with ice, gently shaping the characteristic limestone terraces.

Burren, incidentally, is a very fitting name — it's derived from the Gaelic word meaning "stoney place." Despite the rough geology and lack of significant soil, the Burren plays host to more than 70 percent of Ireland's native plant species. Arctic and alpine plants co-exist alongside Mediterranean species.

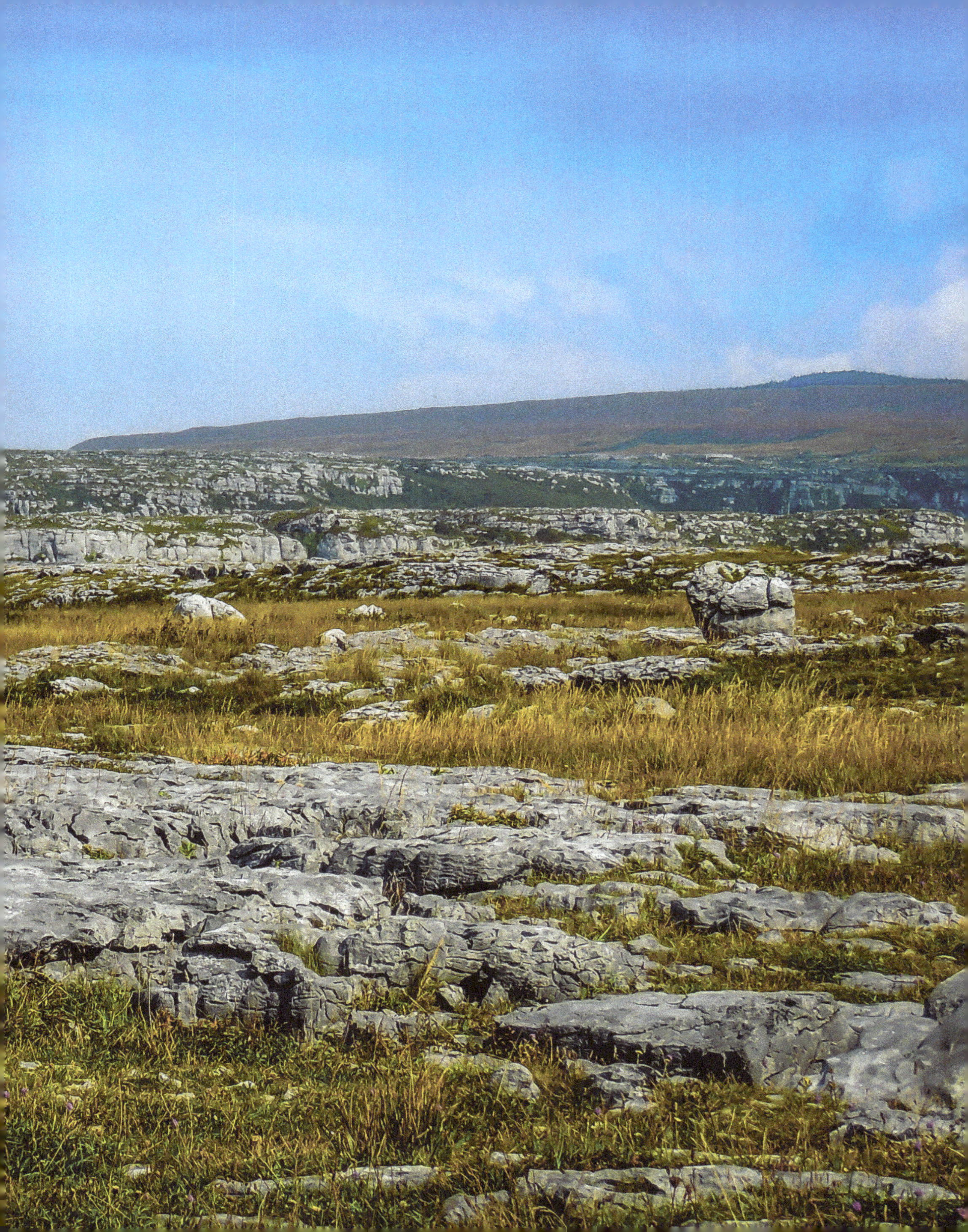

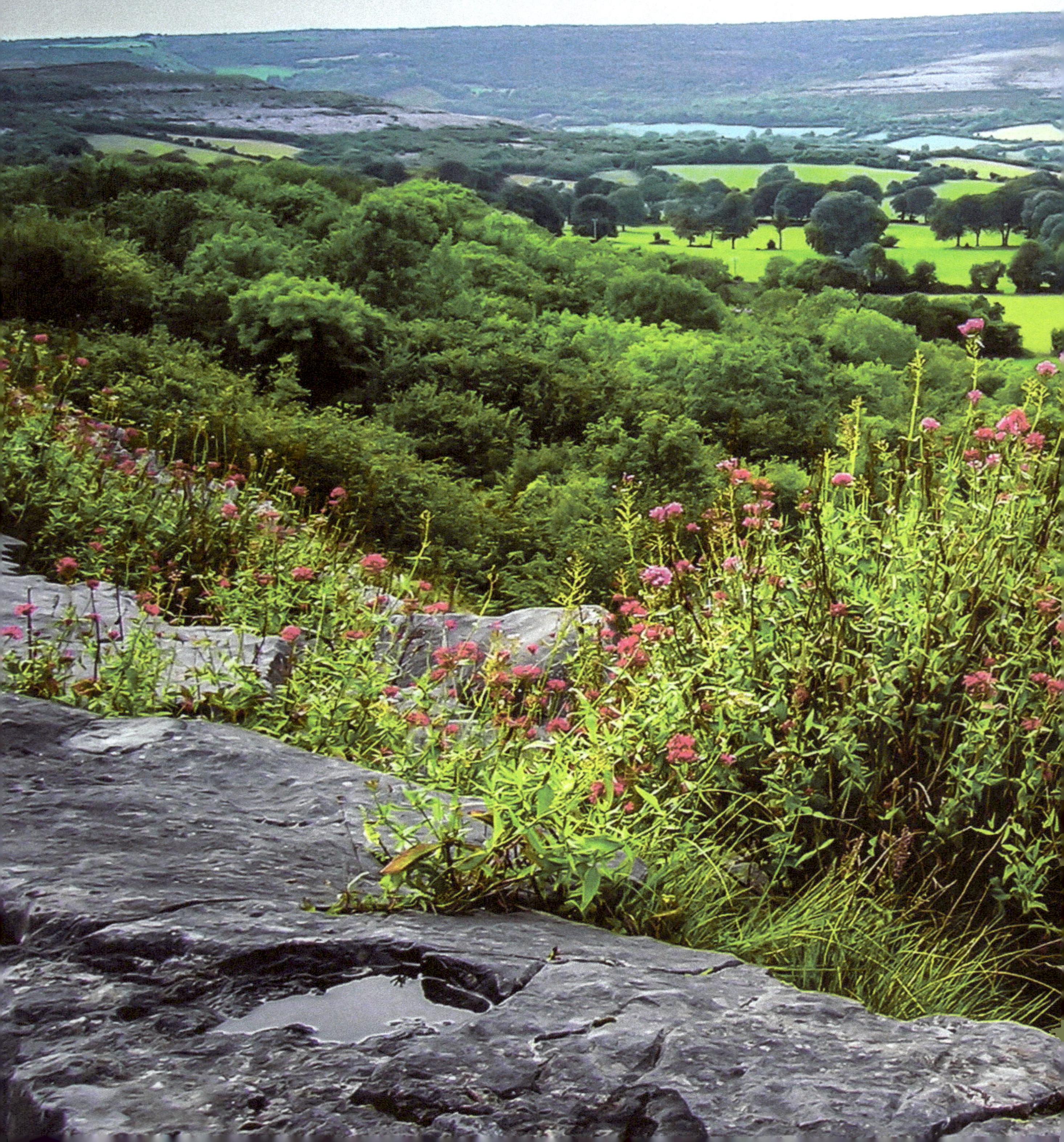

On a sunny late summer day, the crisscrossed pastures of the Burren lowlands offset the trademark gray limestone substrate of Ireland's smallest National Park. This view is from the car park of Aillwee Cave in northwest County Clare.

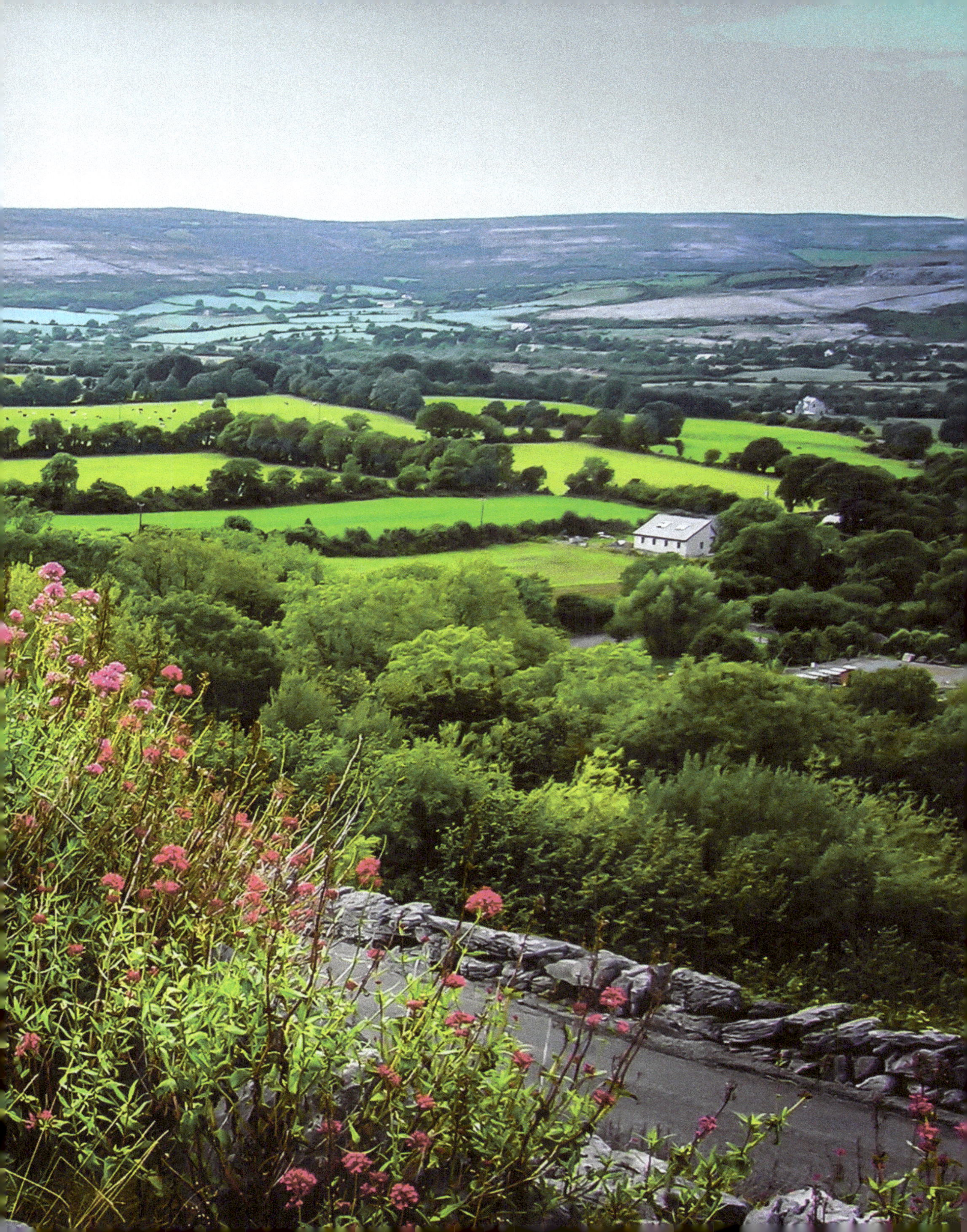

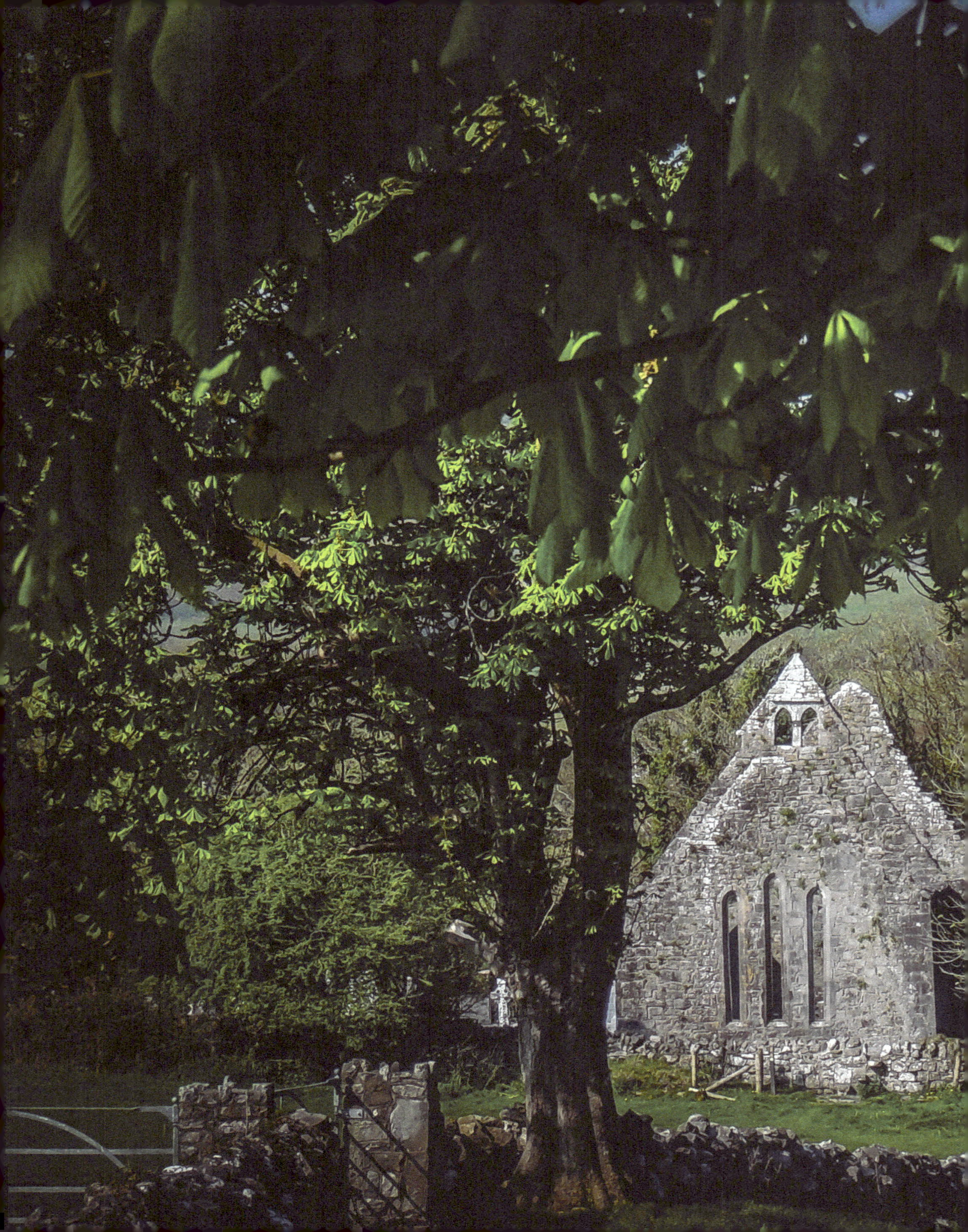

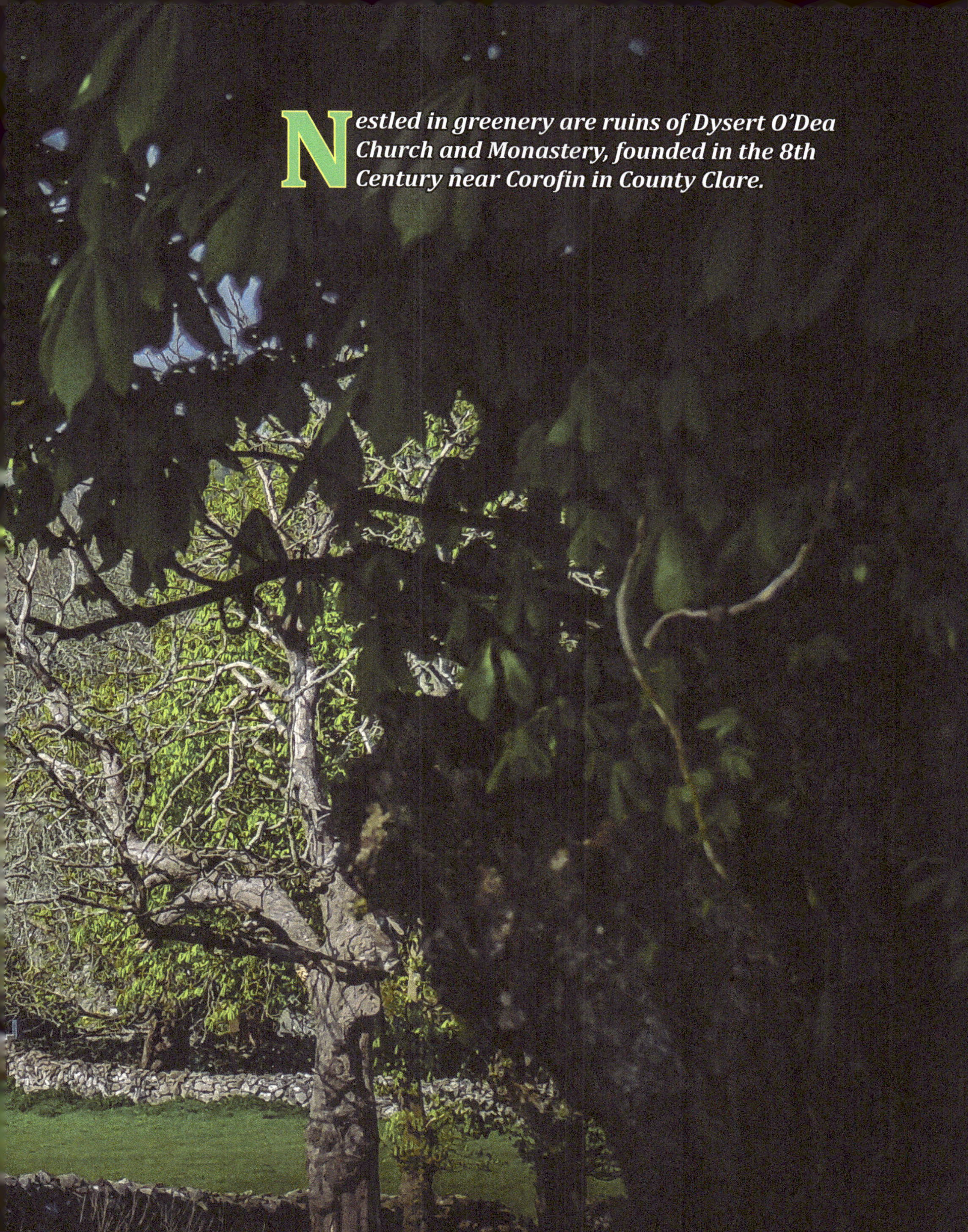

Nestled in greenery are ruins of Dysert O'Dea Church and Monastery, founded in the 8th Century near Corofin in County Clare.

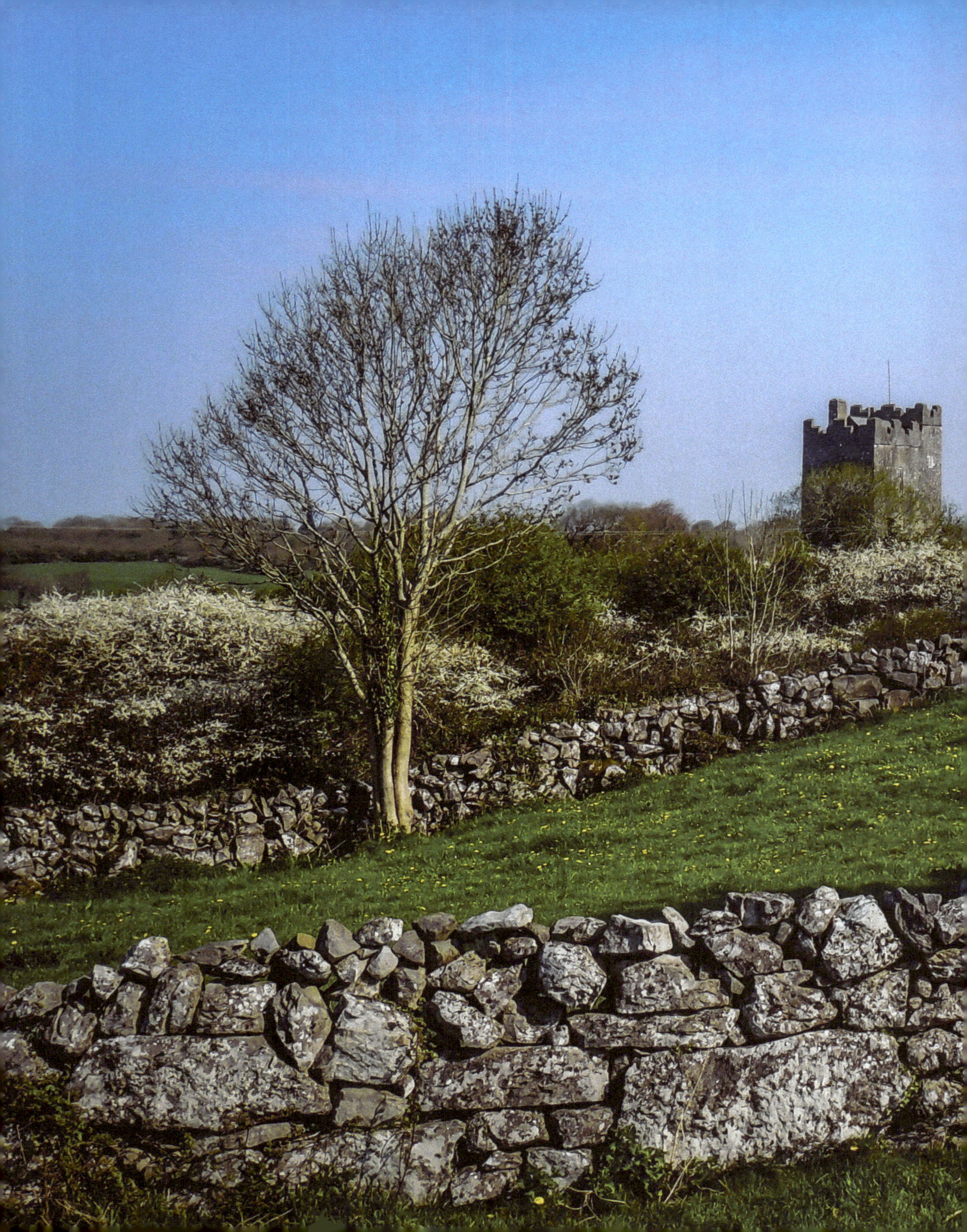

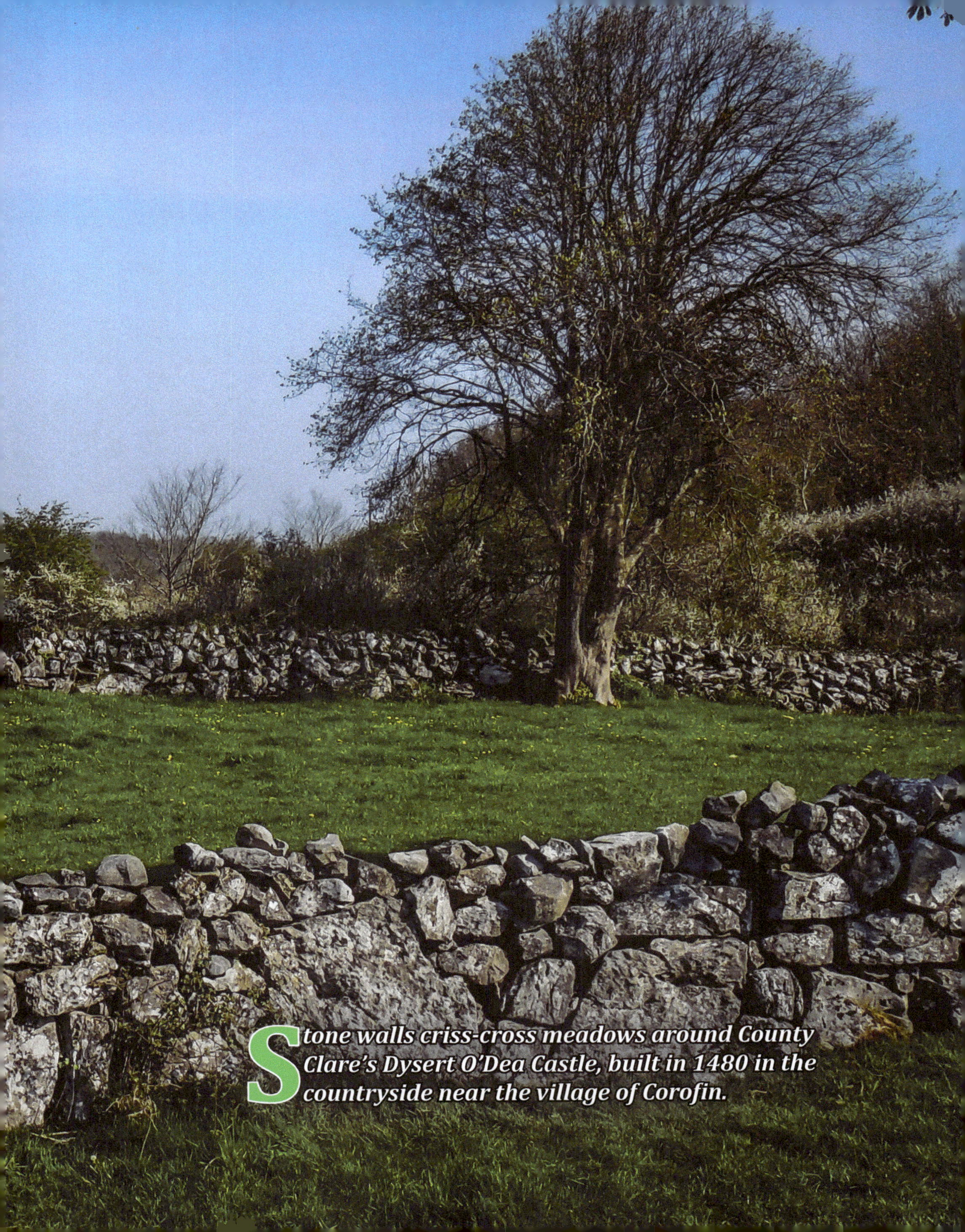

Stone walls criss-cross meadows around County Clare's Dysert O'Dea Castle, built in 1480 in the countryside near the village of Corofin.

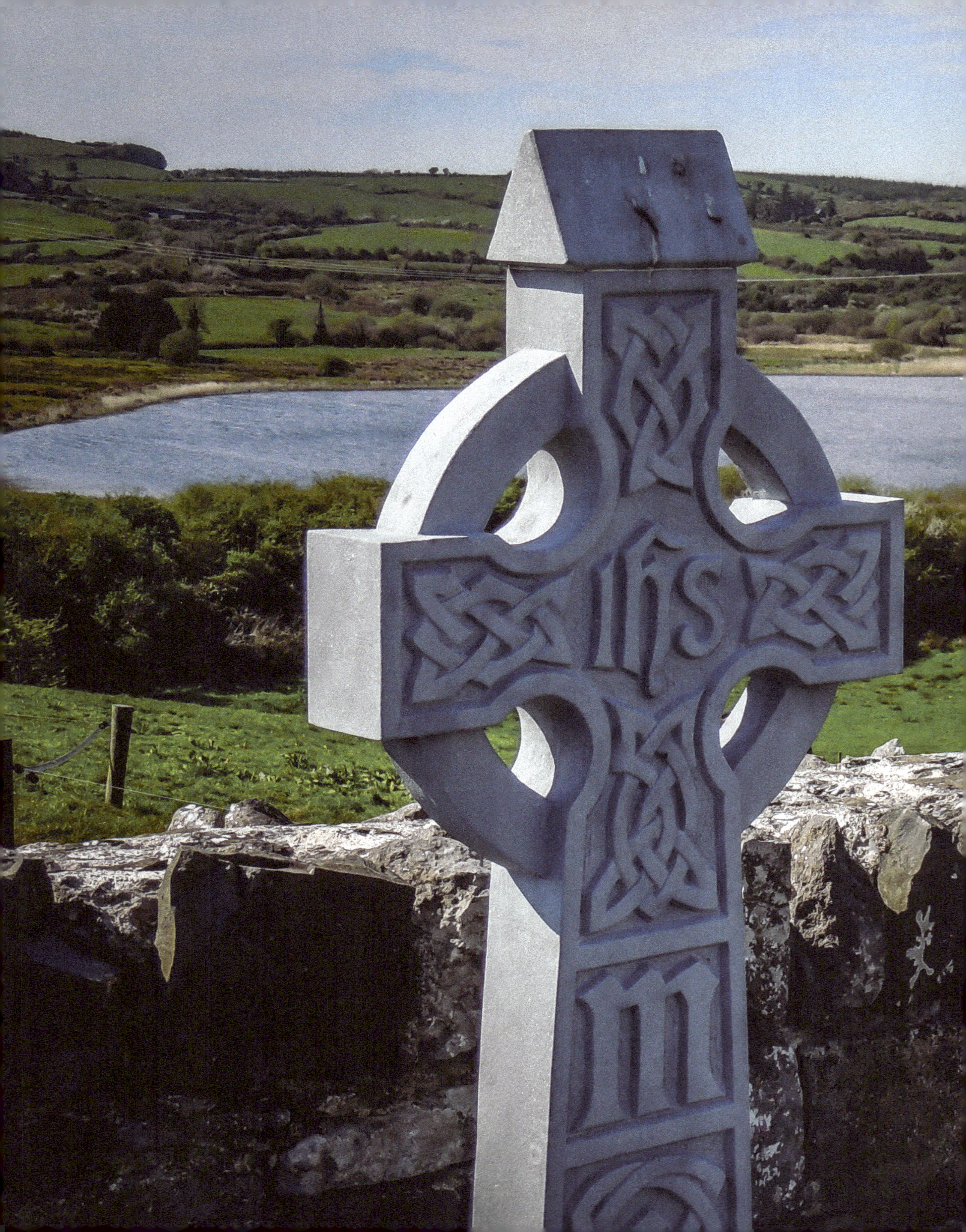

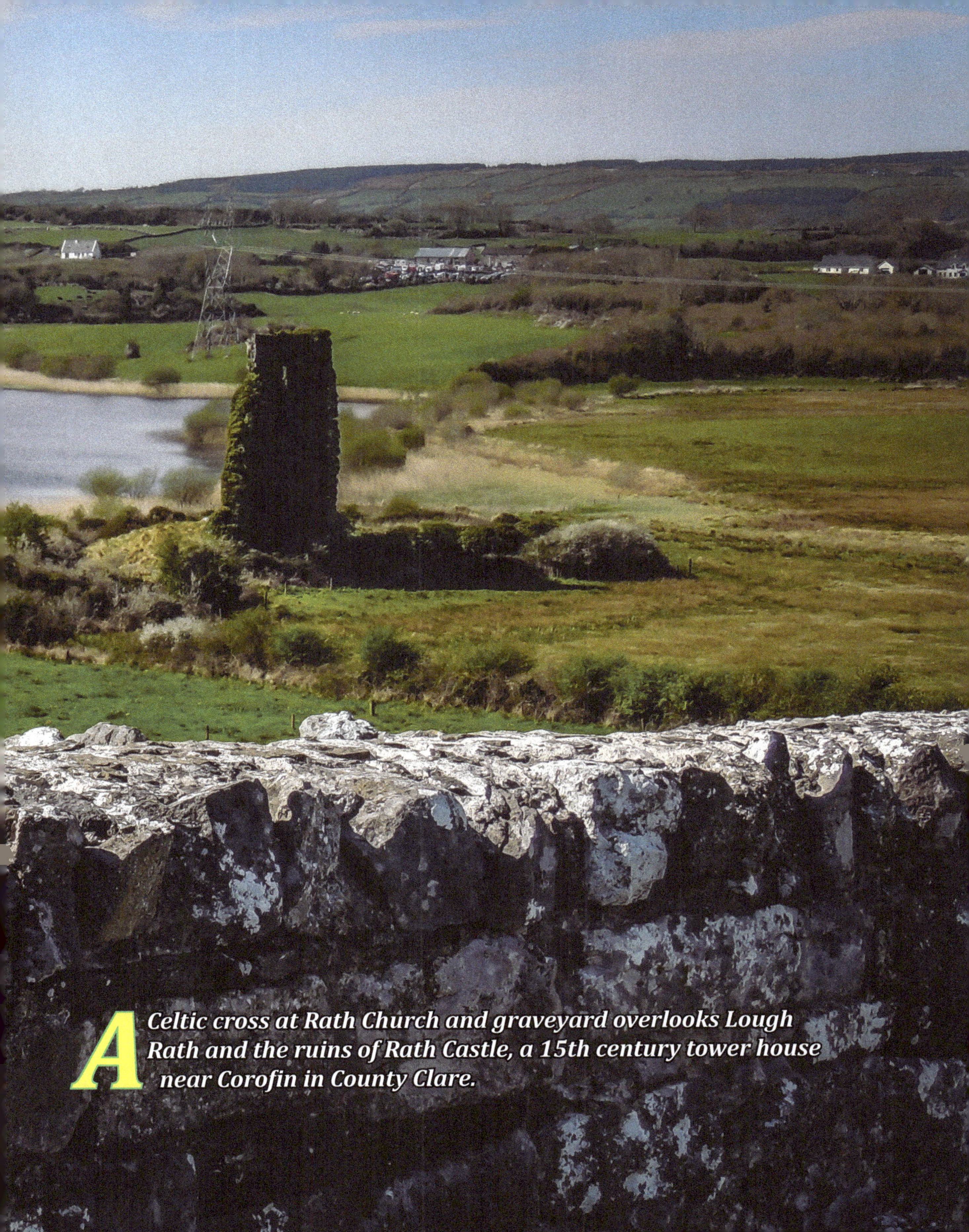

A Celtic cross at Rath Church and graveyard overlooks Lough Rath and the ruins of Rath Castle, a 15th century tower house near Corofin in County Clare.

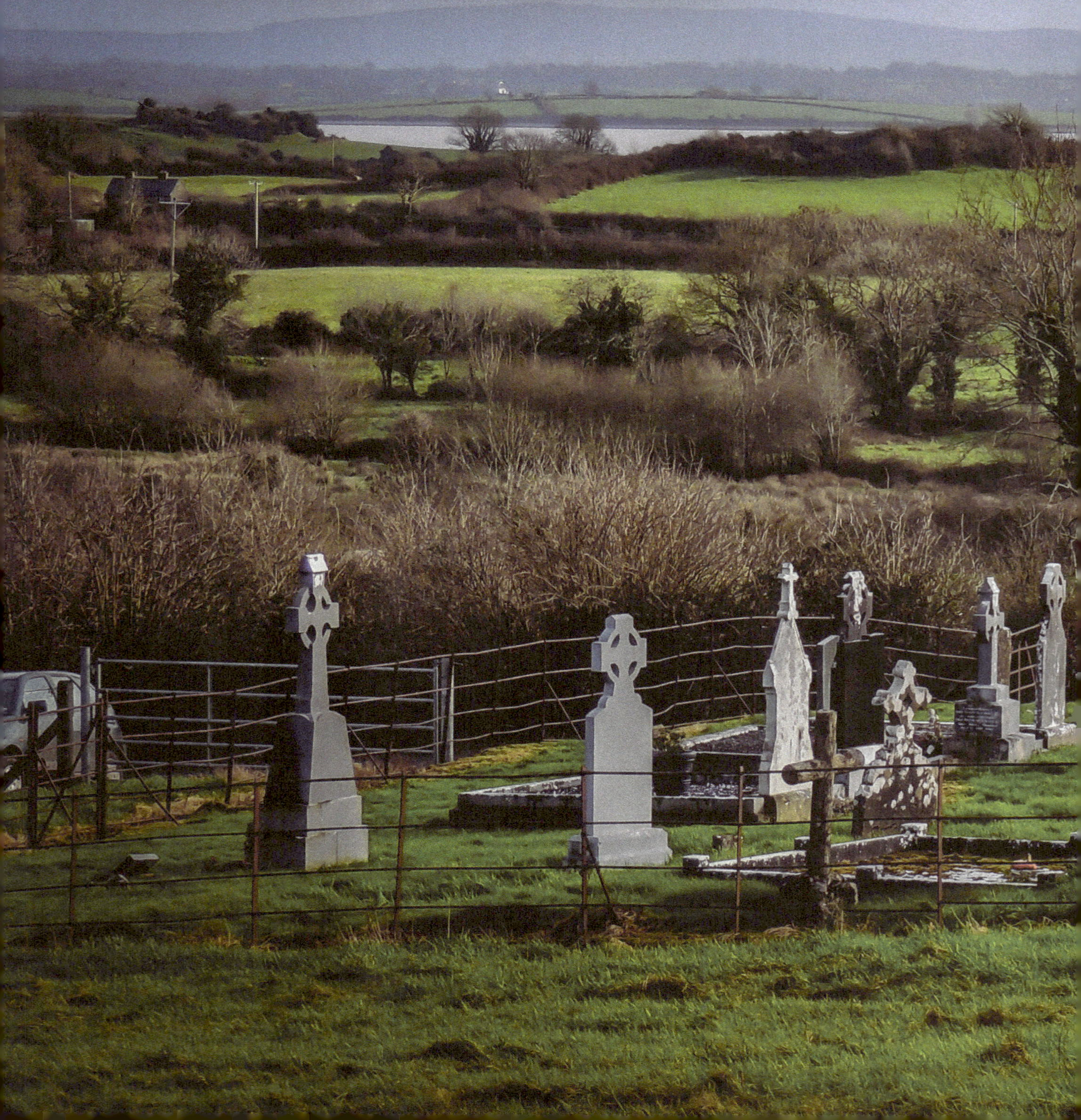
Killea Graveyard, in the County Clare parish of Clondegad, originally was a "Cillín" — a burial ground for unbaptized children. With a stunning view of the Shannon Estuary, it now also is the final resting place for adults, too.

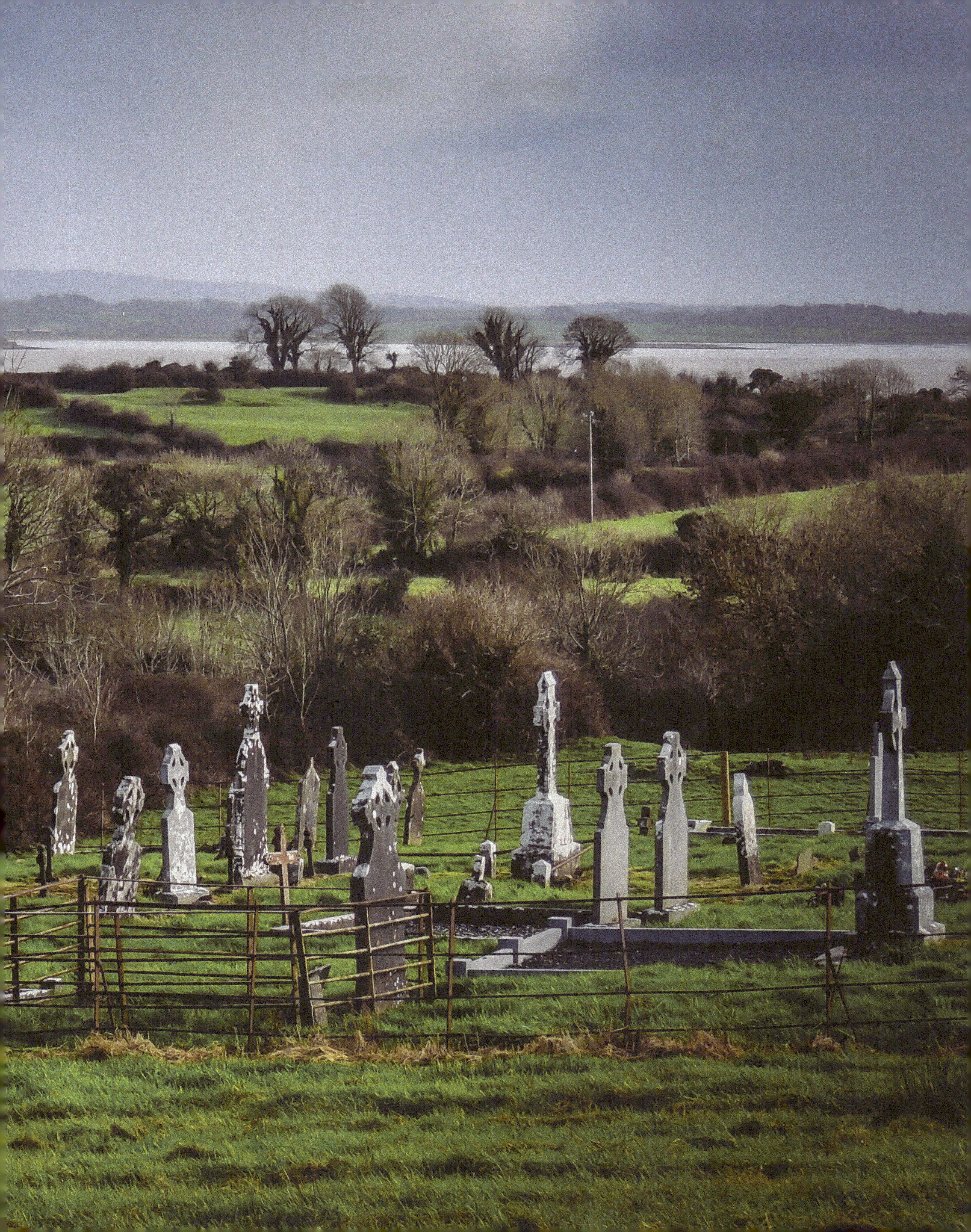

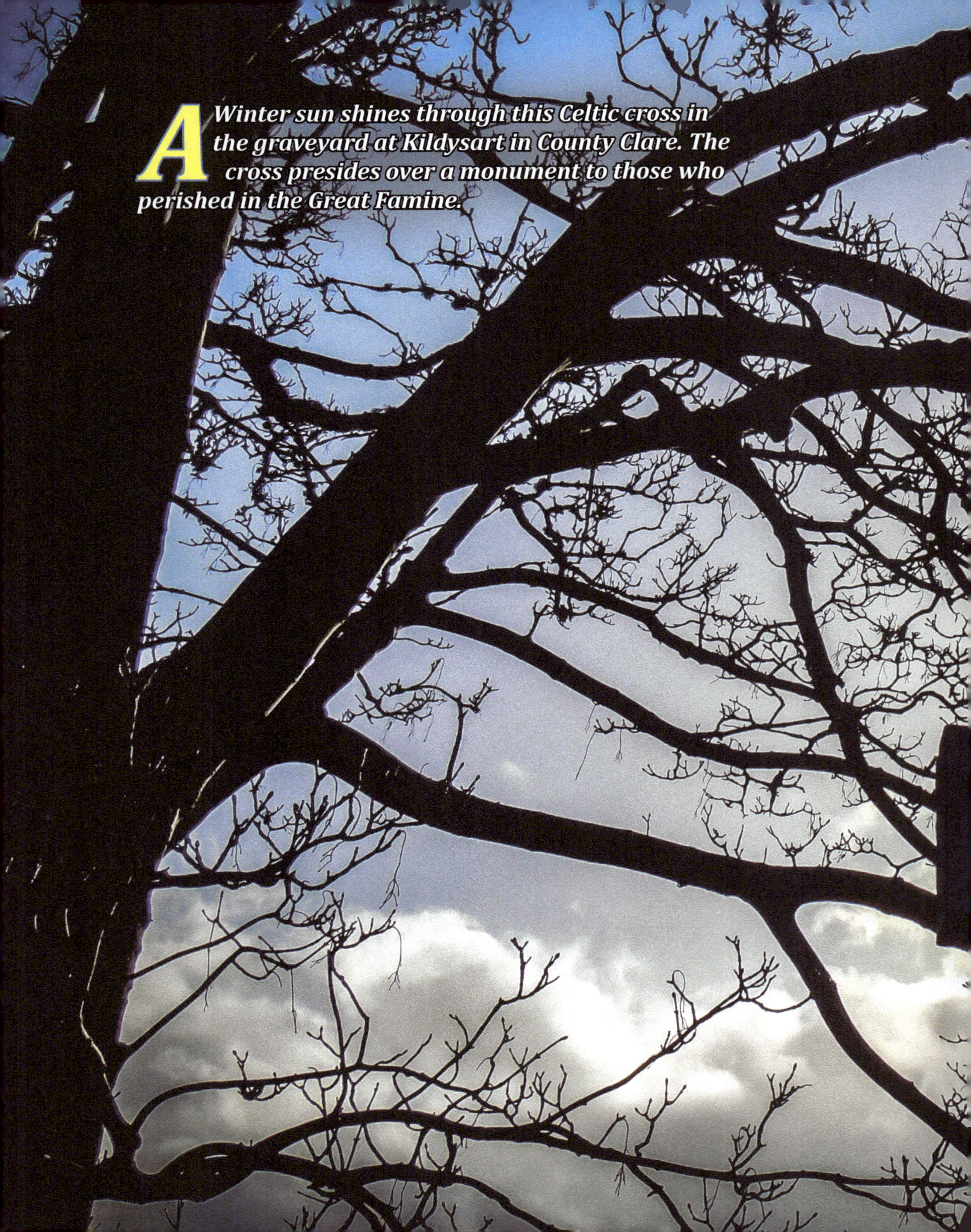

A Winter sun shines through this Celtic cross in the graveyard at Kildysart in County Clare. The cross presides over a monument to those who perished in the Great Famine.

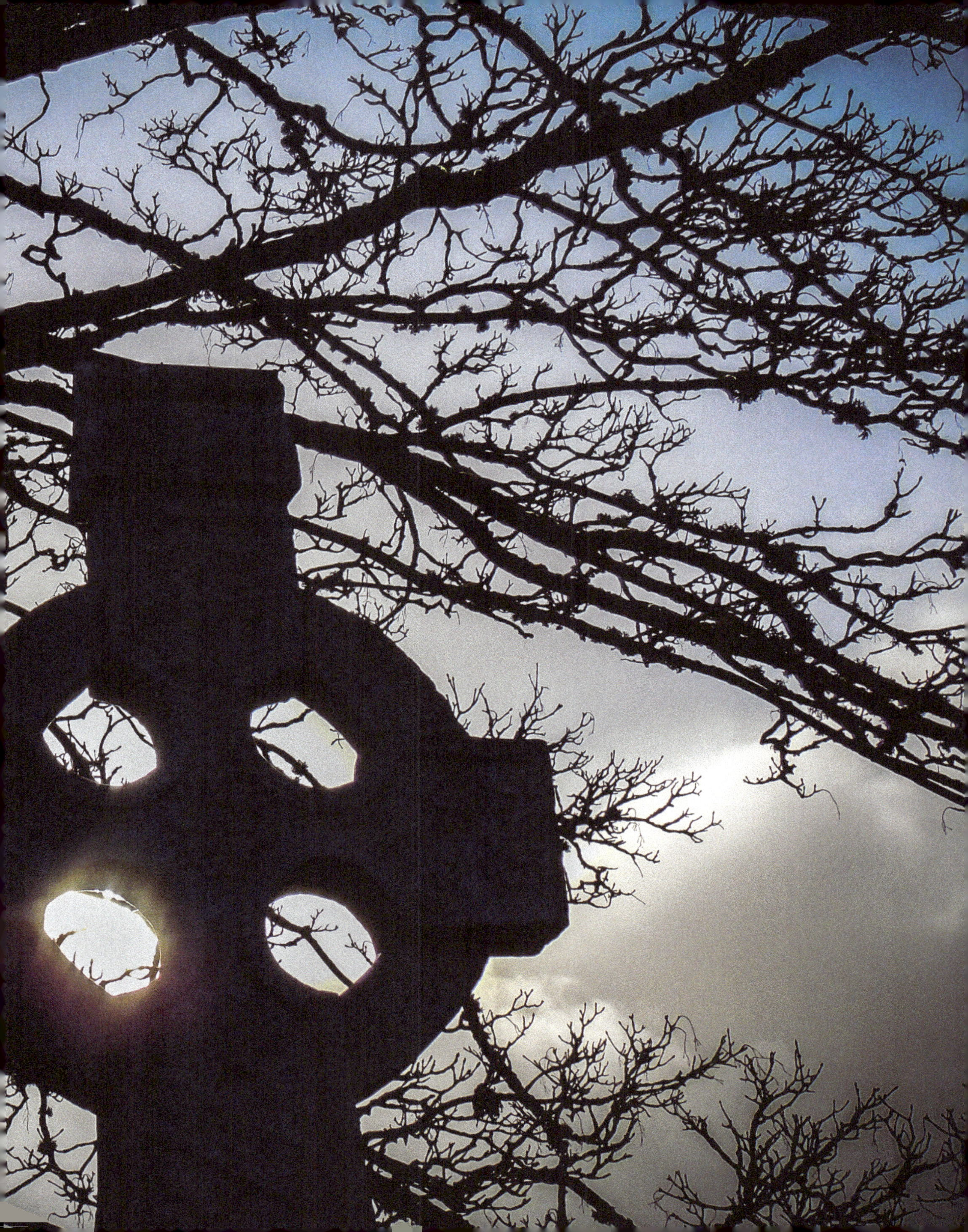

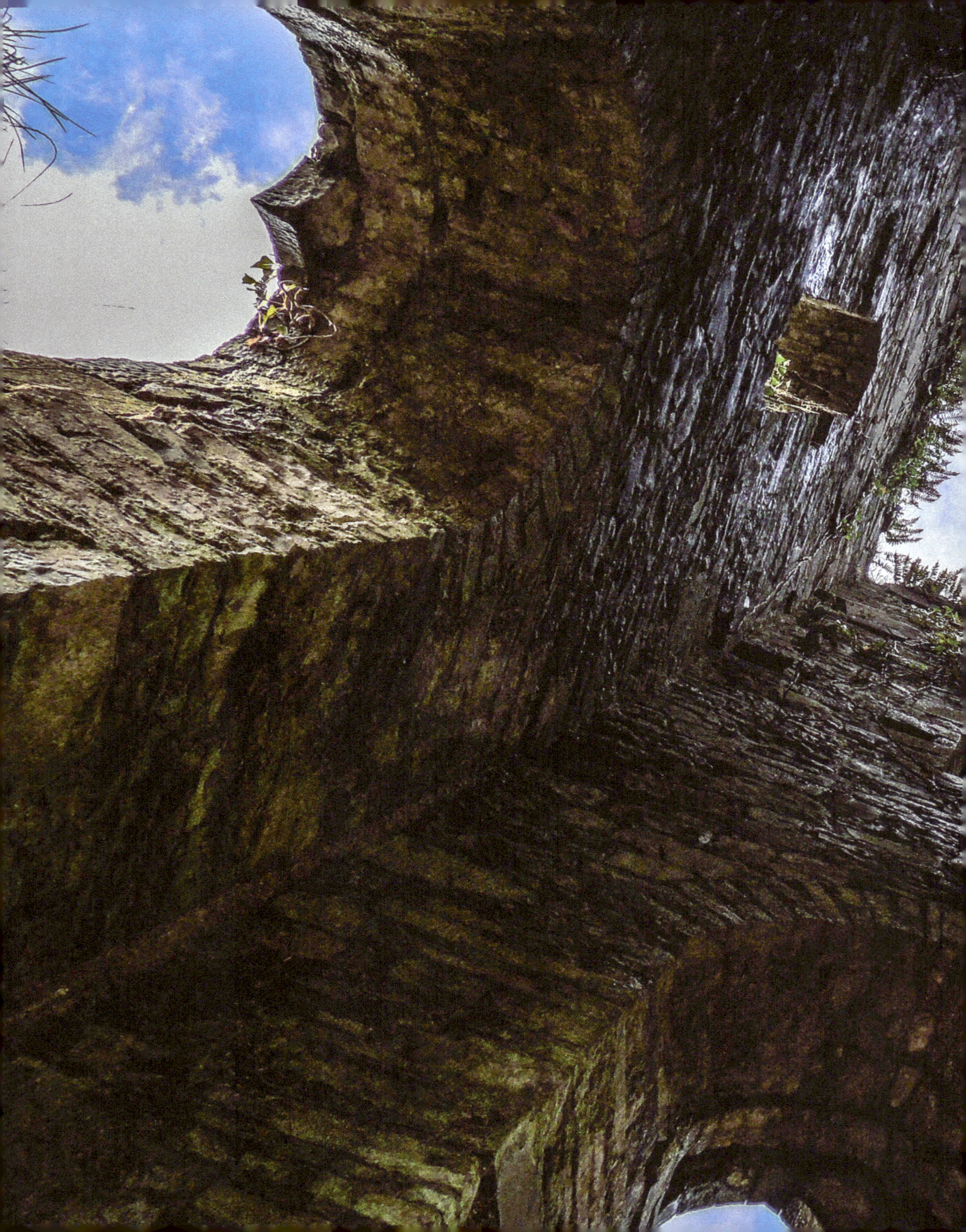

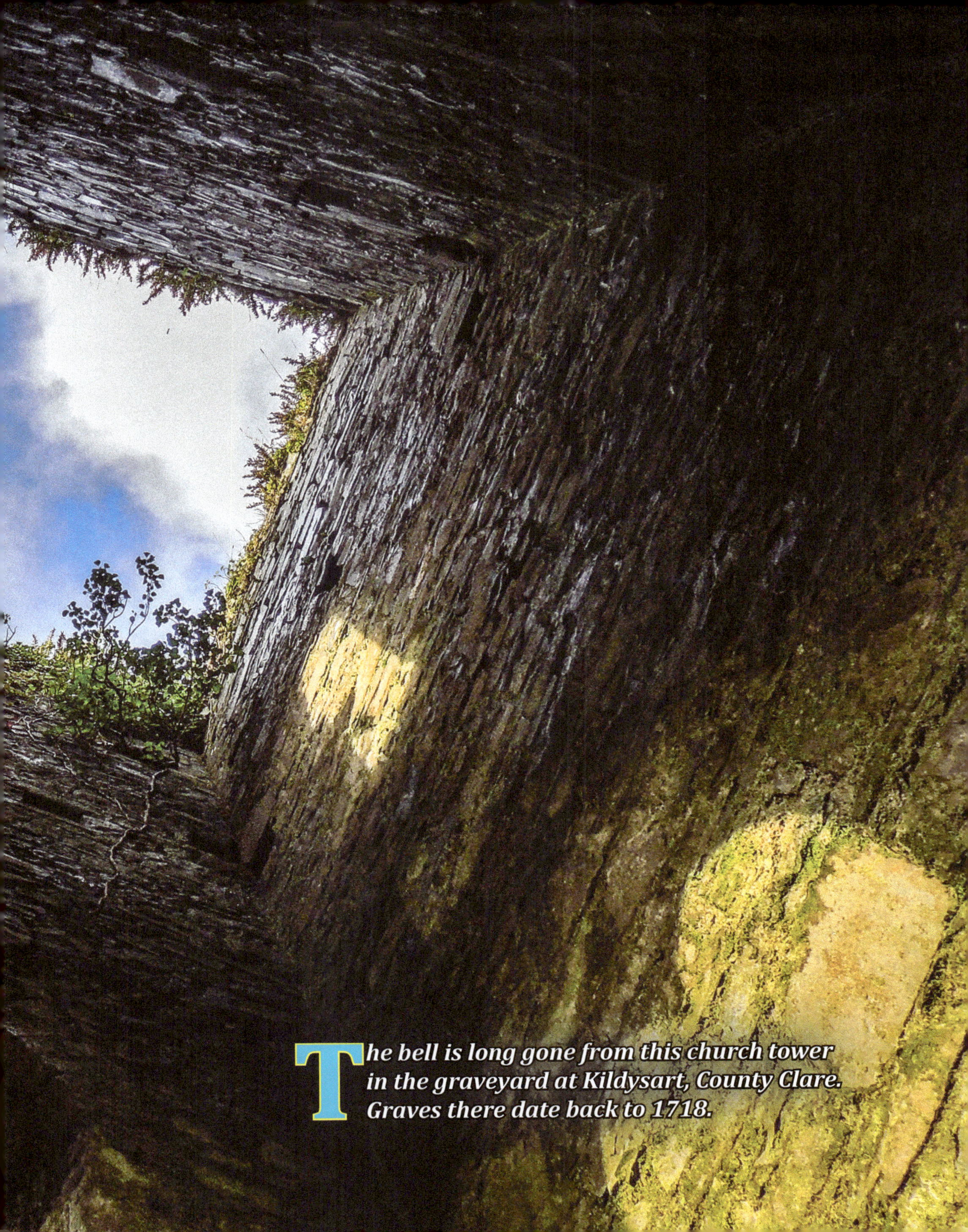

The bell is long gone from this church tower in the graveyard at Kildysart, County Clare. Graves there date back to 1718.

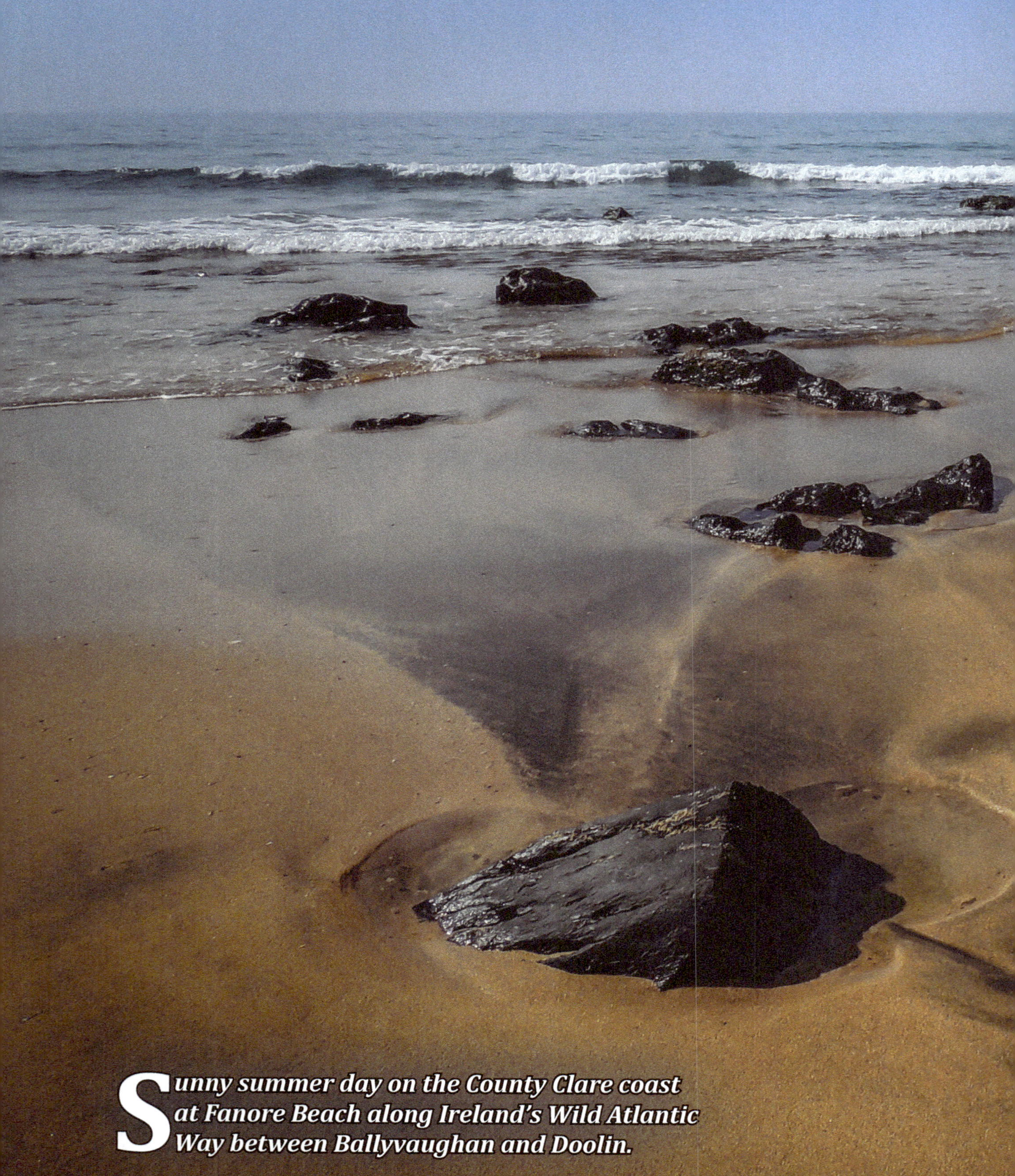

Sunny summer day on the County Clare coast at Fanore Beach along Ireland's Wild Atlantic Way between Ballyvaughan and Doolin.

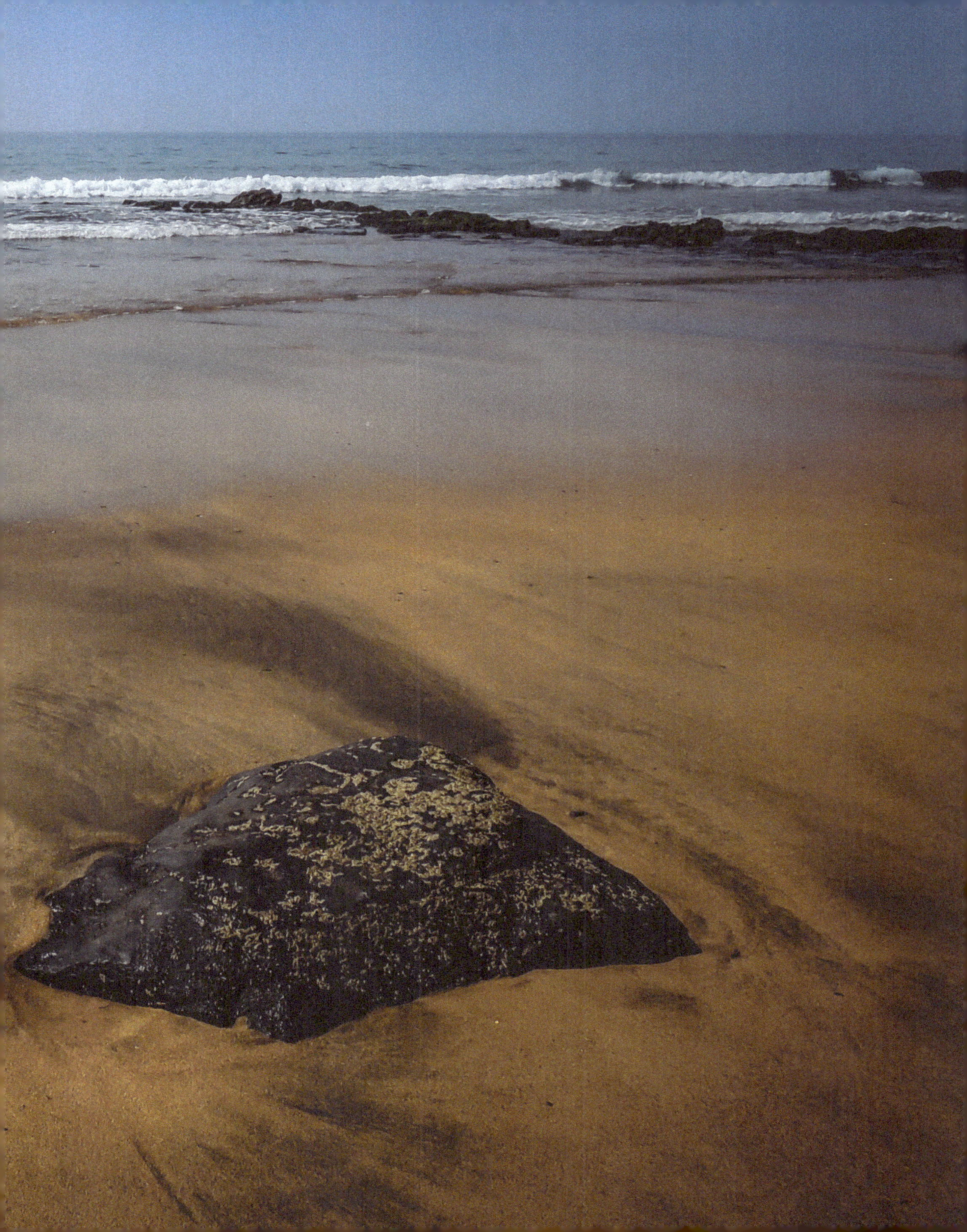

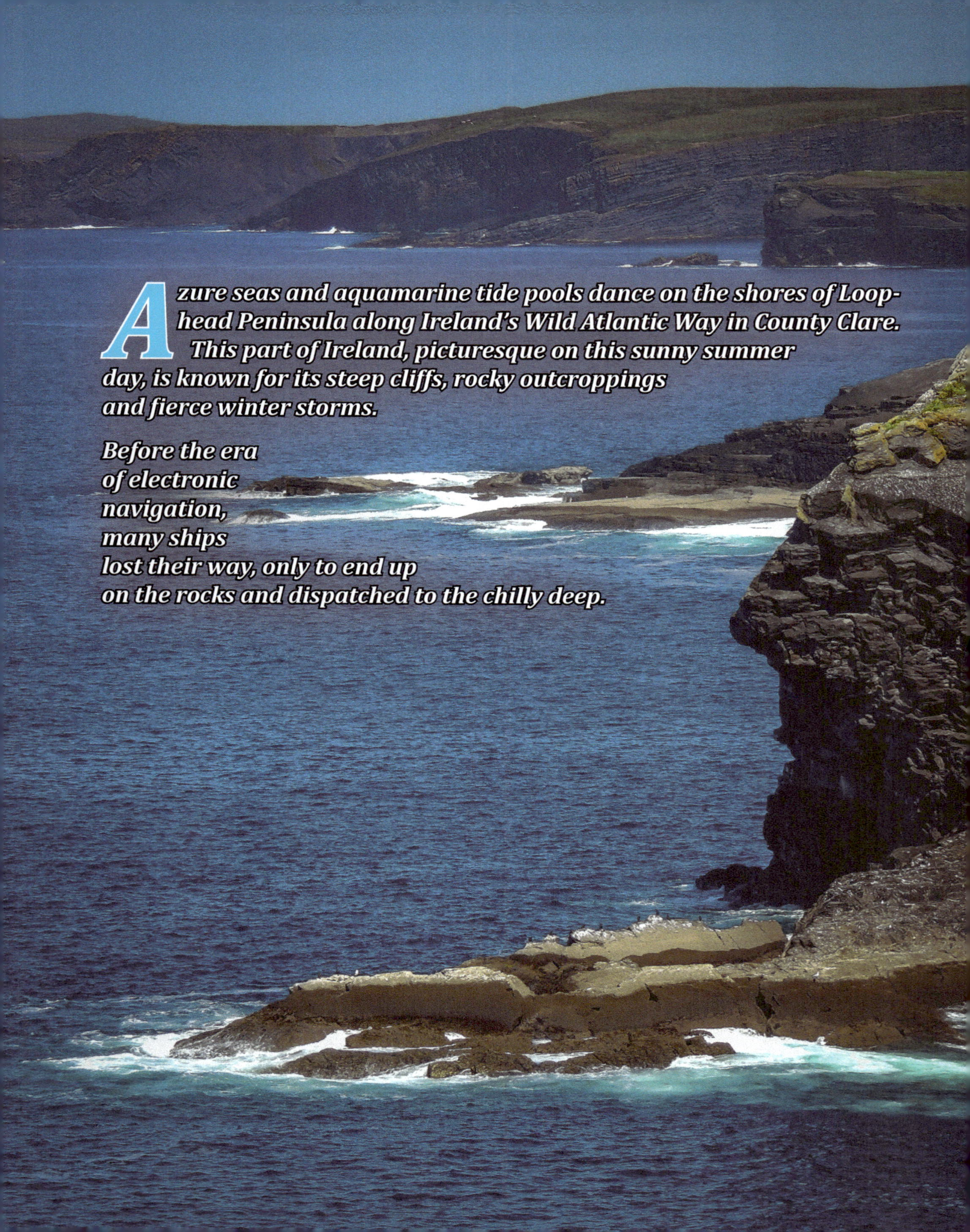

Azure seas and aquamarine tide pools dance on the shores of Loop-head Peninsula along Ireland's Wild Atlantic Way in County Clare. This part of Ireland, picturesque on this sunny summer day, is known for its steep cliffs, rocky outcroppings and fierce winter storms.

Before the era of electronic navigation, many ships lost their way, only to end up on the rocks and dispatched to the chilly deep.

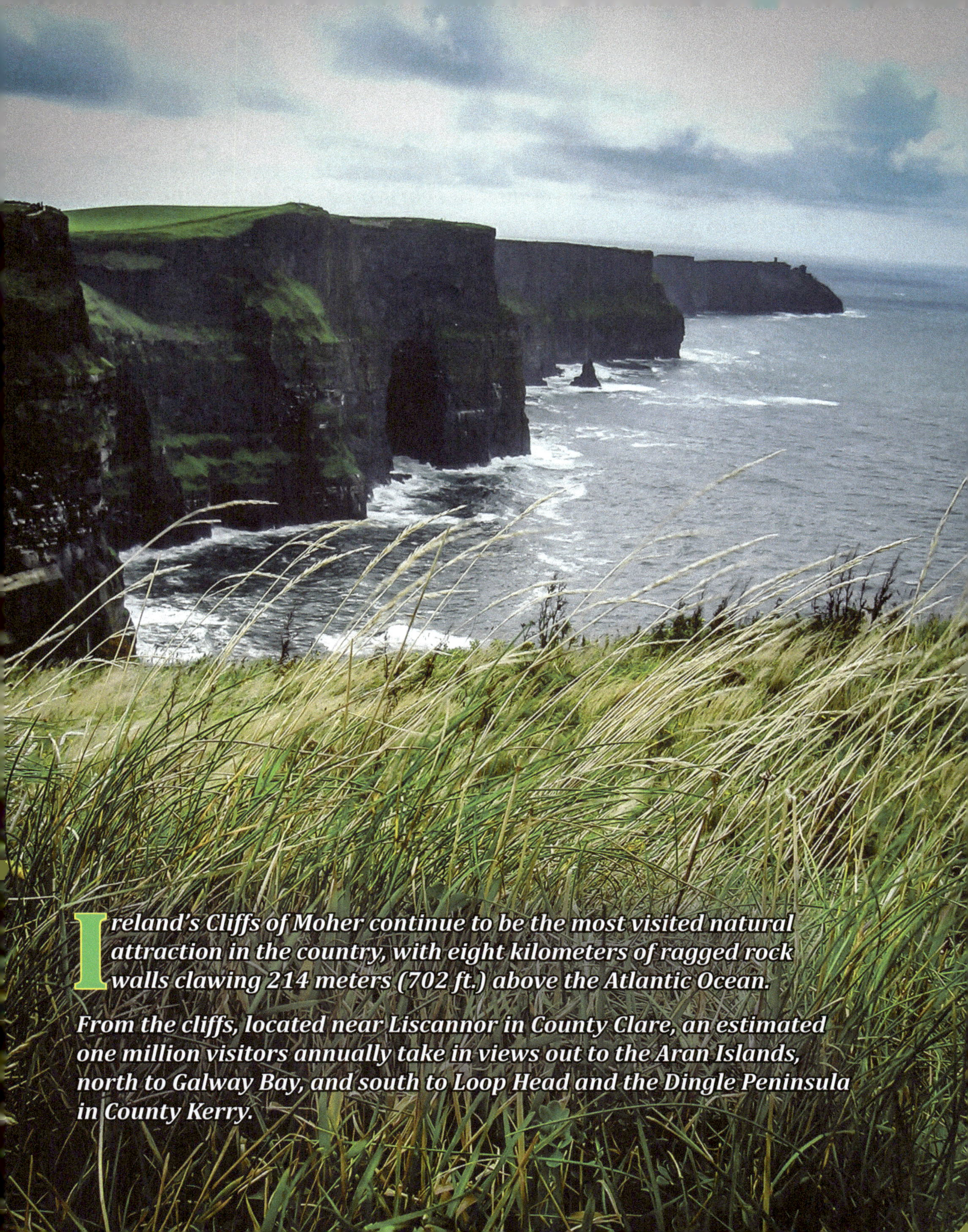

I reland's Cliffs of Moher continue to be the most visited natural attraction in the country, with eight kilometers of ragged rock walls clawing 214 meters (702 ft.) above the Atlantic Ocean.

From the cliffs, located near Liscannor in County Clare, an estimated one million visitors annually take in views out to the Aran Islands, north to Galway Bay, and south to Loop Head and the Dingle Peninsula in County Kerry.

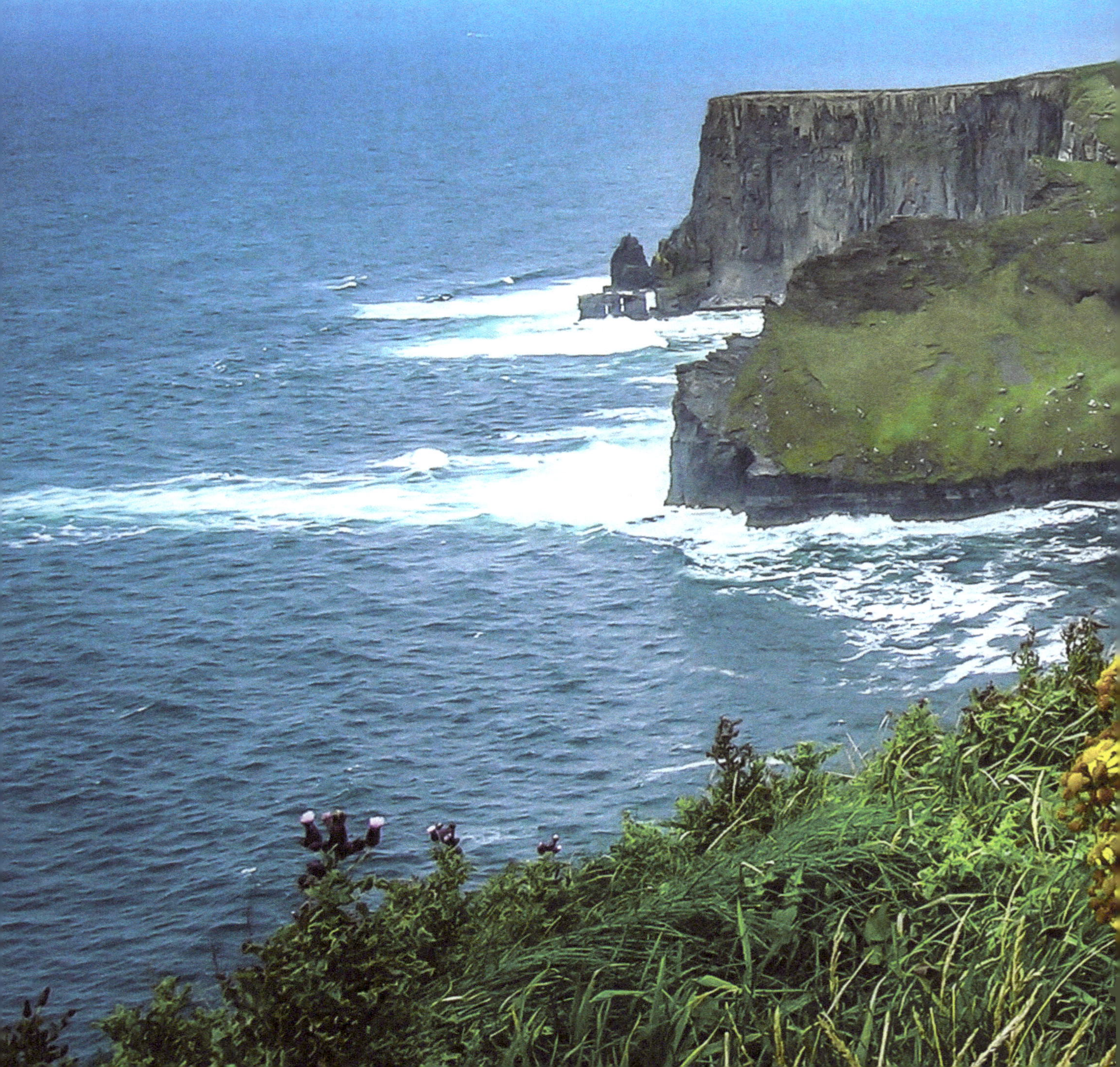

Agem in the crown of the Wild Atlantic Way, the Cliffs of Moher are named after the old Fort Moher, which once stood at Hag's Head at the southern end of the natural wonder.

A €32 million visitor center opened in February 2007. In keeping with an overall plan to preserve the natural surroundings, the earth-sheltered building is integrated into the adjacent hillside.

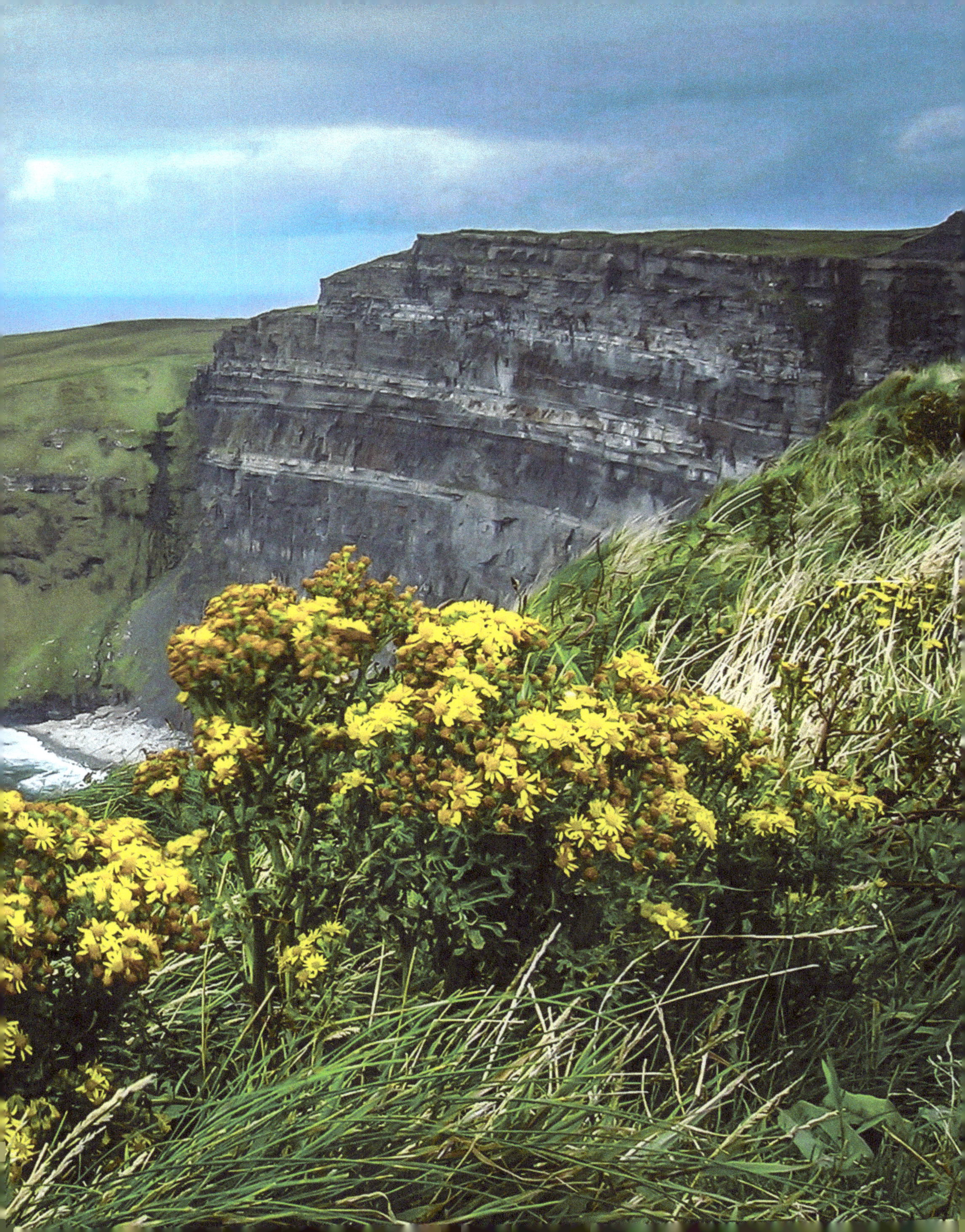

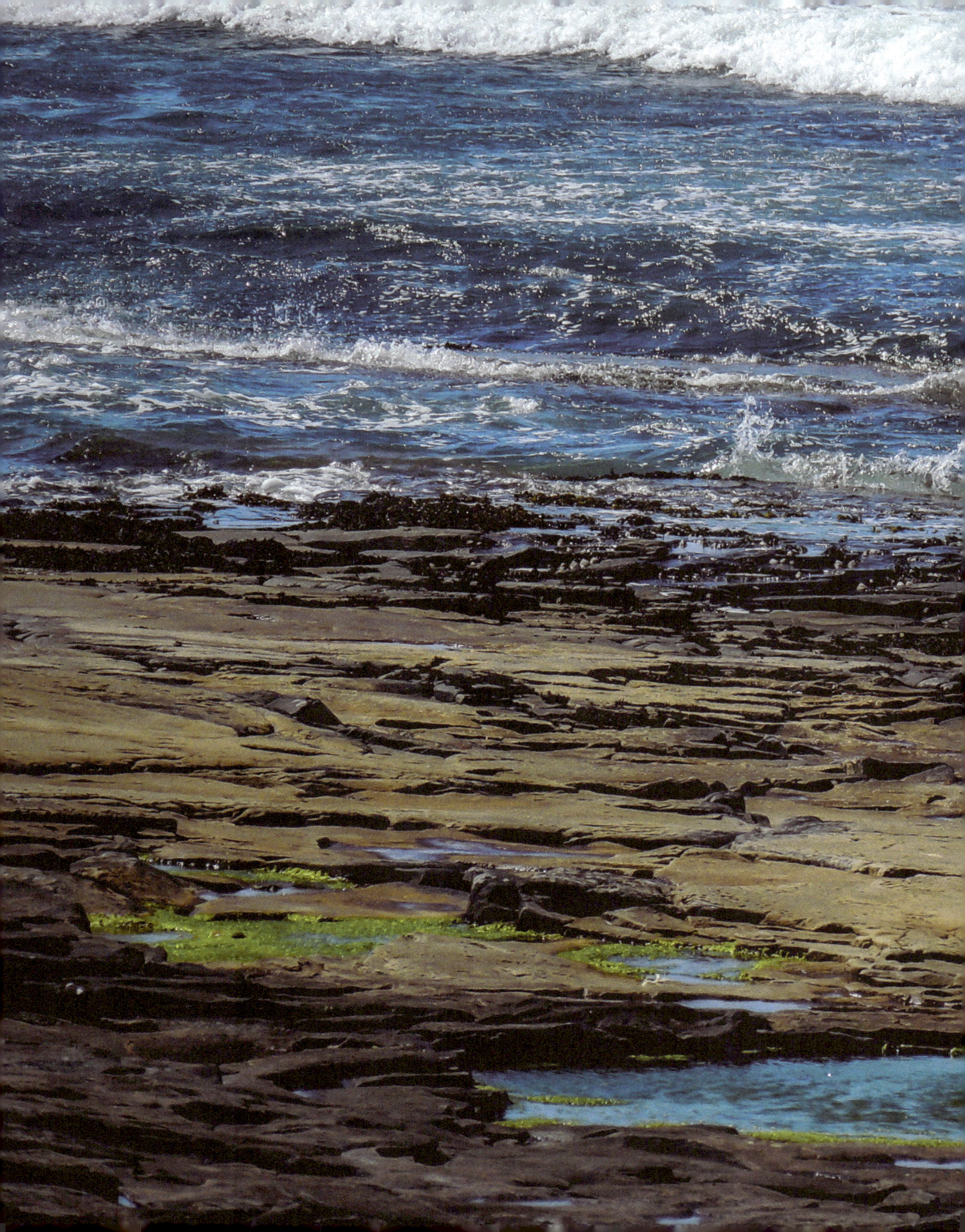

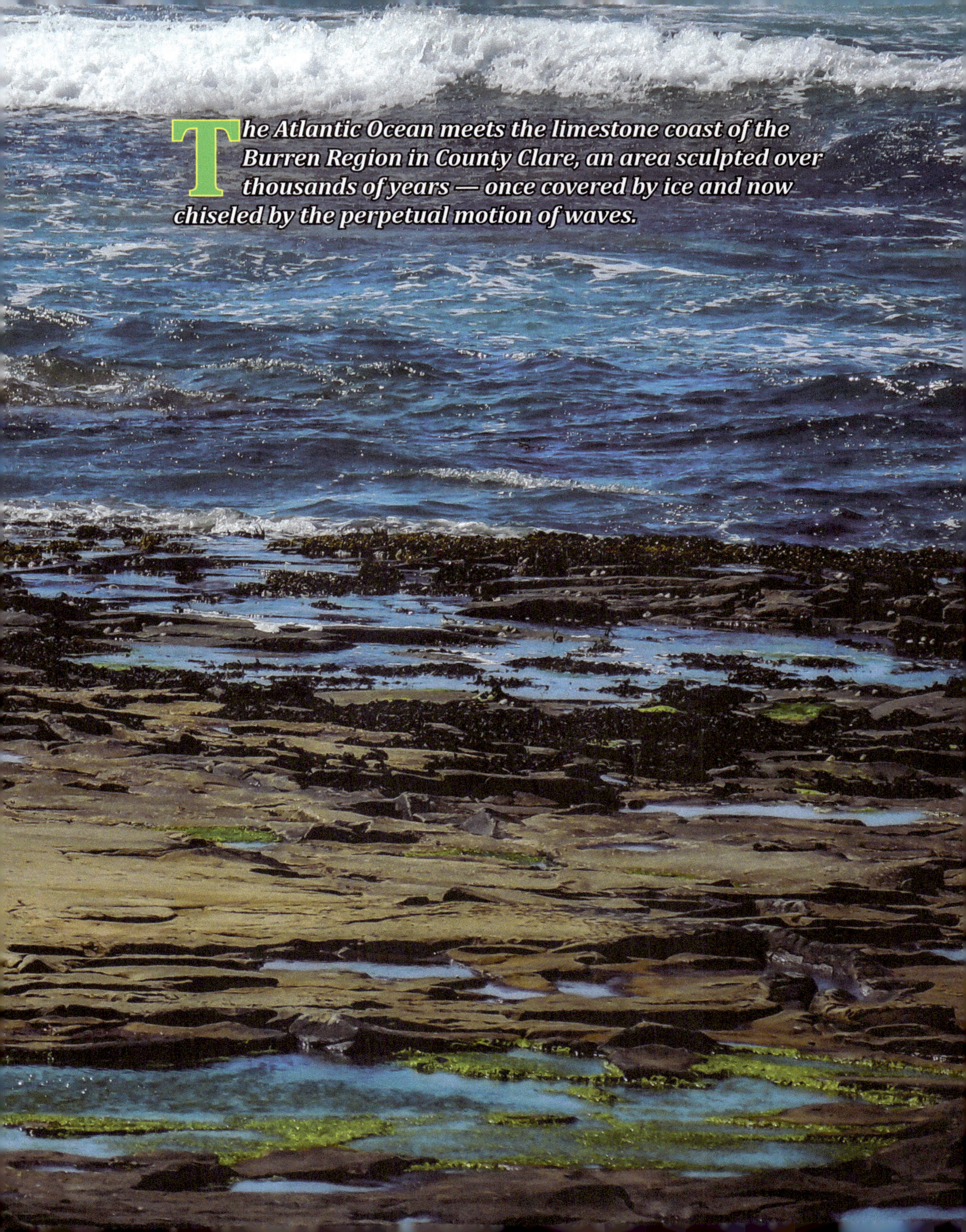

The Atlantic Ocean meets the limestone coast of the Burren Region in County Clare, an area sculpted over thousands of years — once covered by ice and now chiseled by the perpetual motion of waves.

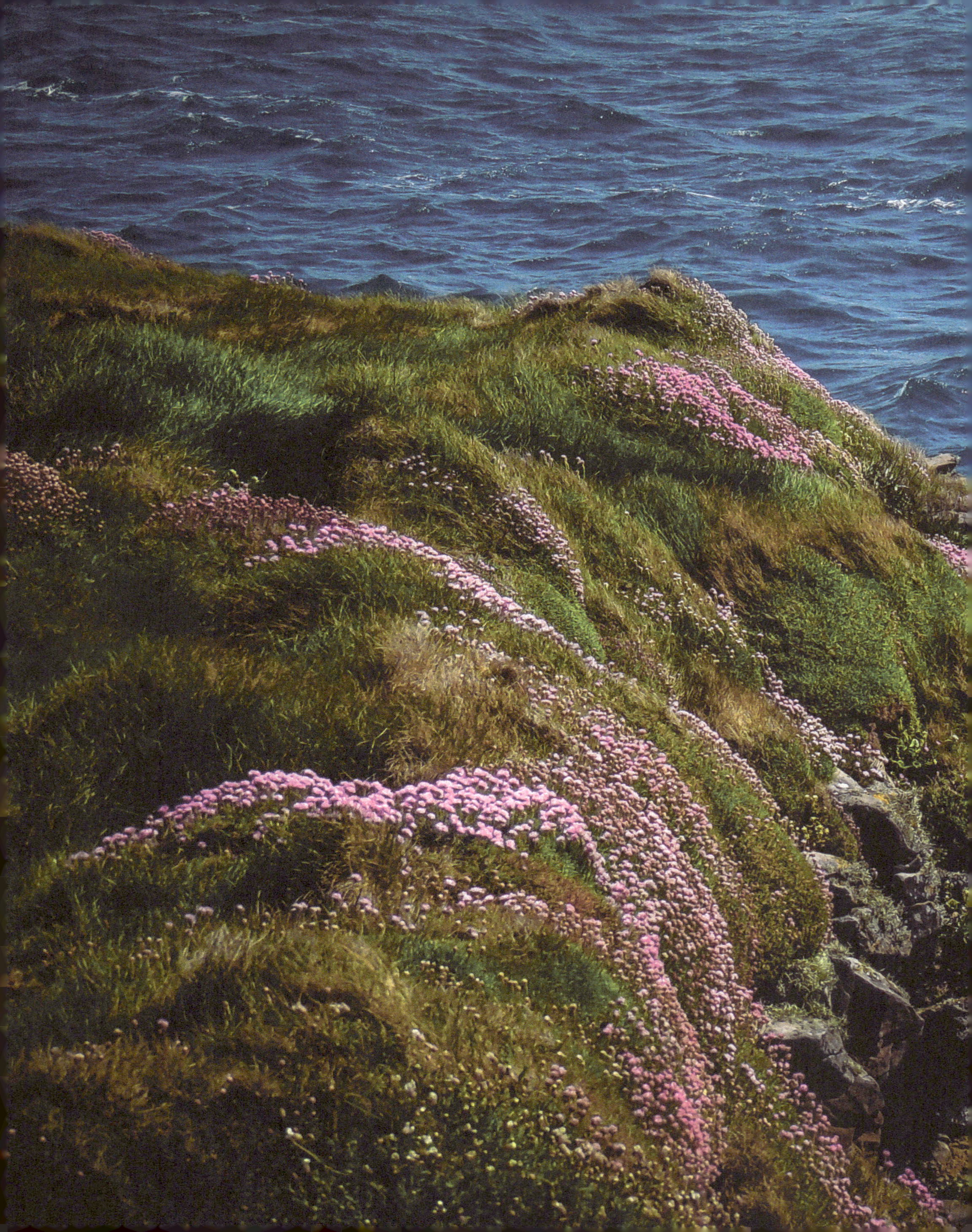

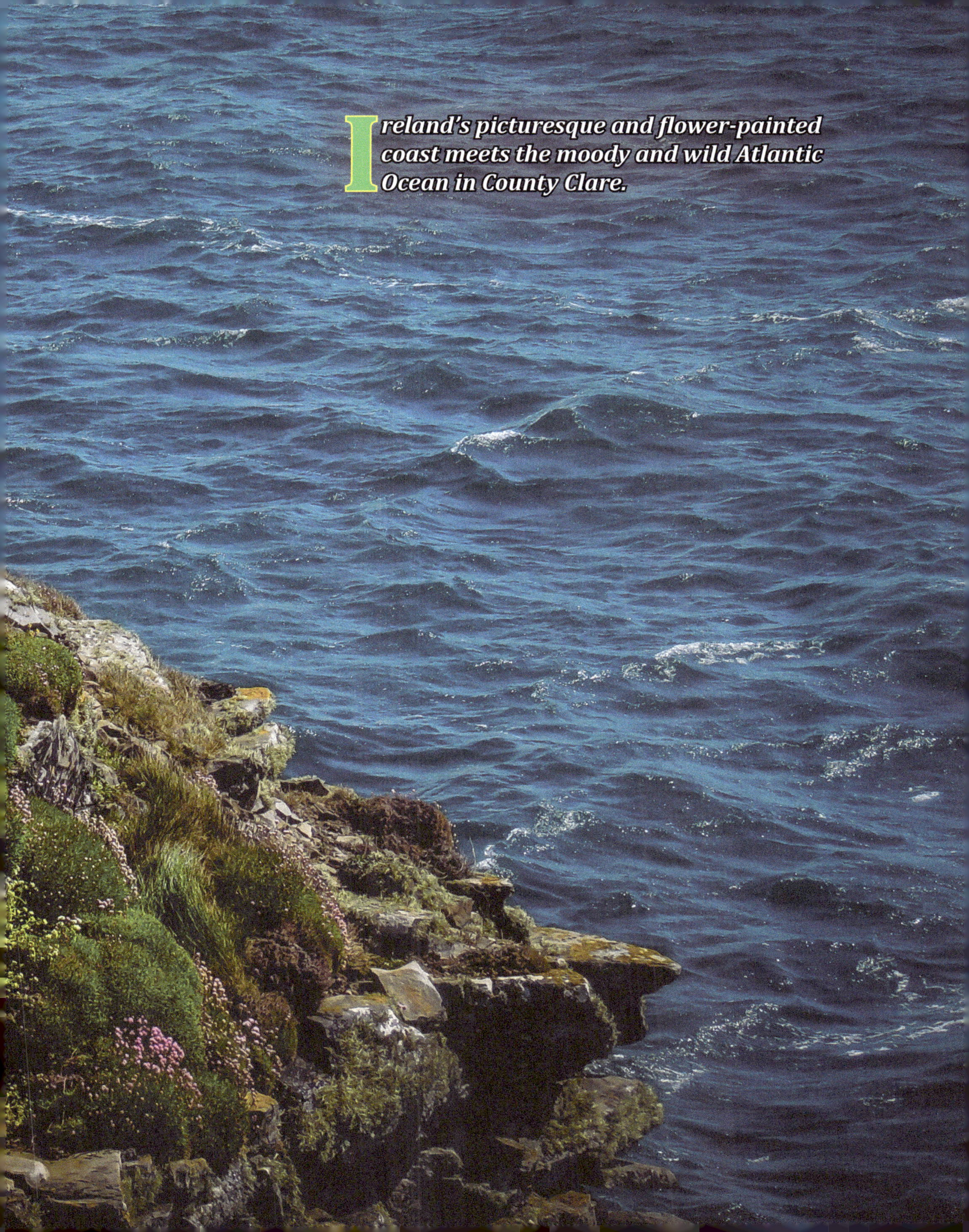

Ireland's picturesque and flower-painted coast meets the moody and wild Atlantic Ocean in County Clare.

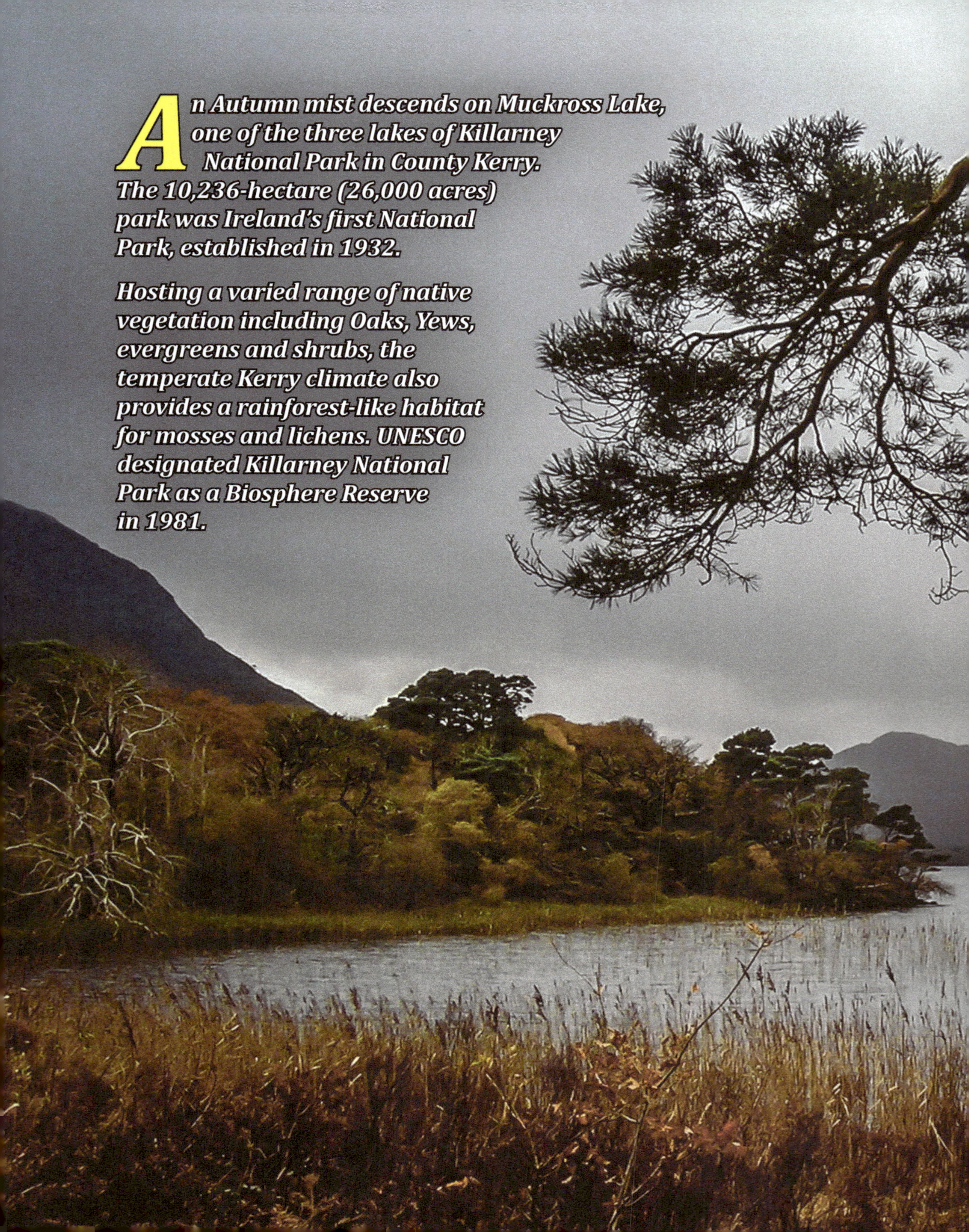

An Autumn mist descends on Muckross Lake, one of the three lakes of Killarney National Park in County Kerry. The 10,236-hectare (26,000 acres) park was Ireland's first National Park, established in 1932.

Hosting a varied range of native vegetation including Oaks, Yews, evergreens and shrubs, the temperate Kerry climate also provides a rainforest-like habitat for mosses and lichens. UNESCO designated Killarney National Park as a Biosphere Reserve in 1981.

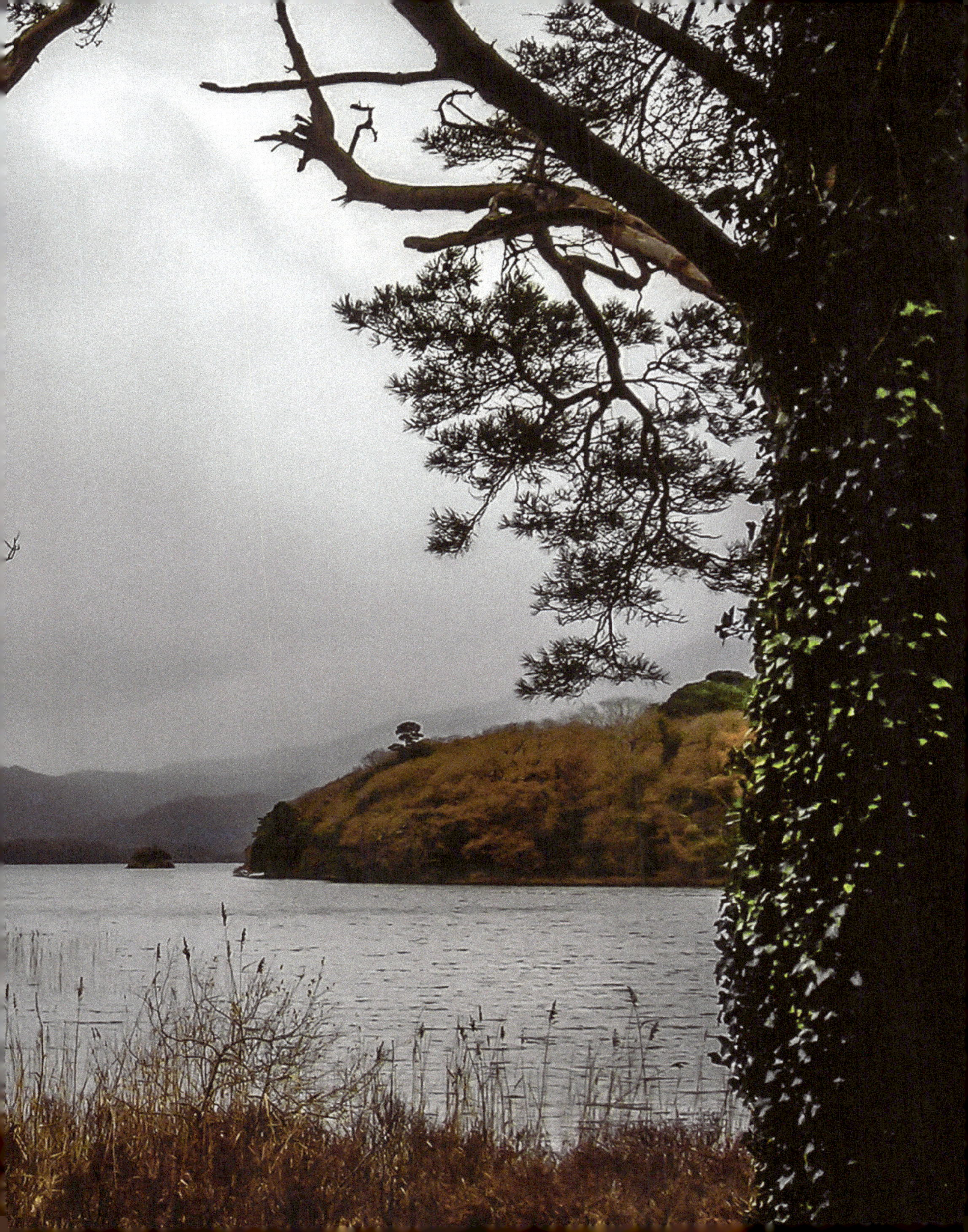

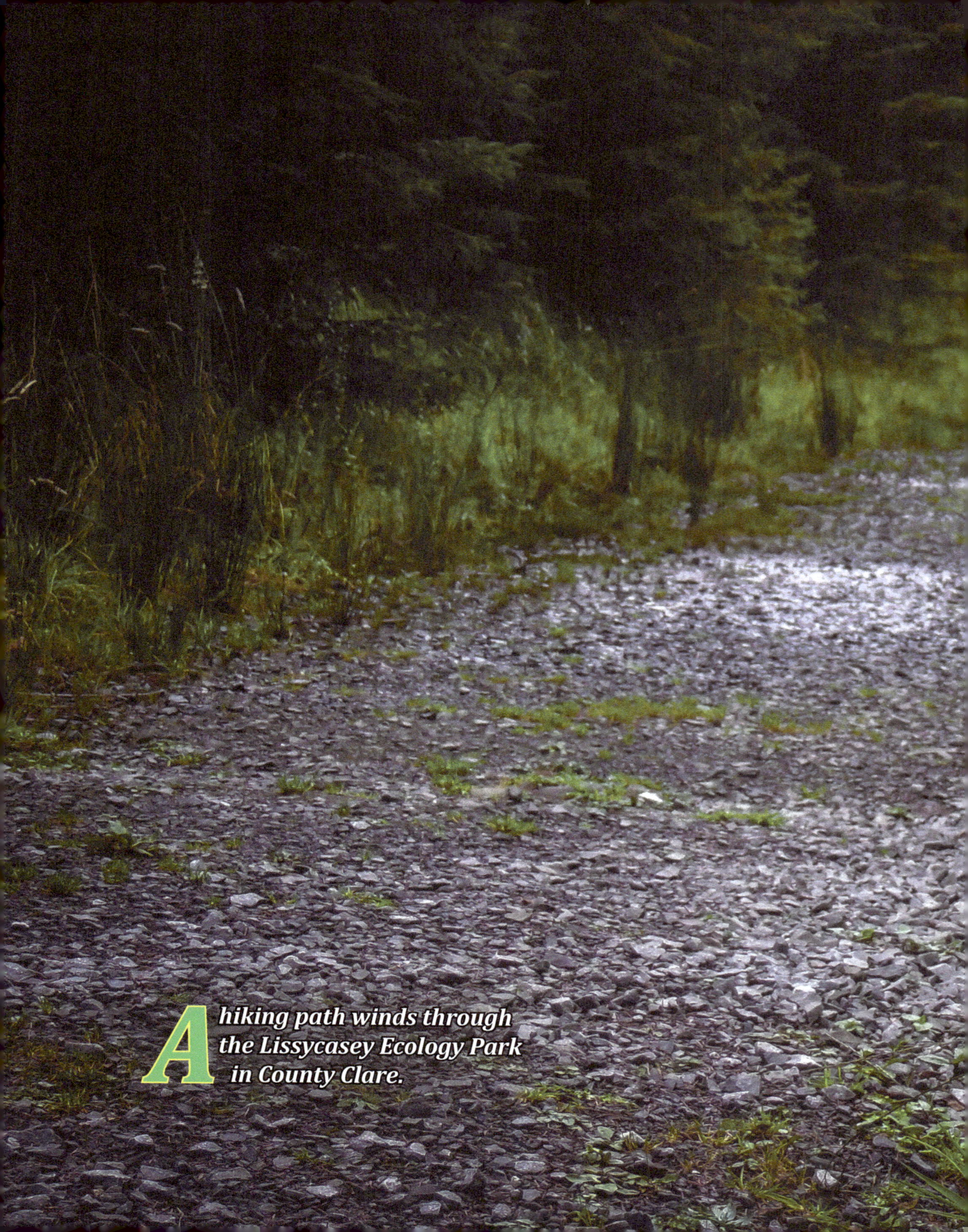
A hiking path winds through
the Lissycasey Ecology Park
in County Clare.

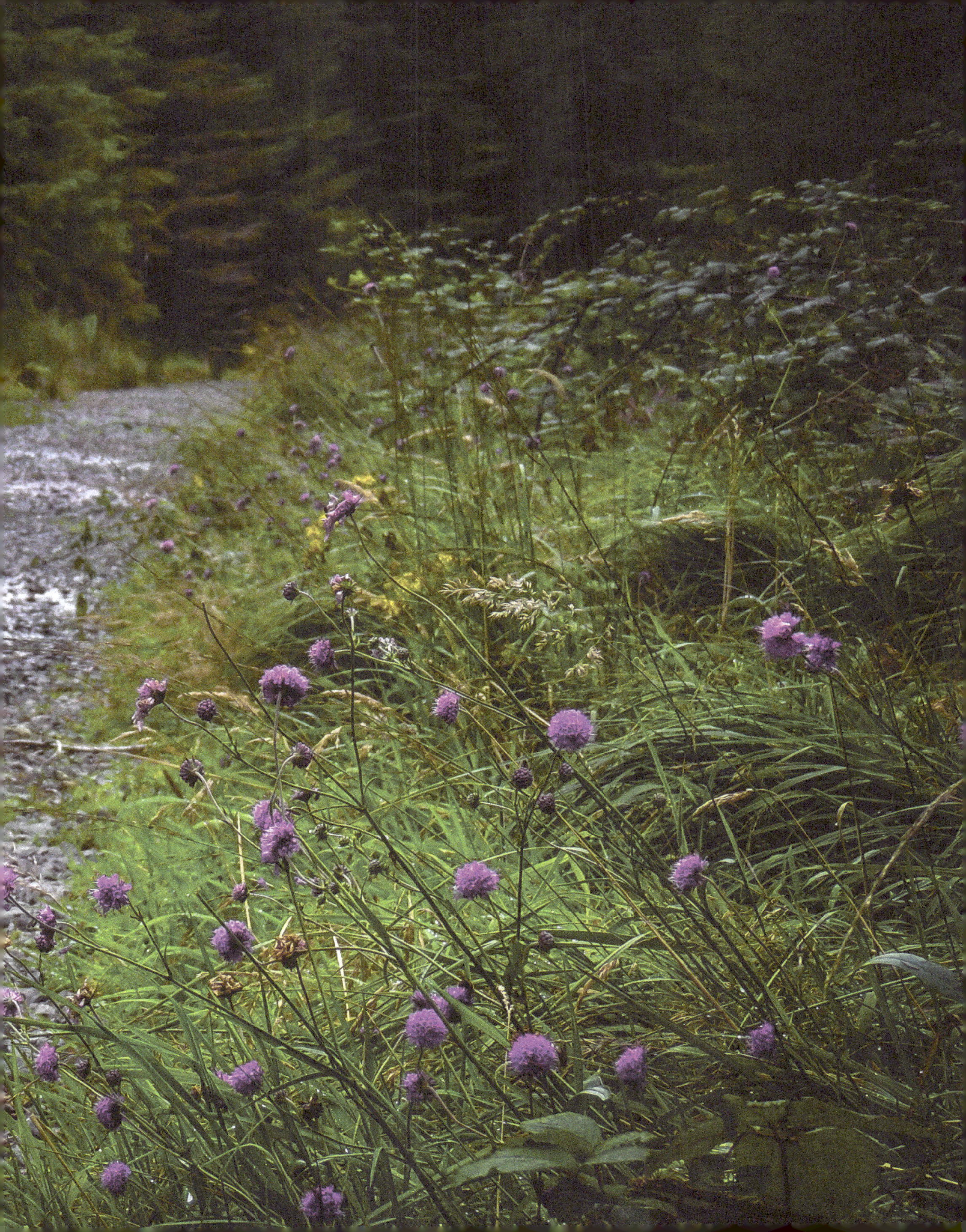

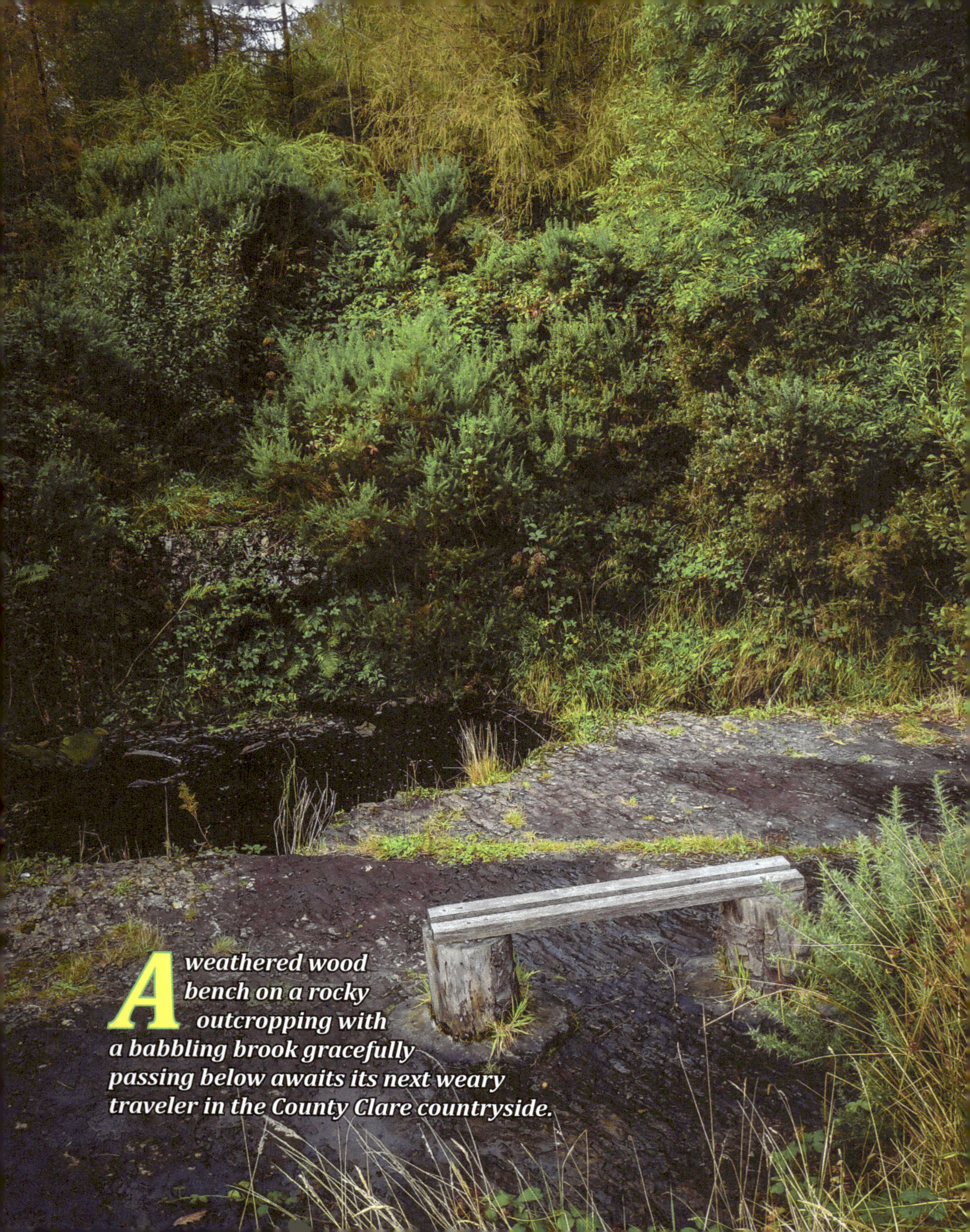
A weathered wood bench on a rocky outcropping with a babbling brook gracefully passing below awaits its next weary traveler in the County Clare countryside.

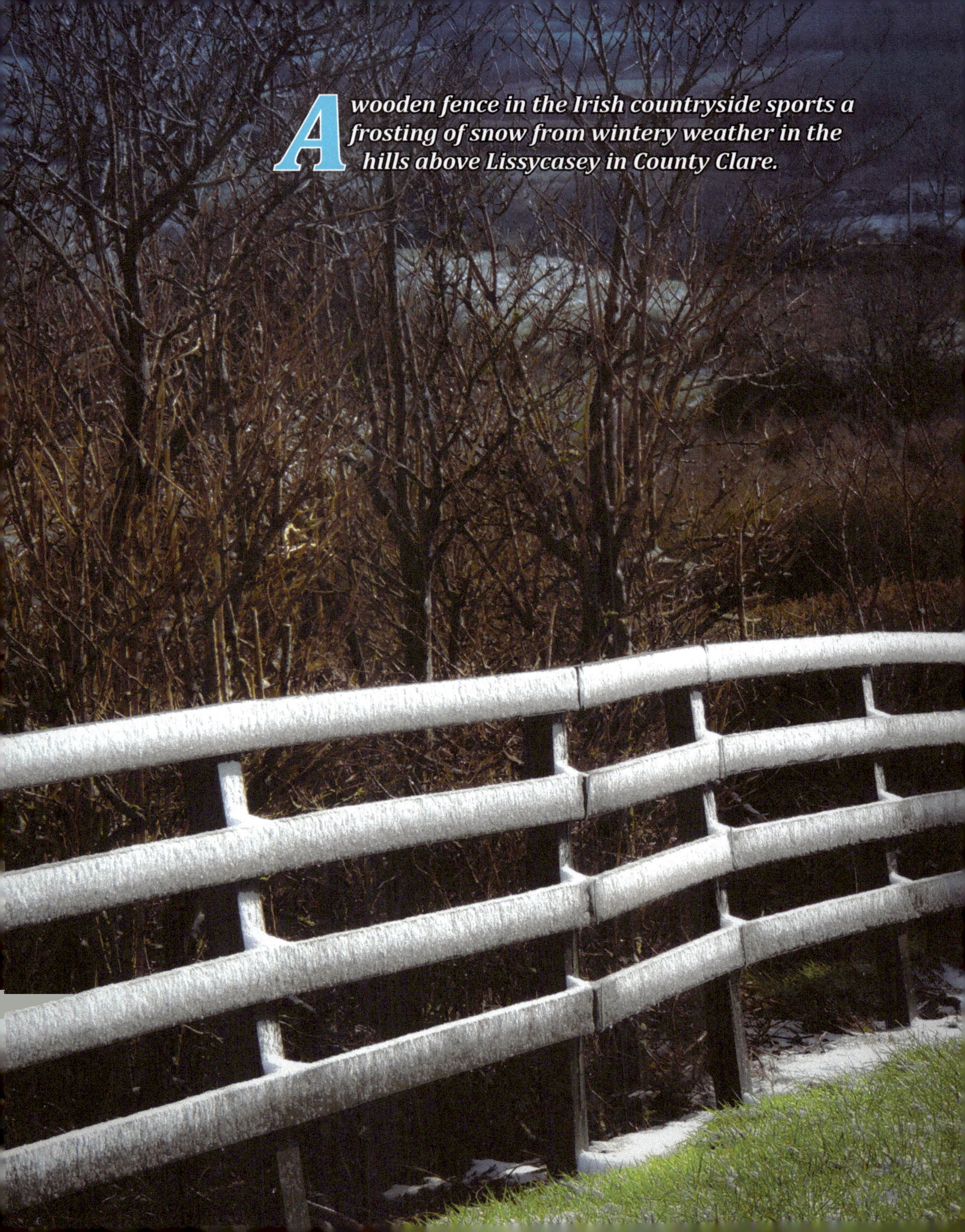

A wooden fence in the Irish countryside sports a frosting of snow from wintery weather in the hills above Lissycasey in County Clare.

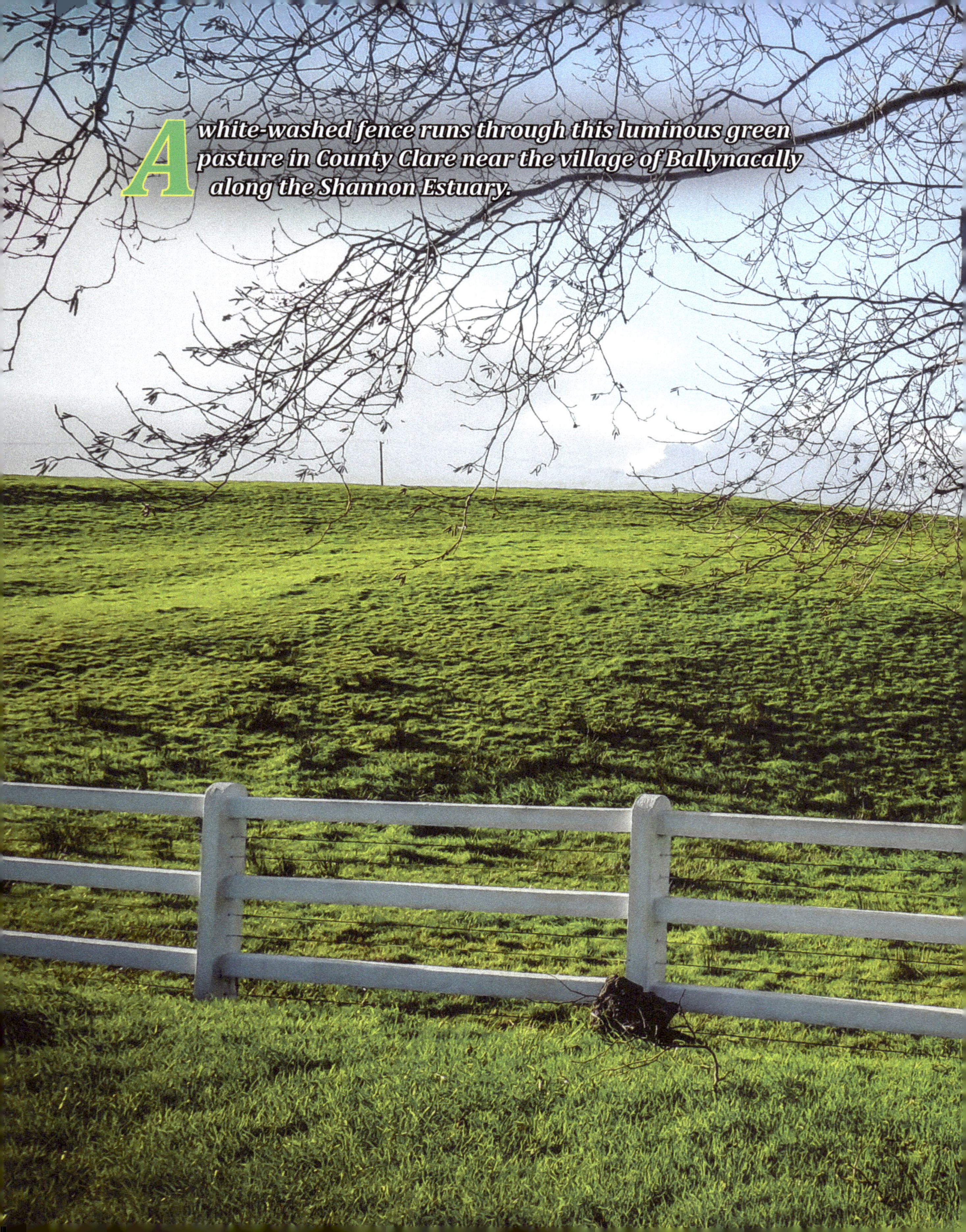

A white-washed fence runs through this luminous green pasture in County Clare near the village of Ballynacally along the Shannon Estuary.

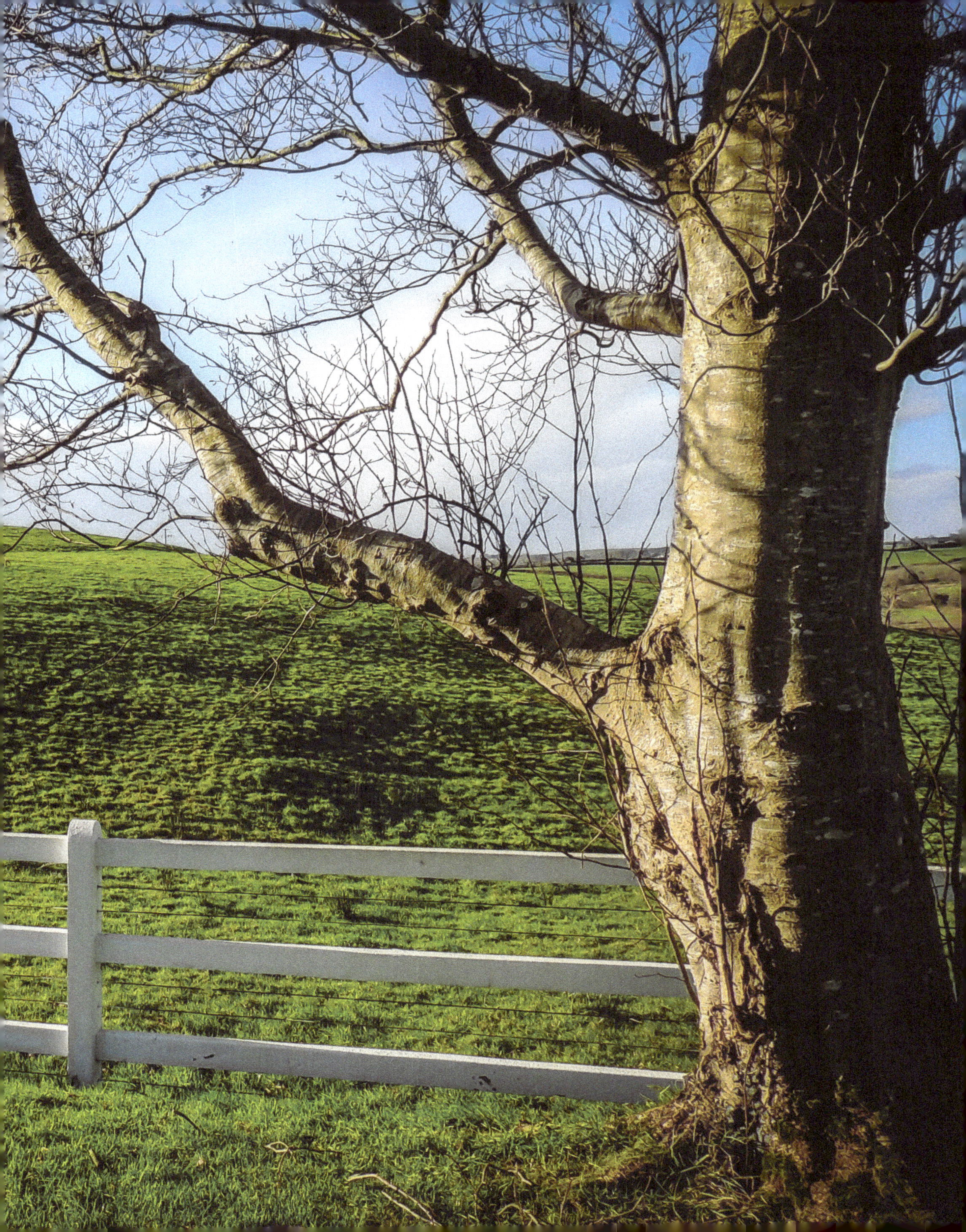

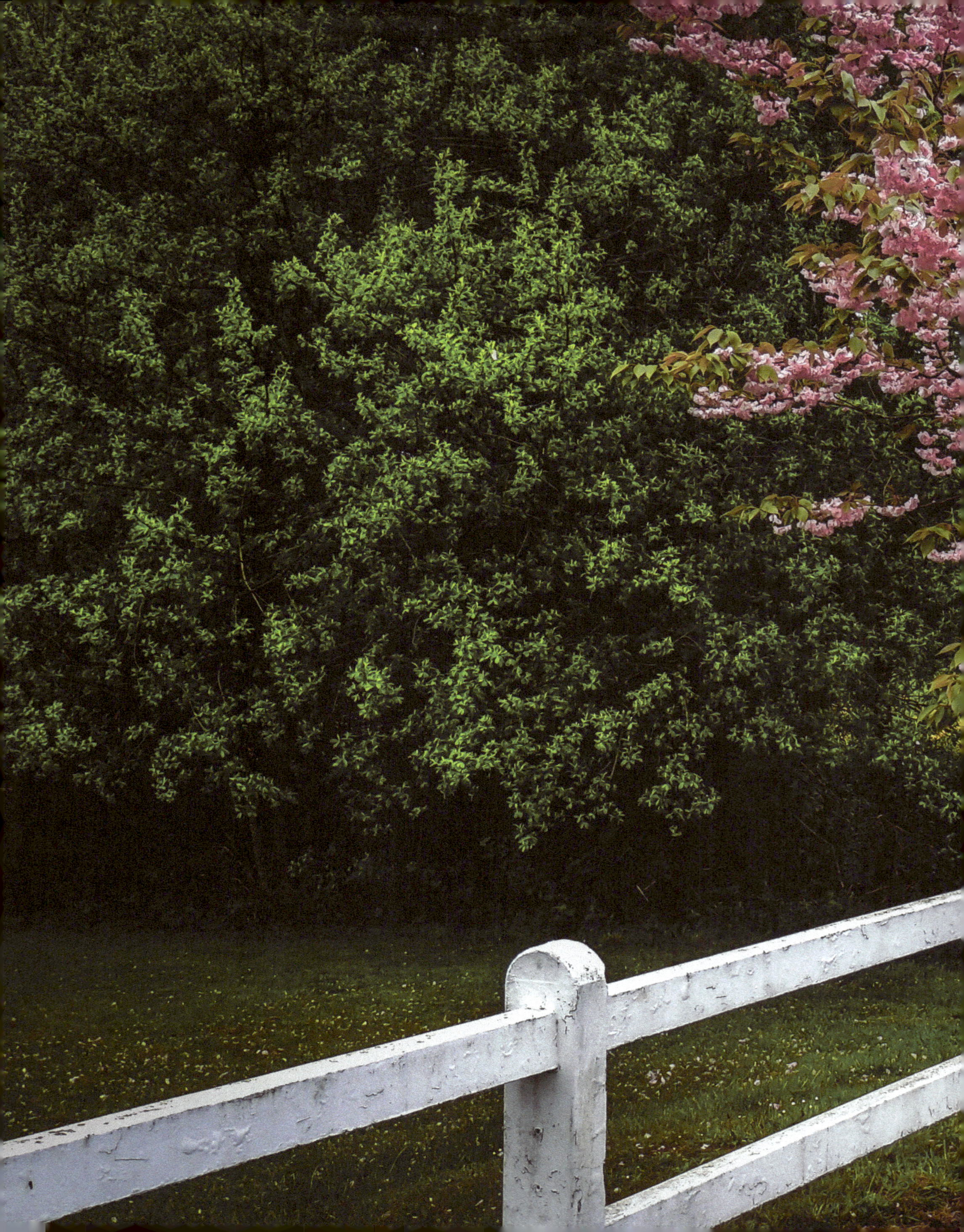

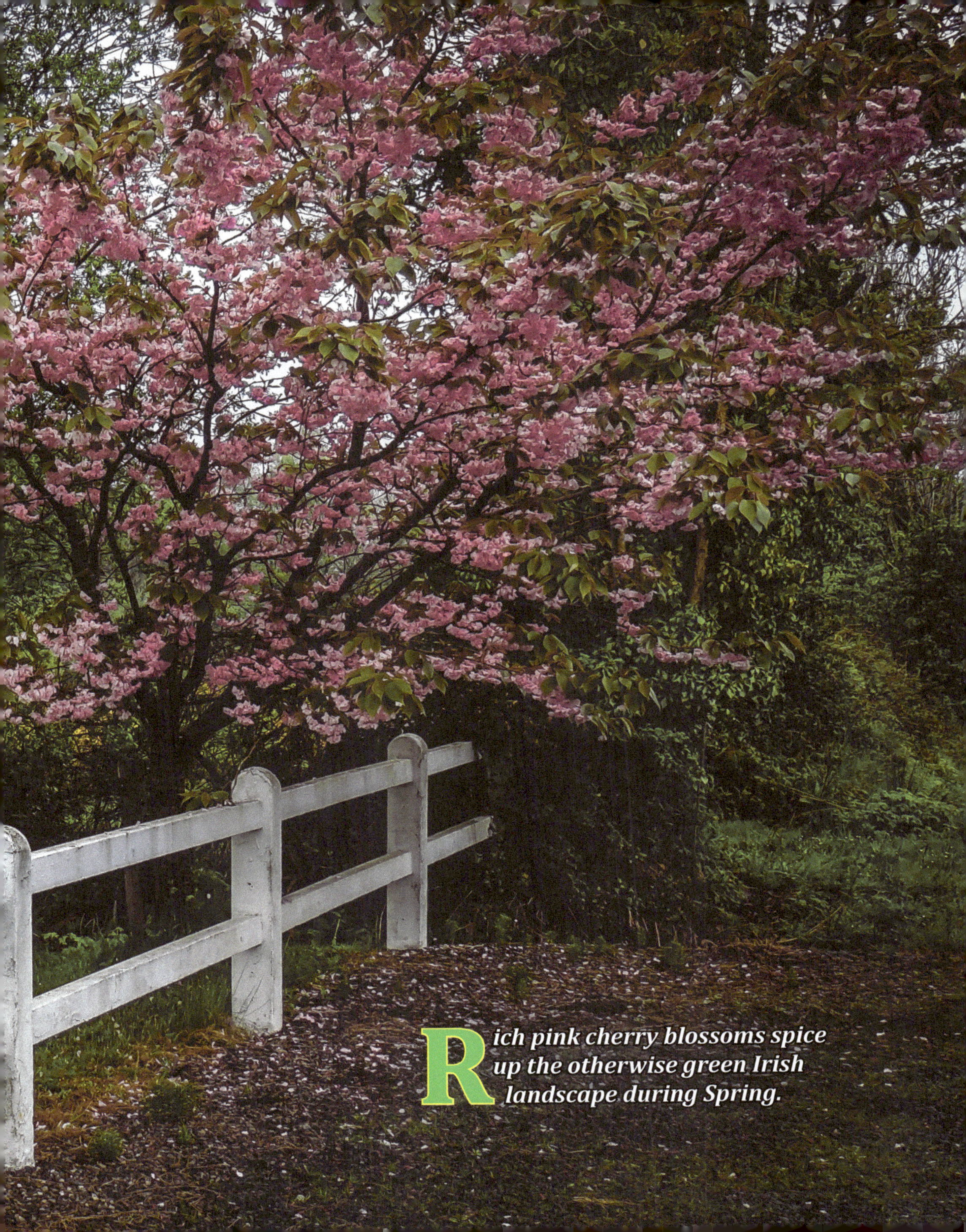

Rich pink cherry blossoms spice up the otherwise green Irish landscape during Spring.

The "Lions of March" mustered forces over Ireland's Shannon River Valley in County Clare, with hail storms, high winds, thunder and lightening. Many homes were without power as this pre-Spring 2015 storm swept through with winds reaching 100 kph in some areas.

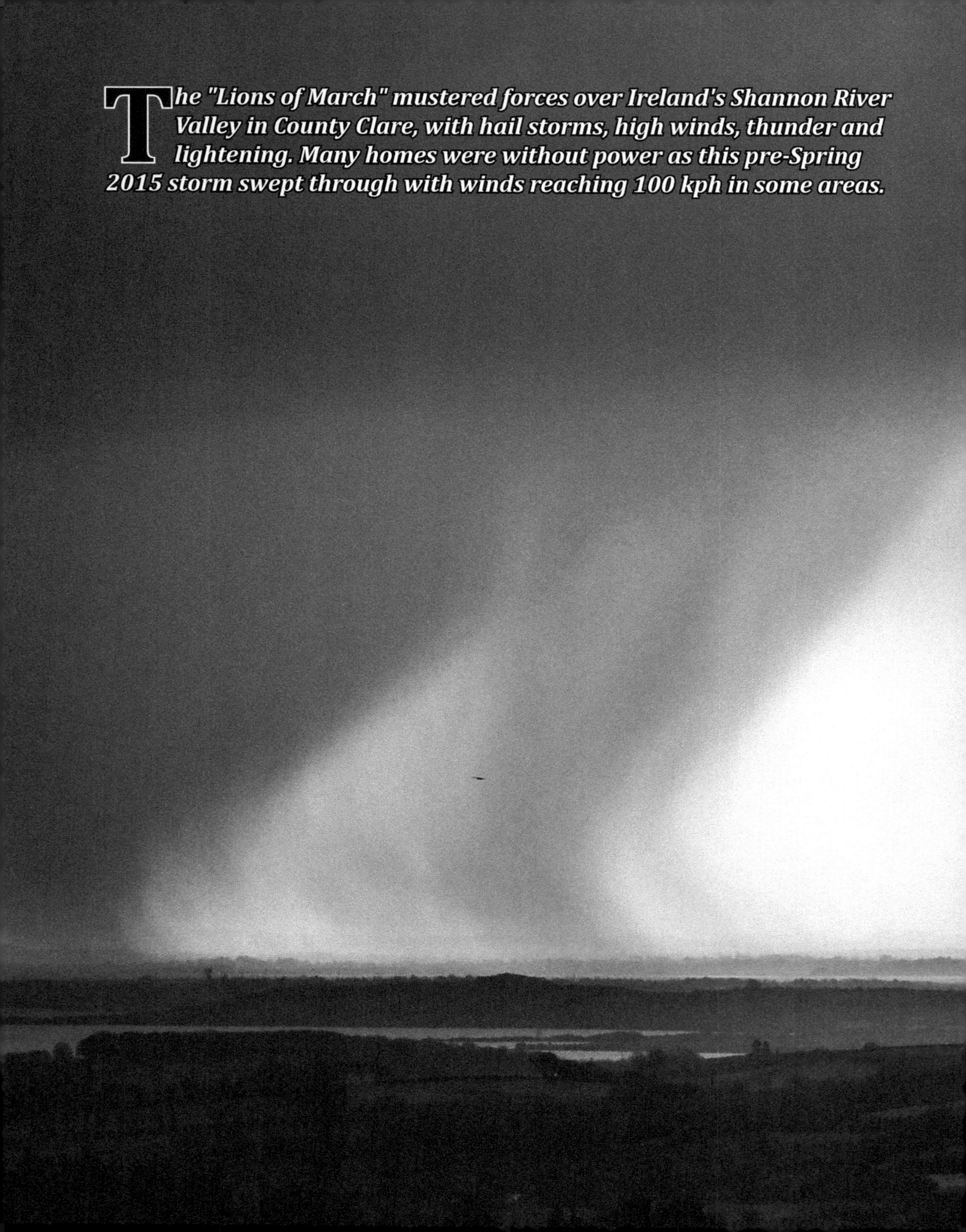

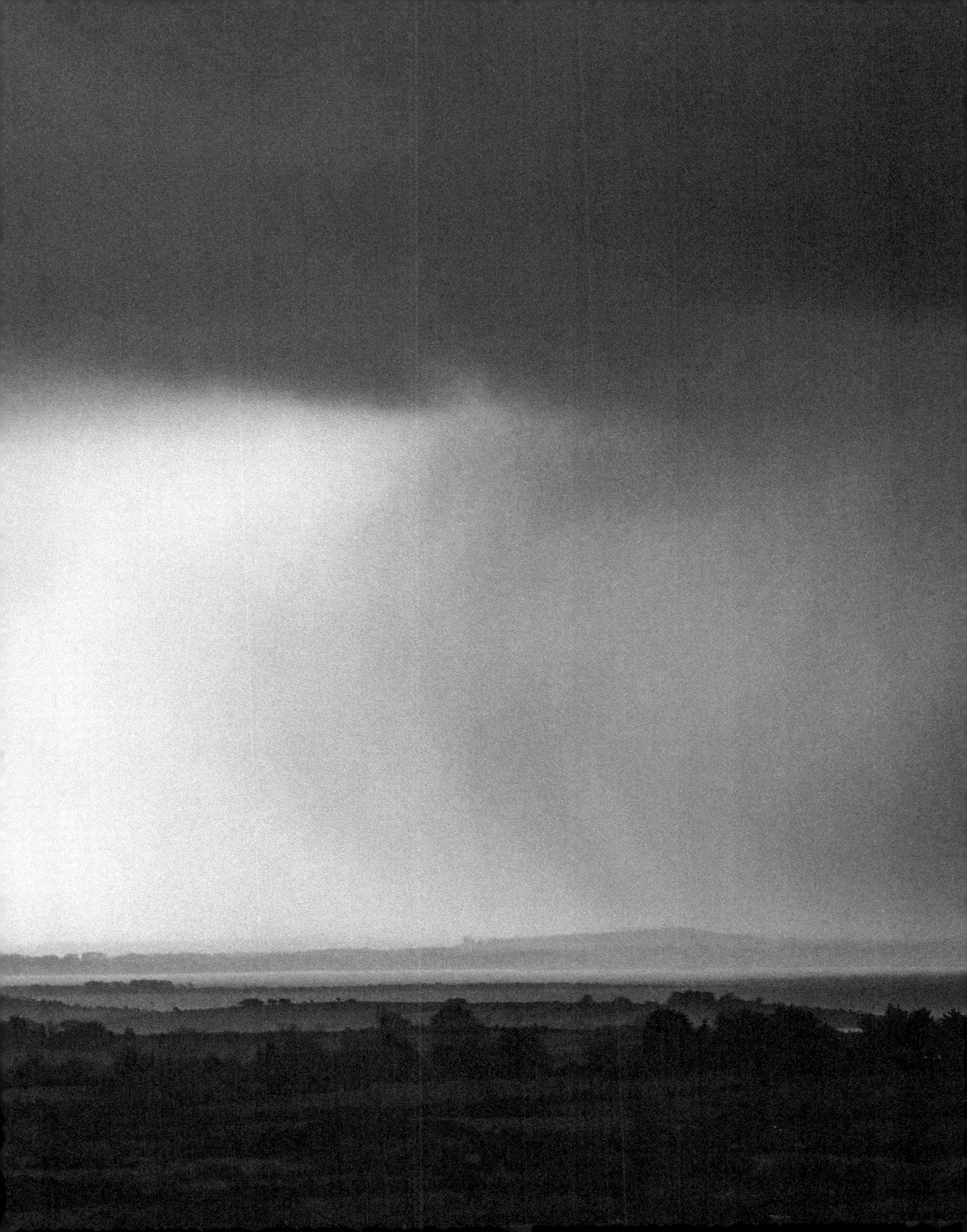

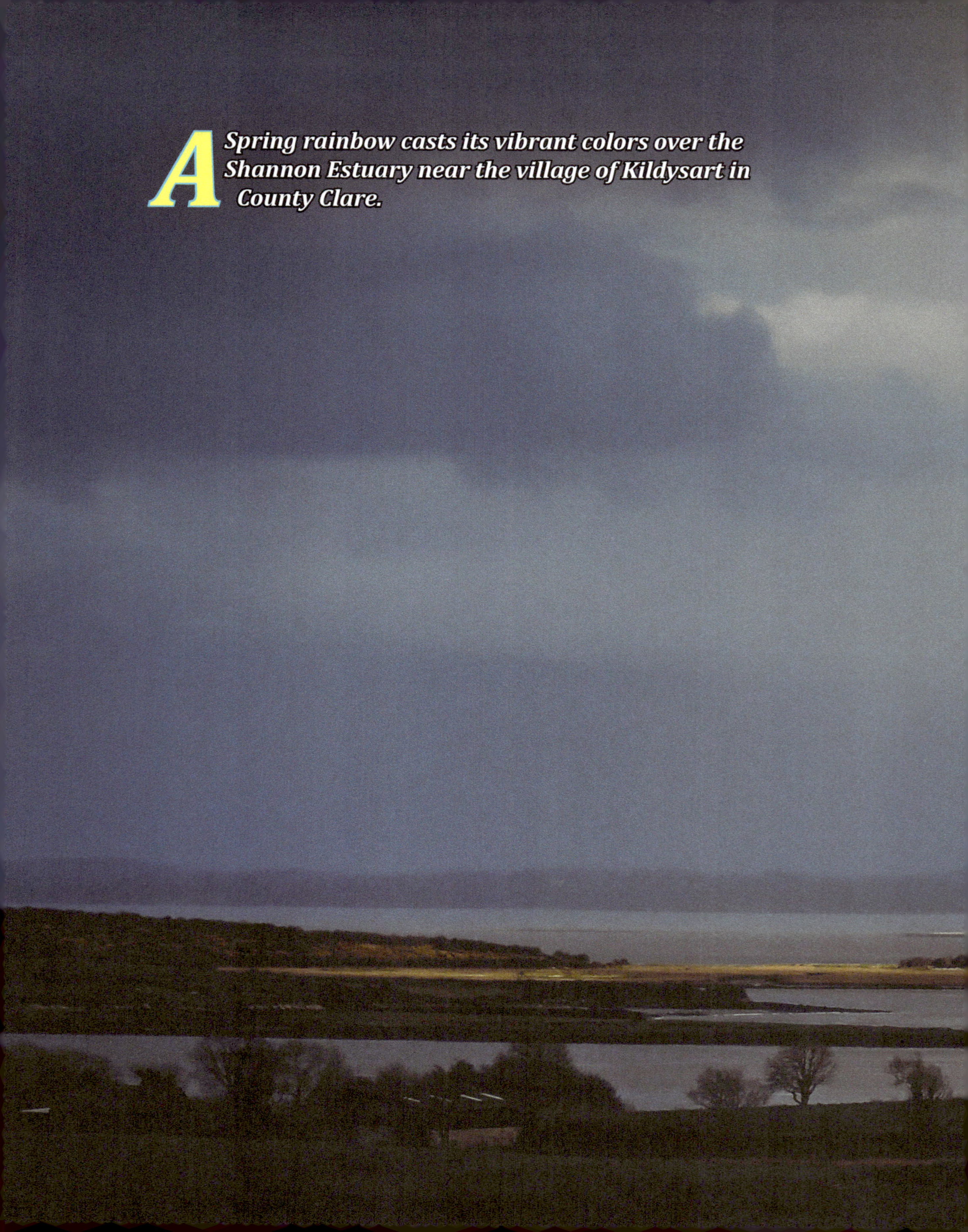

A Spring rainbow casts its vibrant colors over the Shannon Estuary near the village of Kildysart in County Clare.

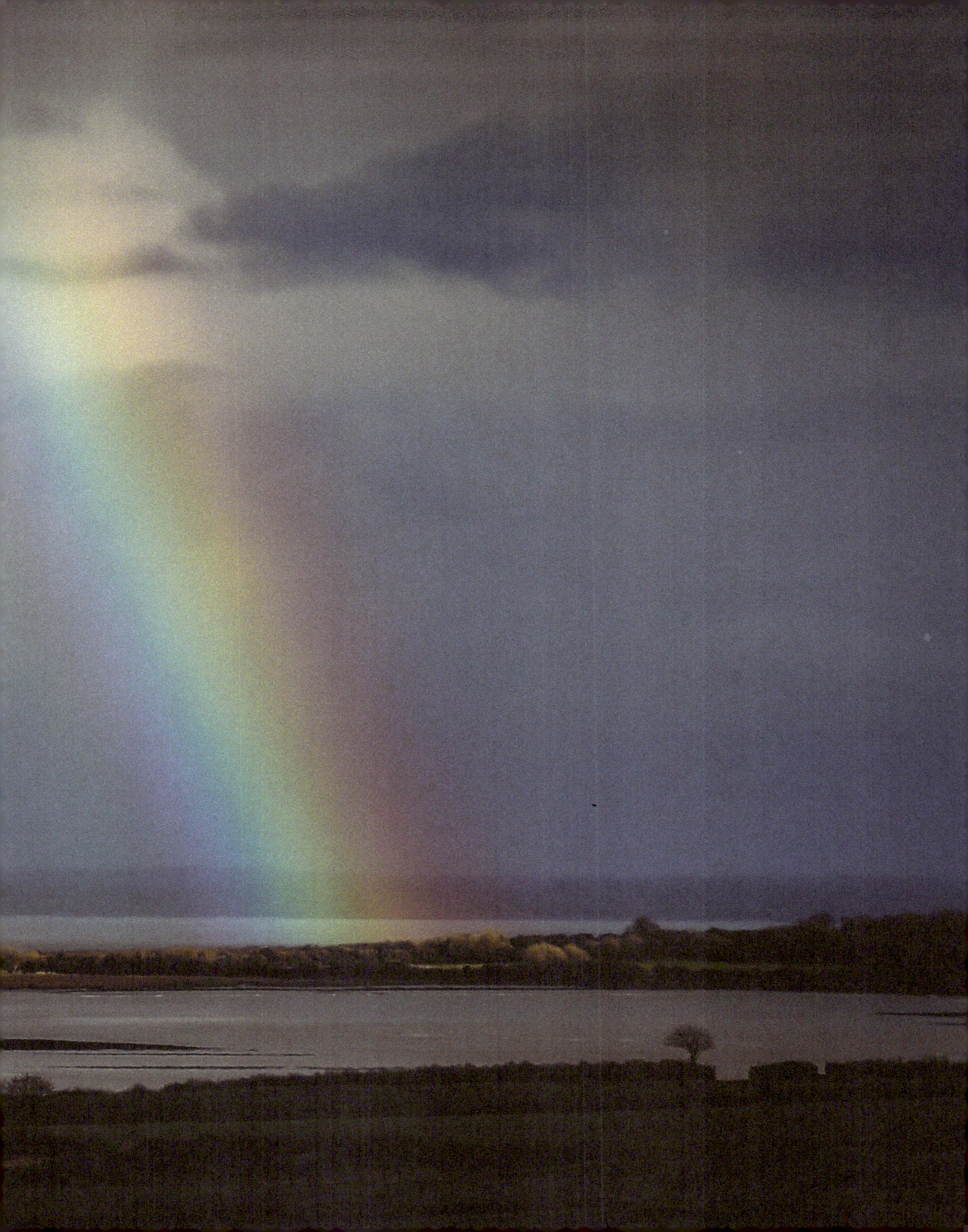

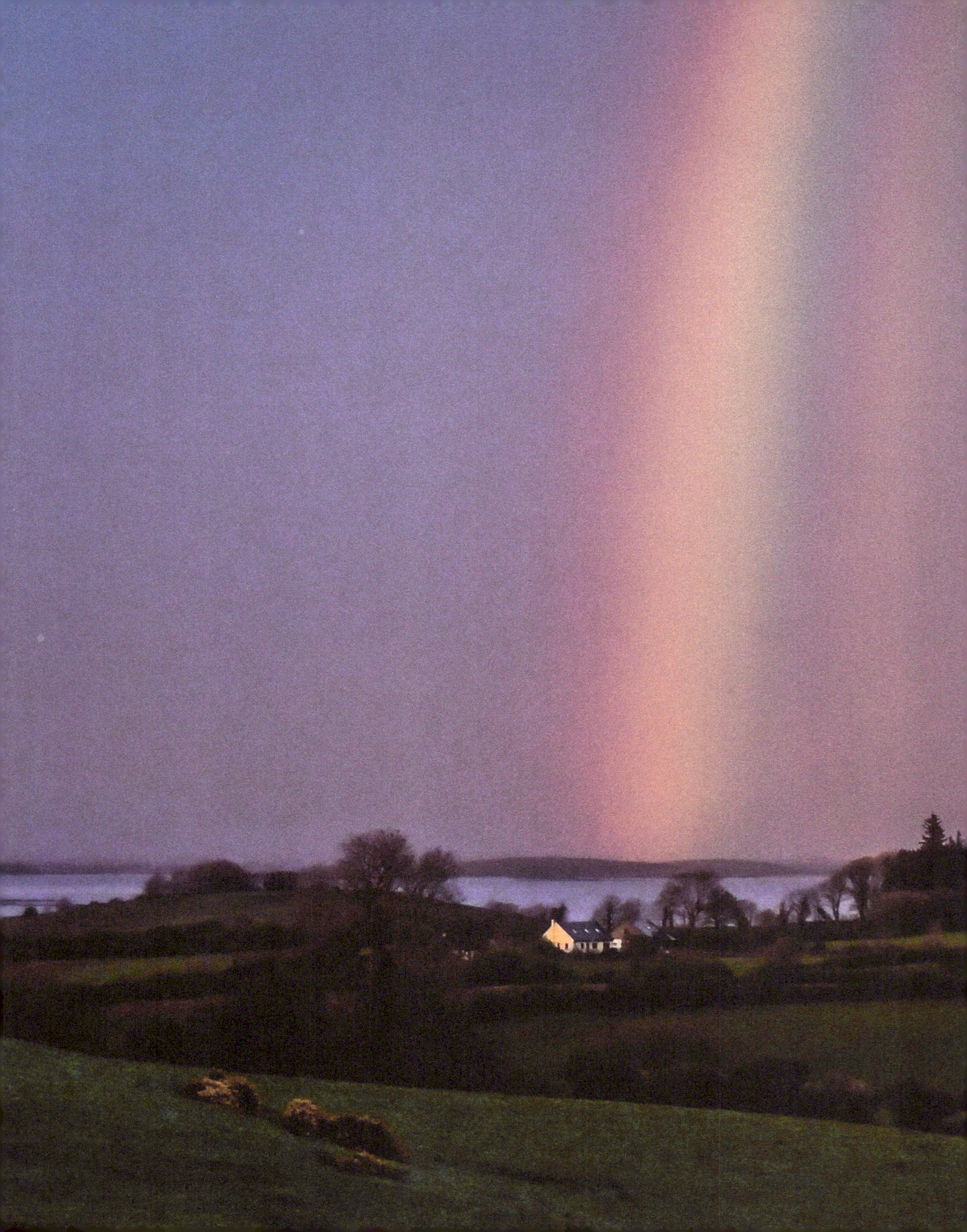

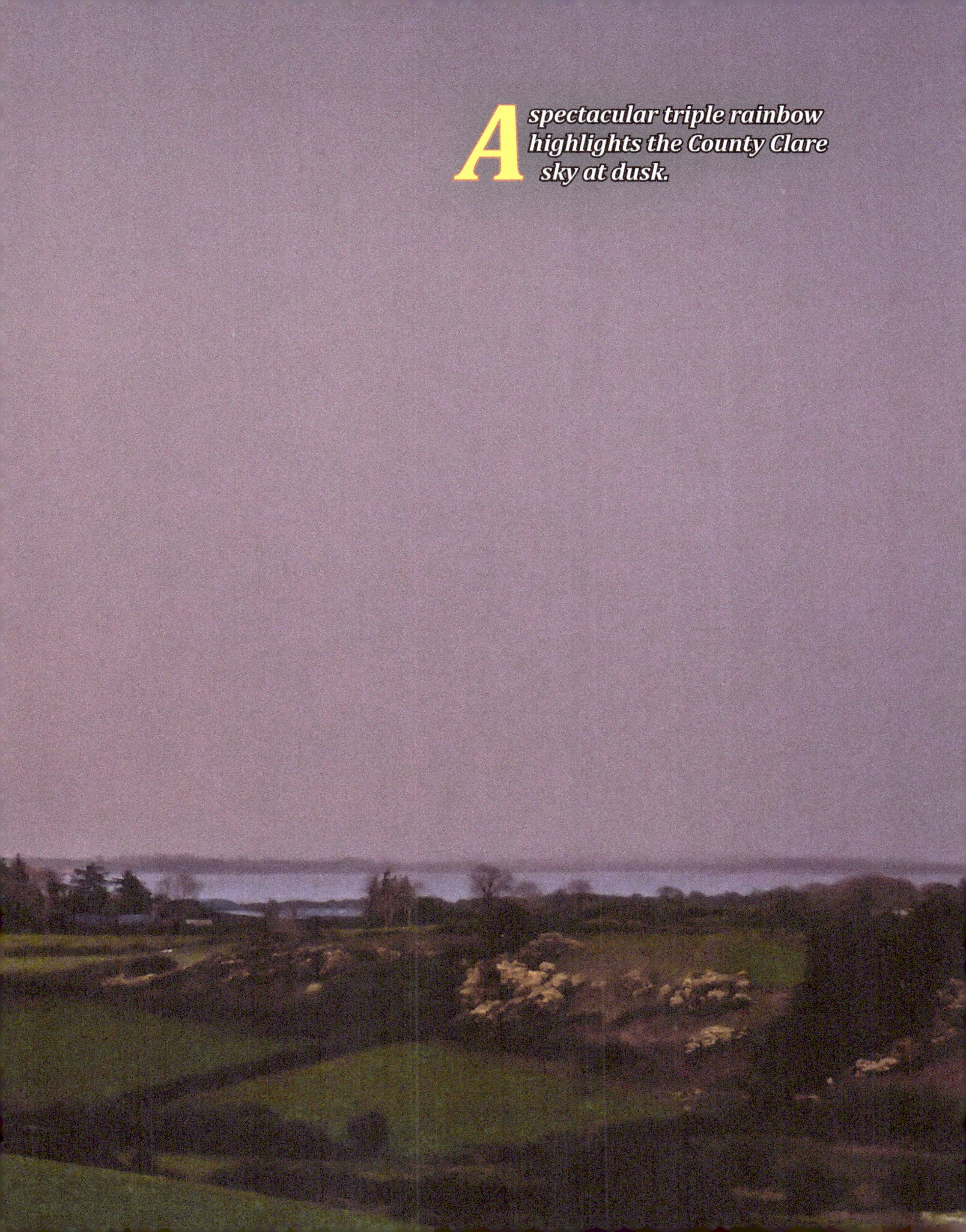

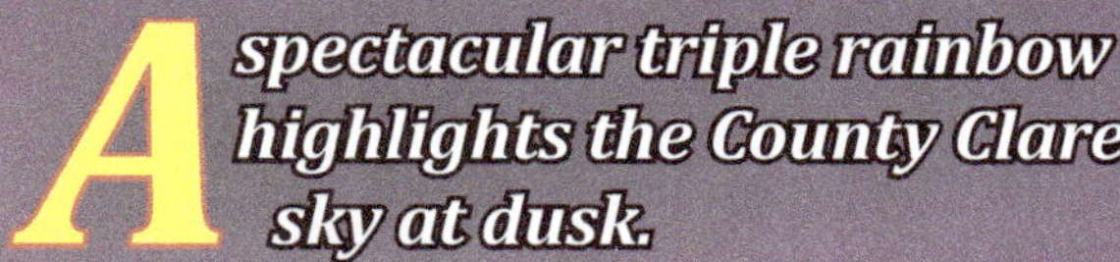

A spectacular triple rainbow highlights the County Clare sky at dusk.

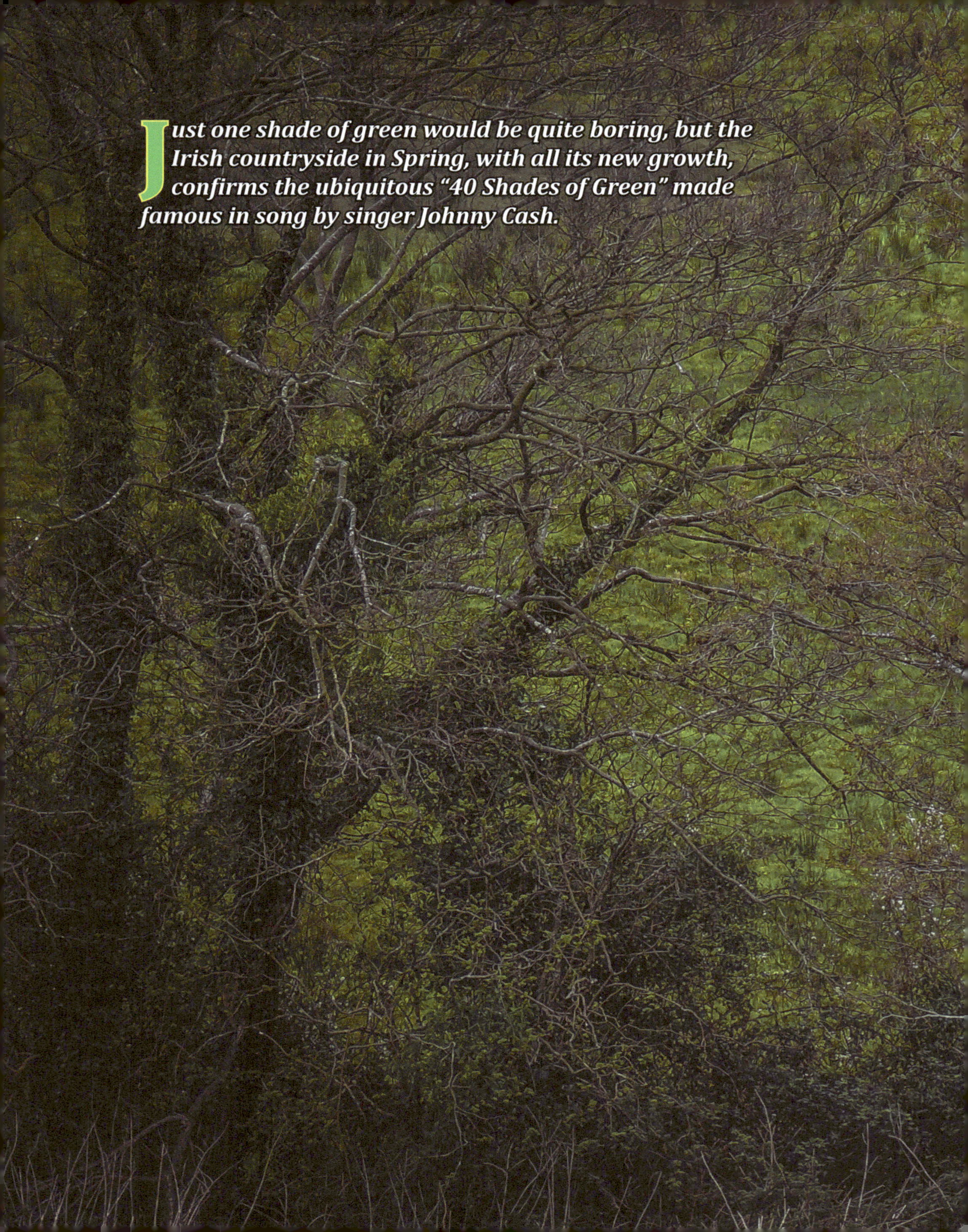
Just one shade of green would be quite boring, but the Irish countryside in Spring, with all its new growth, confirms the ubiquitous "40 Shades of Green" made famous in song by singer Johnny Cash.

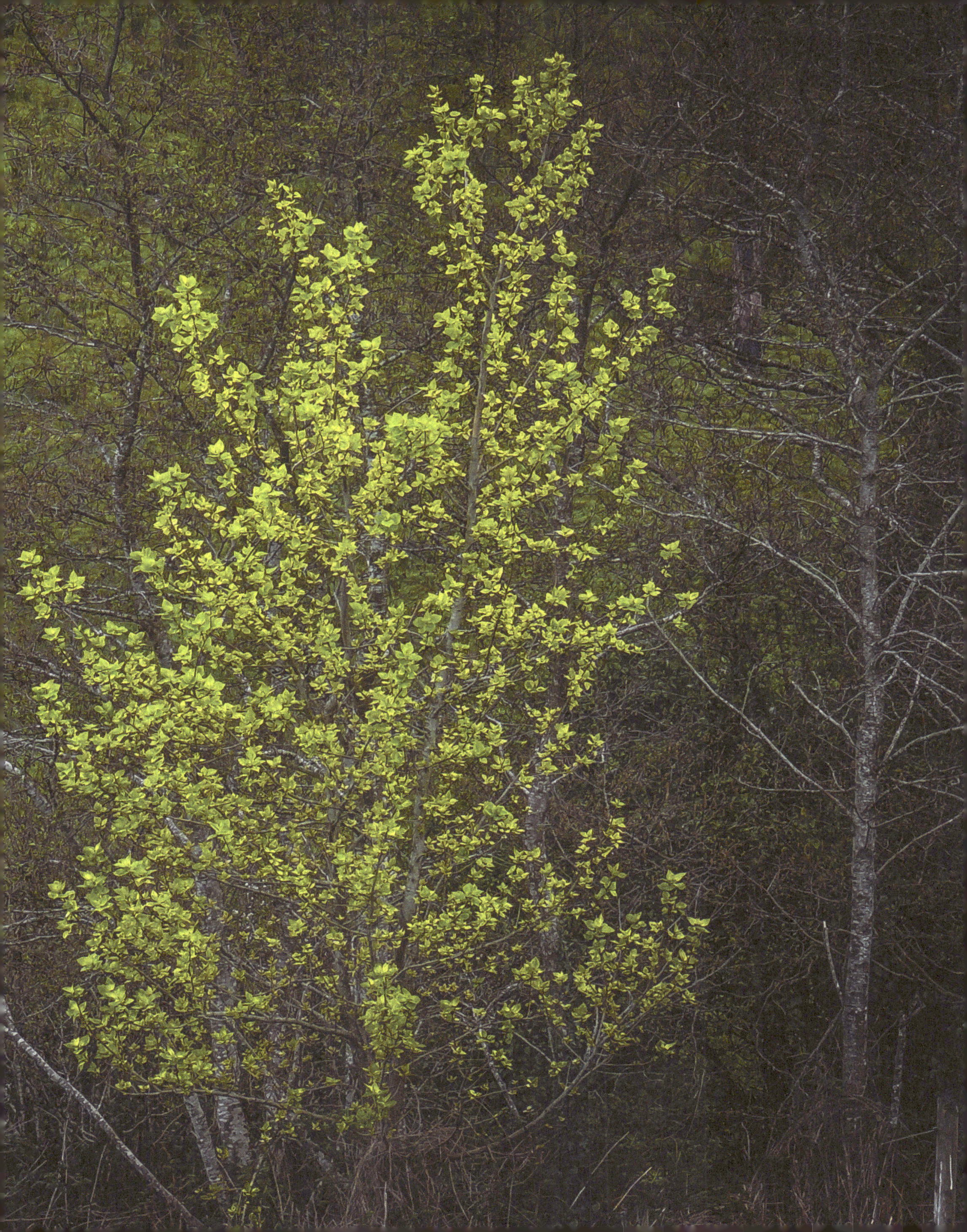

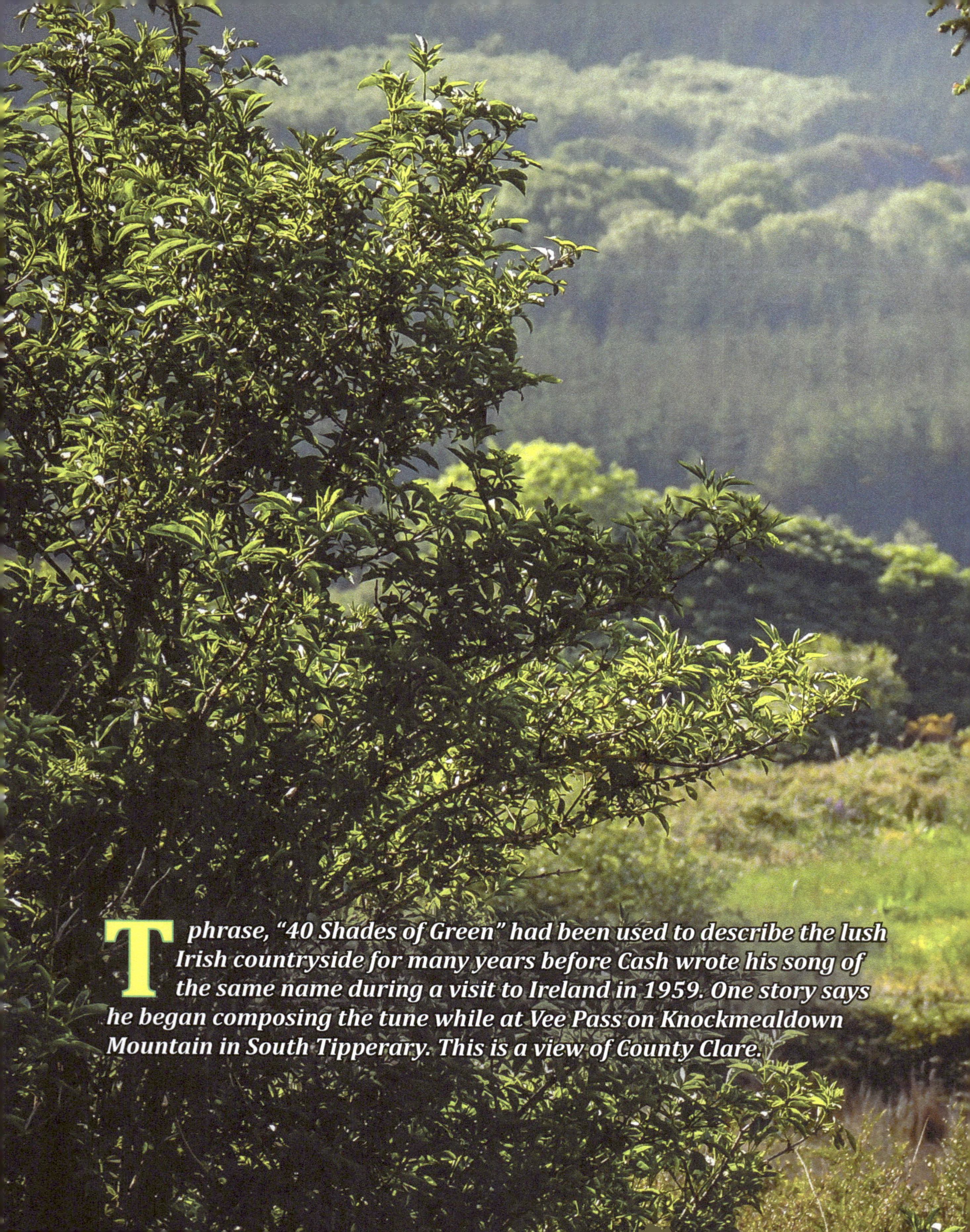

The phrase, "40 Shades of Green" had been used to describe the lush Irish countryside for many years before Cash wrote his song of the same name during a visit to Ireland in 1959. One story says he began composing the tune while at Vee Pass on Knockmealdown Mountain in South Tipperary. This is a view of County Clare.

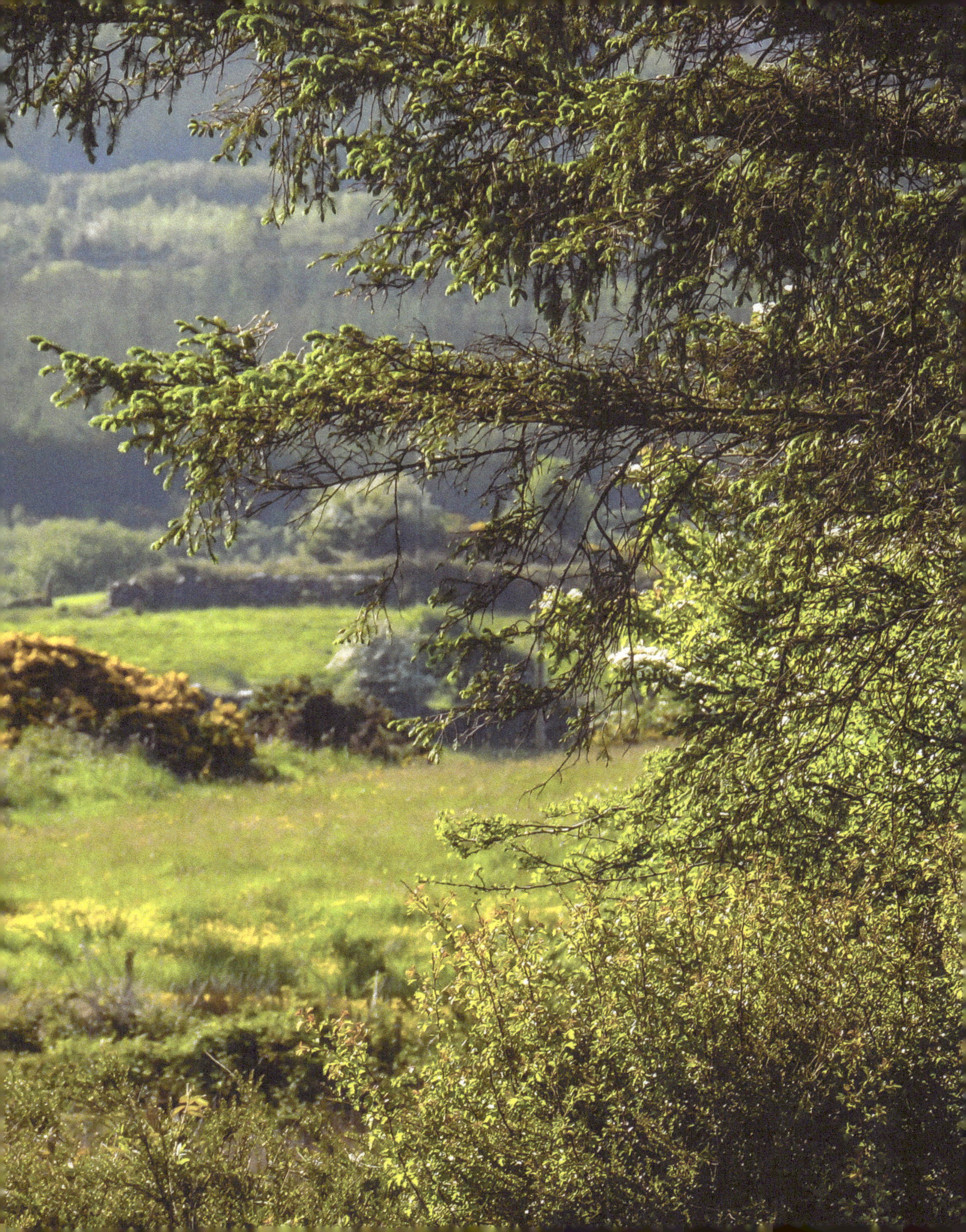

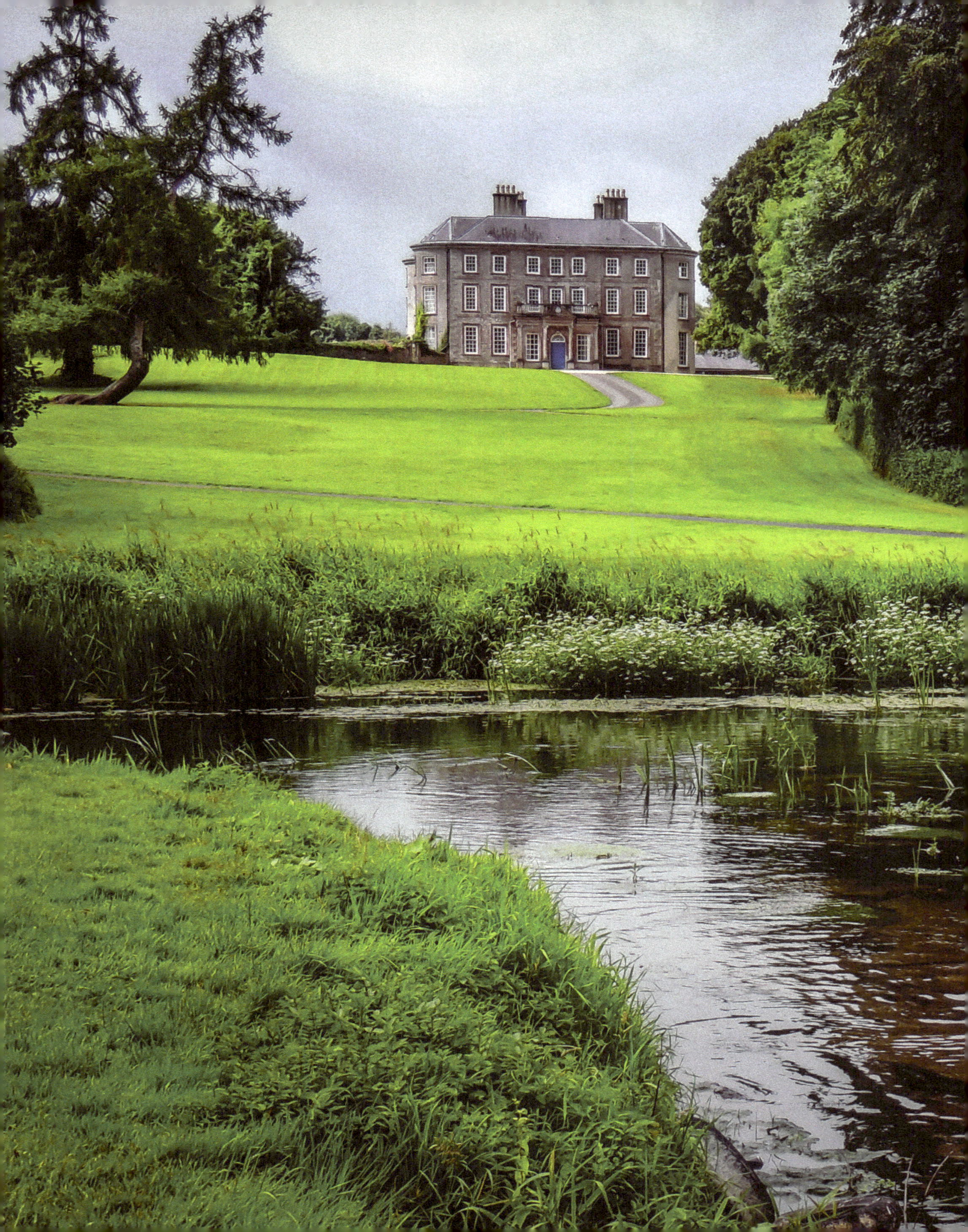

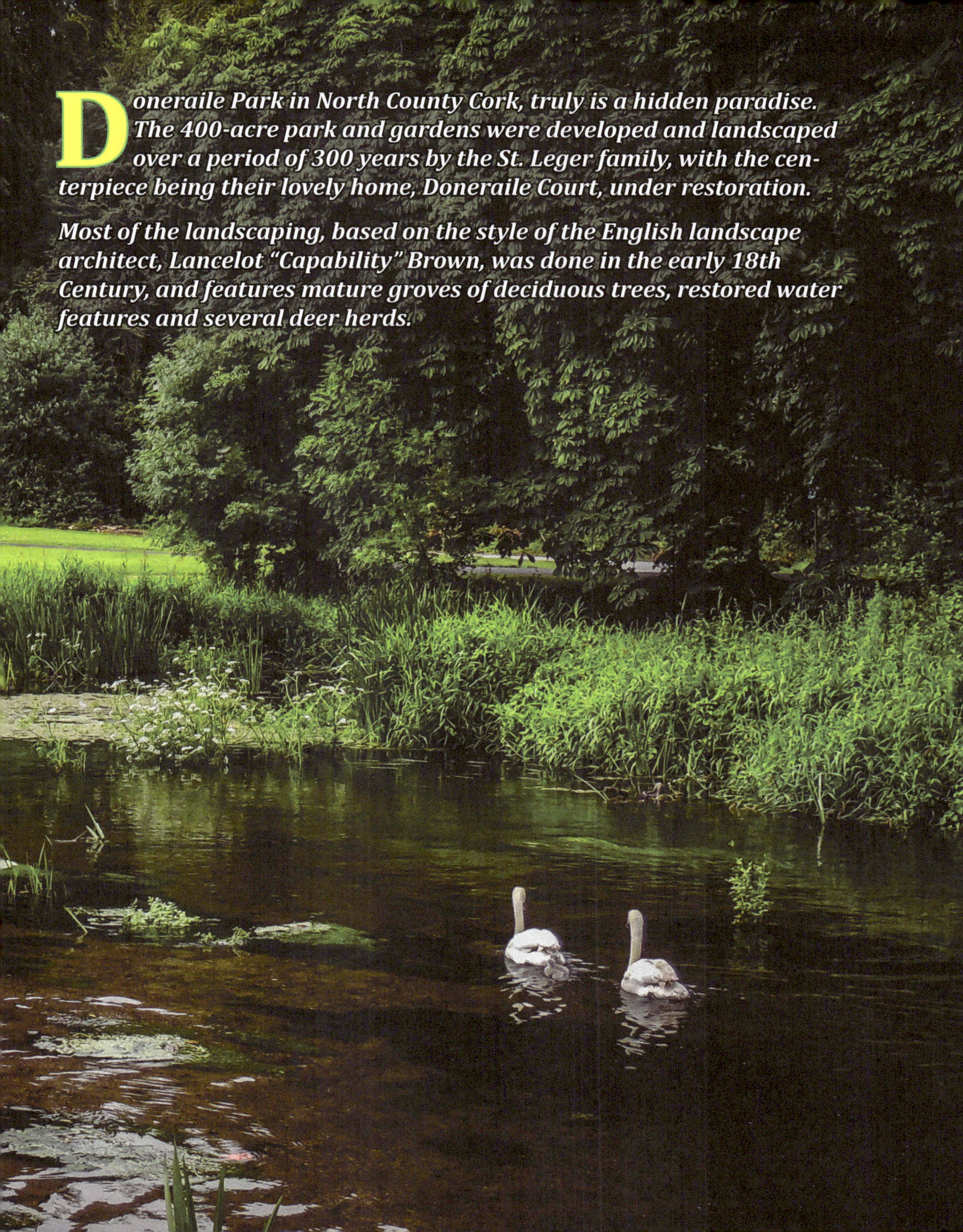

Doneraile Park in North County Cork, truly is a hidden paradise. The 400-acre park and gardens were developed and landscaped over a period of 300 years by the St. Leger family, with the centerpiece being their lovely home, Doneraile Court, under restoration.

Most of the landscaping, based on the style of the English landscape architect, Lancelot "Capability" Brown, was done in the early 18th Century, and features mature groves of deciduous trees, restored water features and several deer herds.

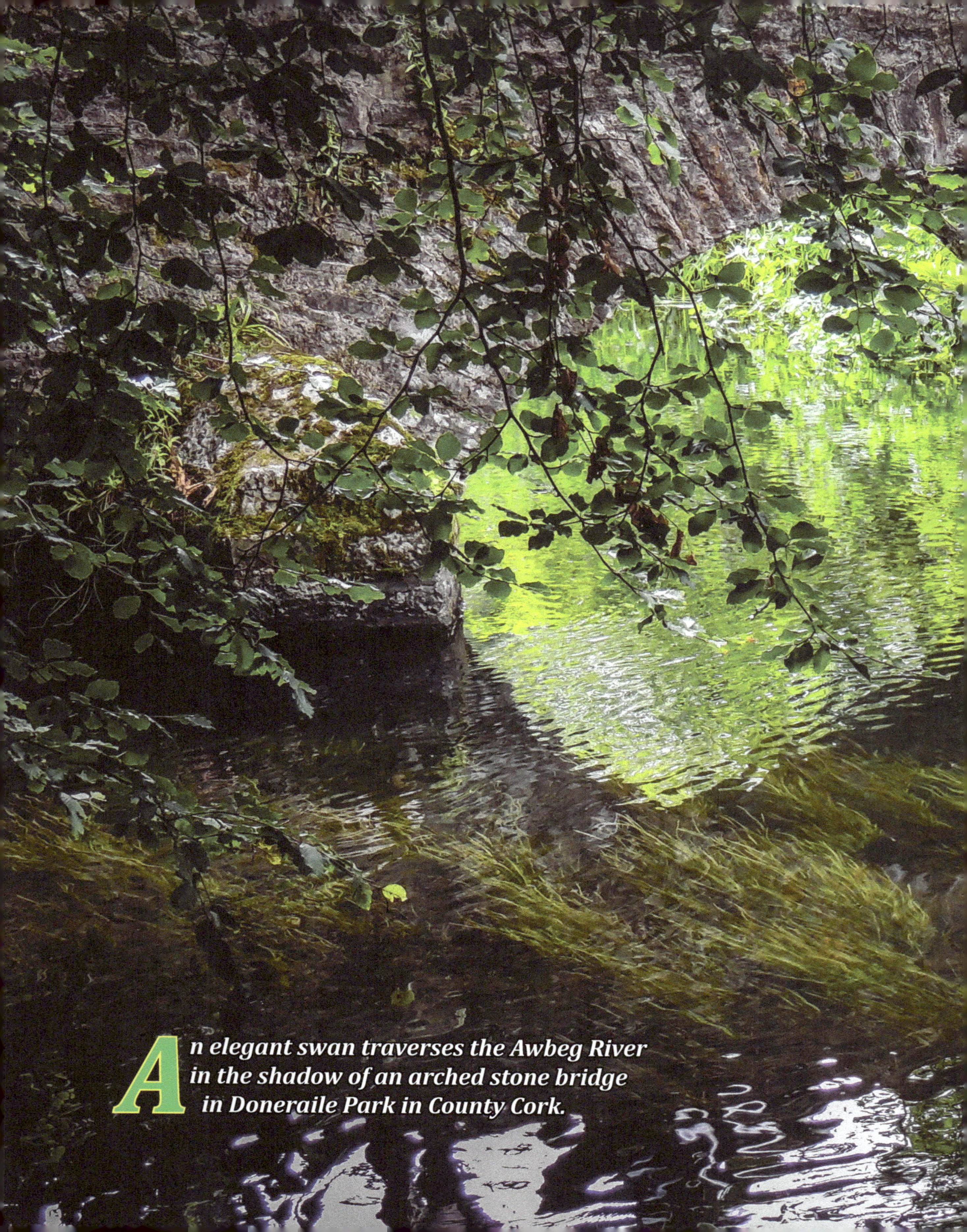

An elegant swan traverses the Awbeg River in the shadow of an arched stone bridge in Doneraile Park in County Cork.

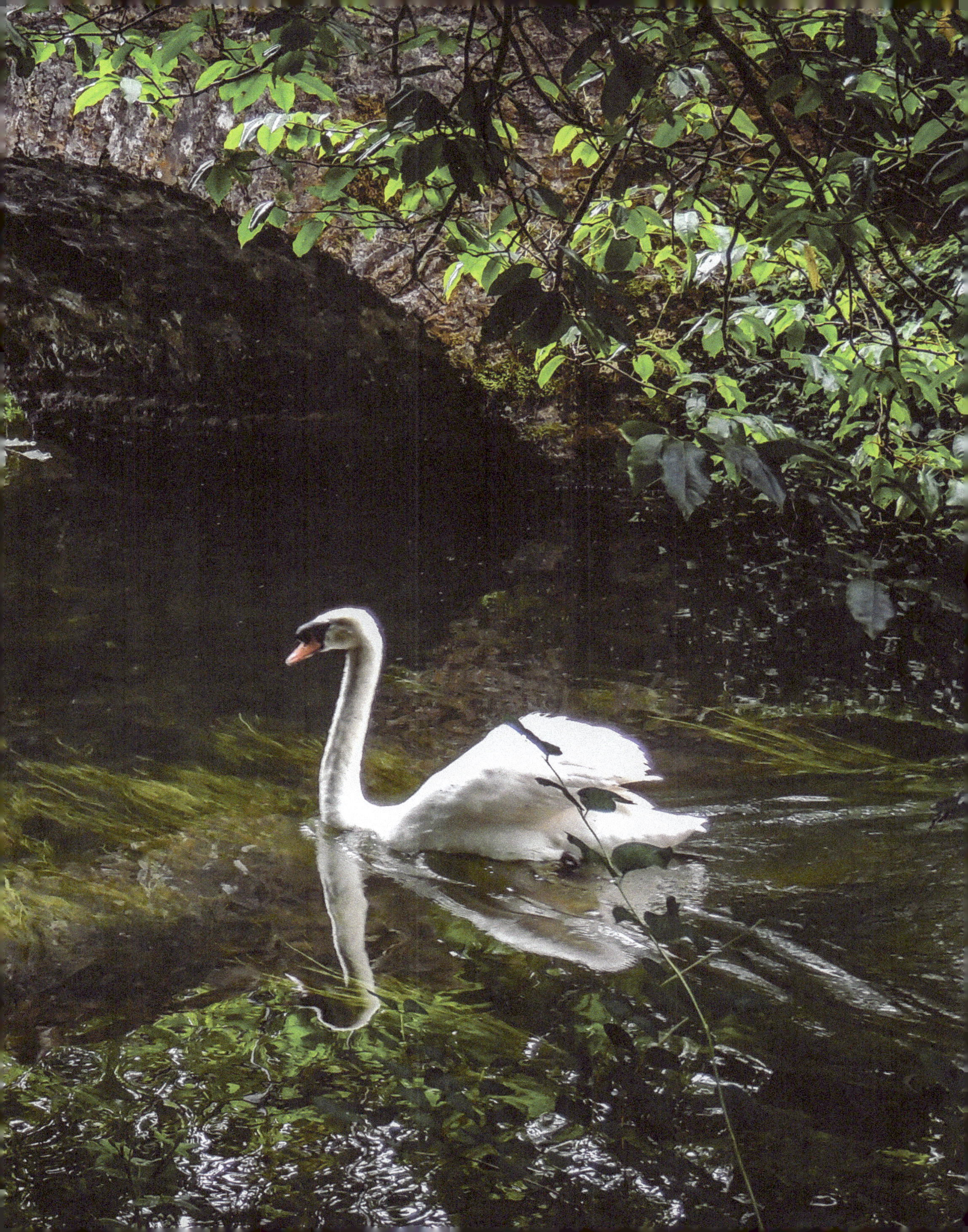

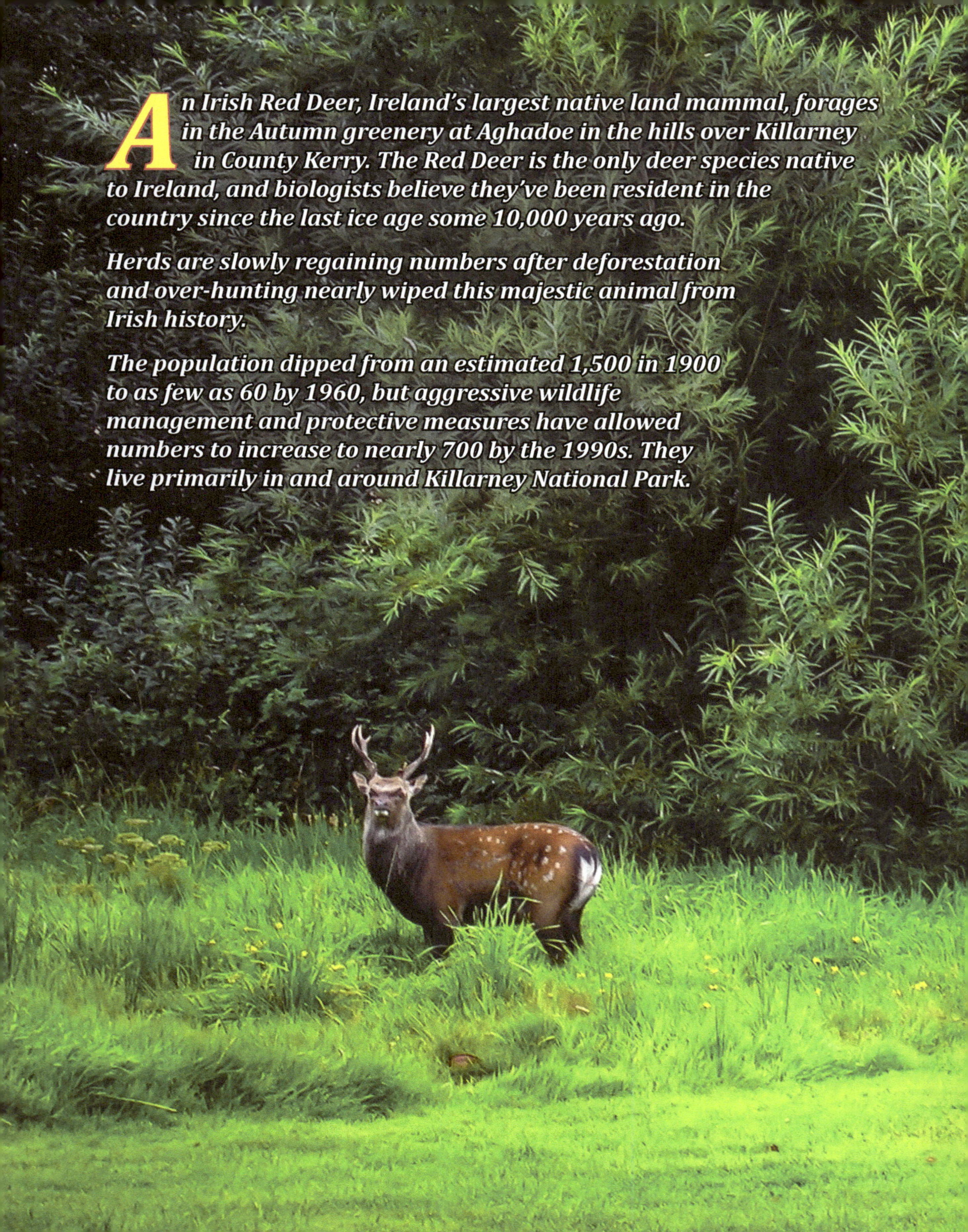
An Irish Red Deer, Ireland's largest native land mammal, forages in the Autumn greenery at Aghadoe in the hills over Killarney in County Kerry. The Red Deer is the only deer species native to Ireland, and biologists believe they've been resident in the country since the last ice age some 10,000 years ago.

Herds are slowly regaining numbers after deforestation and over-hunting nearly wiped this majestic animal from Irish history.

The population dipped from an estimated 1,500 in 1900 to as few as 60 by 1960, but aggressive wildlife management and protective measures have allowed numbers to increase to nearly 700 by the 1990s. They live primarily in and around Killarney National Park.

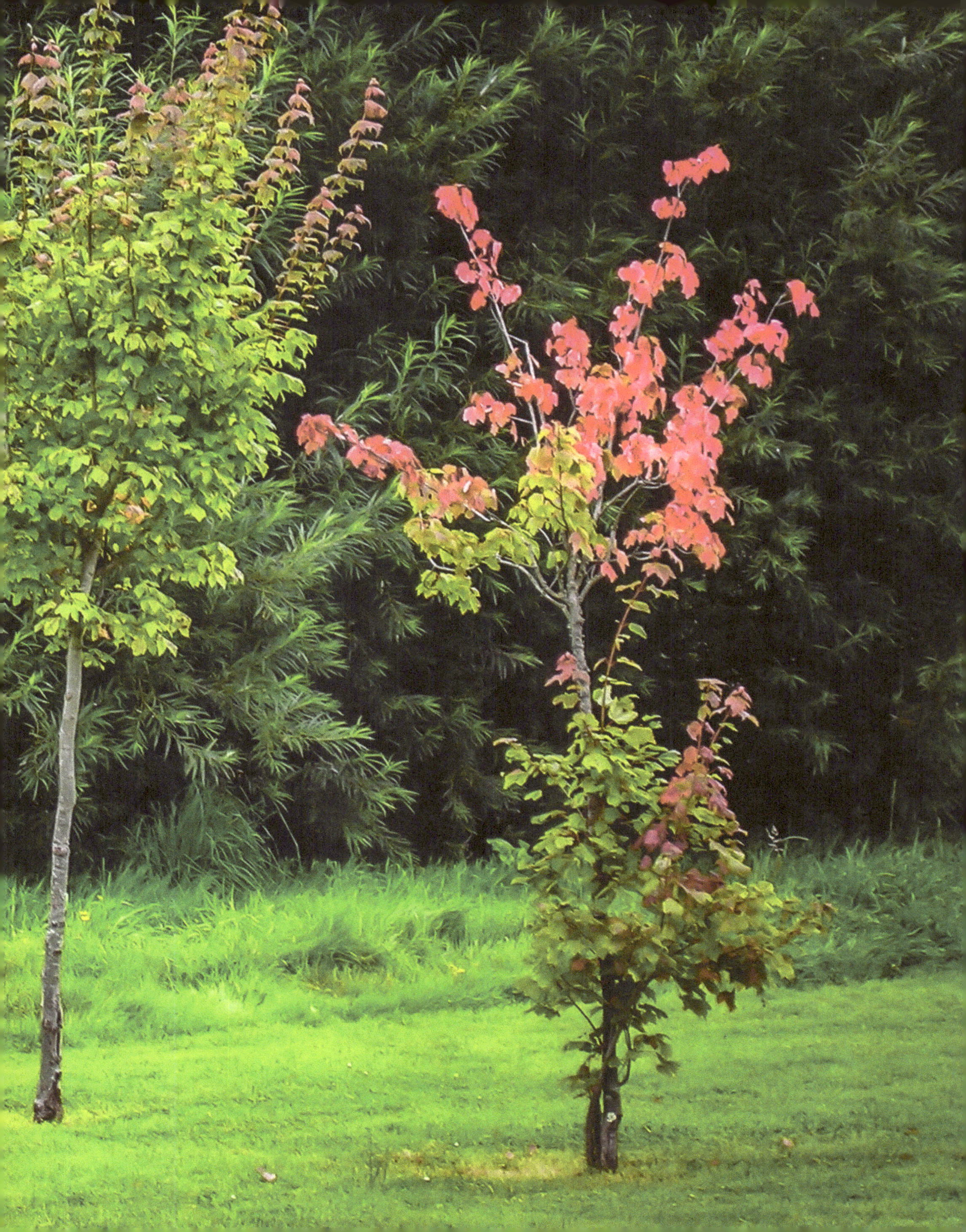

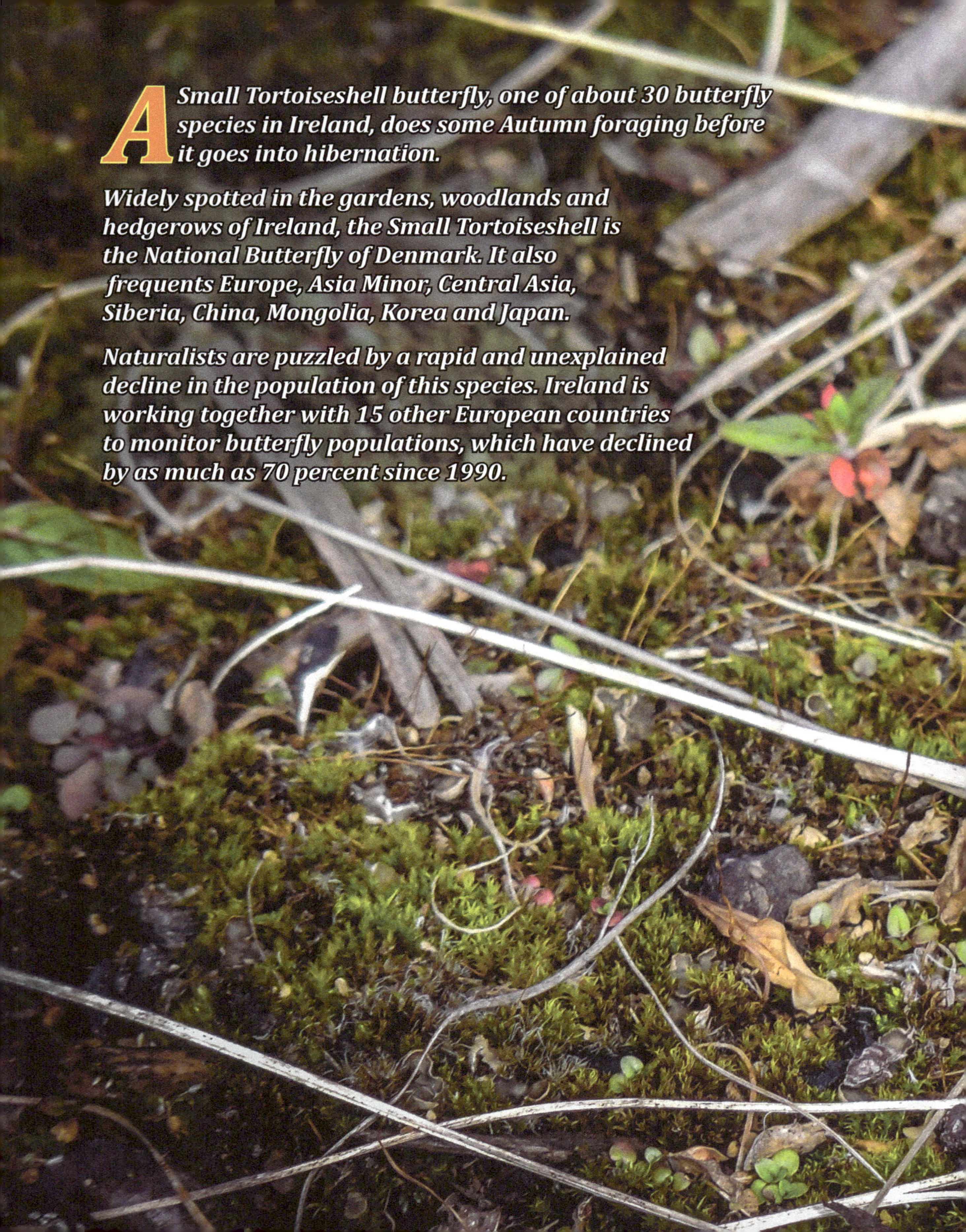

A Small Tortoiseshell butterfly, one of about 30 butterfly species in Ireland, does some Autumn foraging before it goes into hibernation.

Widely spotted in the gardens, woodlands and hedgerows of Ireland, the Small Tortoiseshell is the National Butterfly of Denmark. It also frequents Europe, Asia Minor, Central Asia, Siberia, China, Mongolia, Korea and Japan.

Naturalists are puzzled by a rapid and unexplained decline in the population of this species. Ireland is working together with 15 other European countries to monitor butterfly populations, which have declined by as much as 70 percent since 1990.

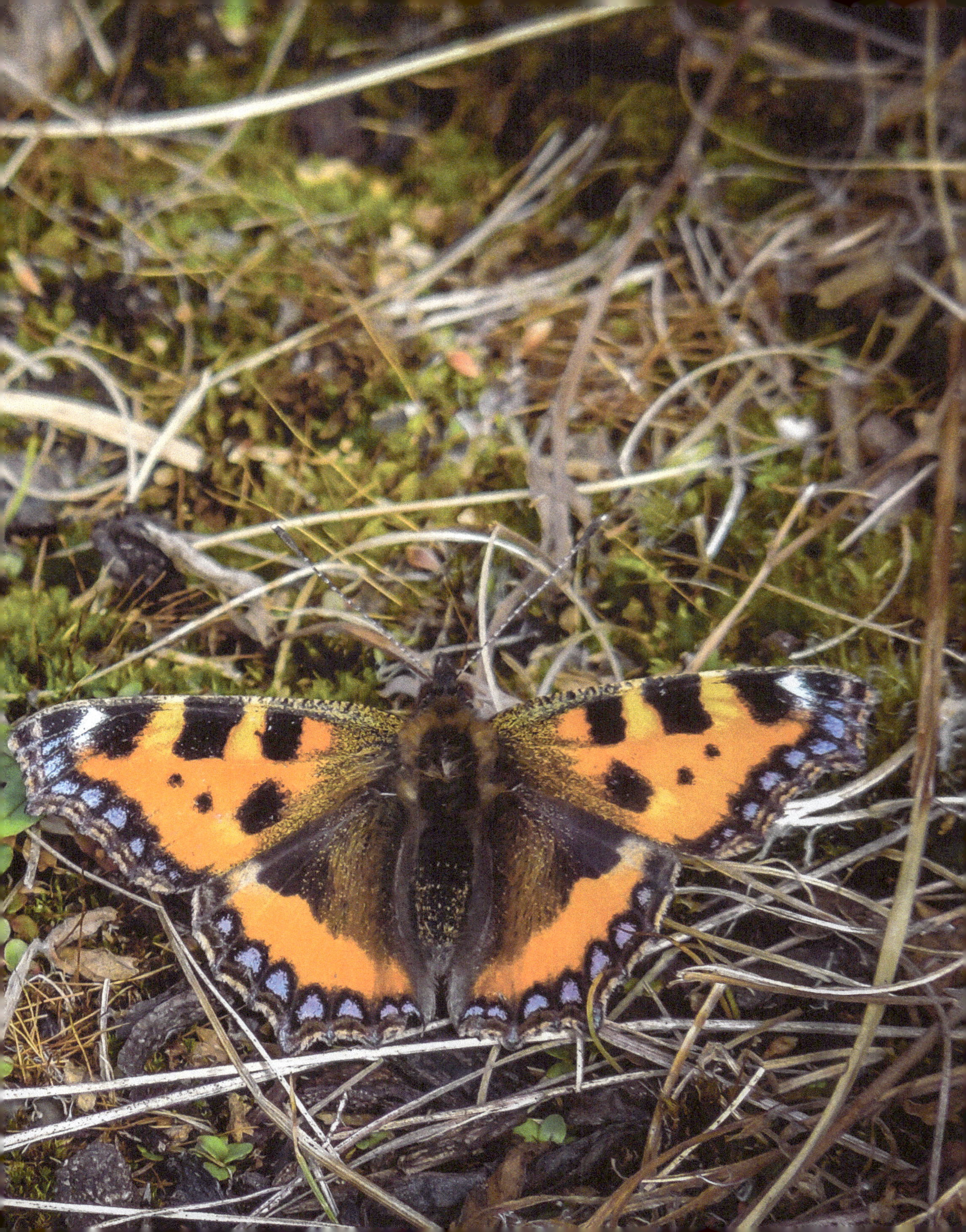

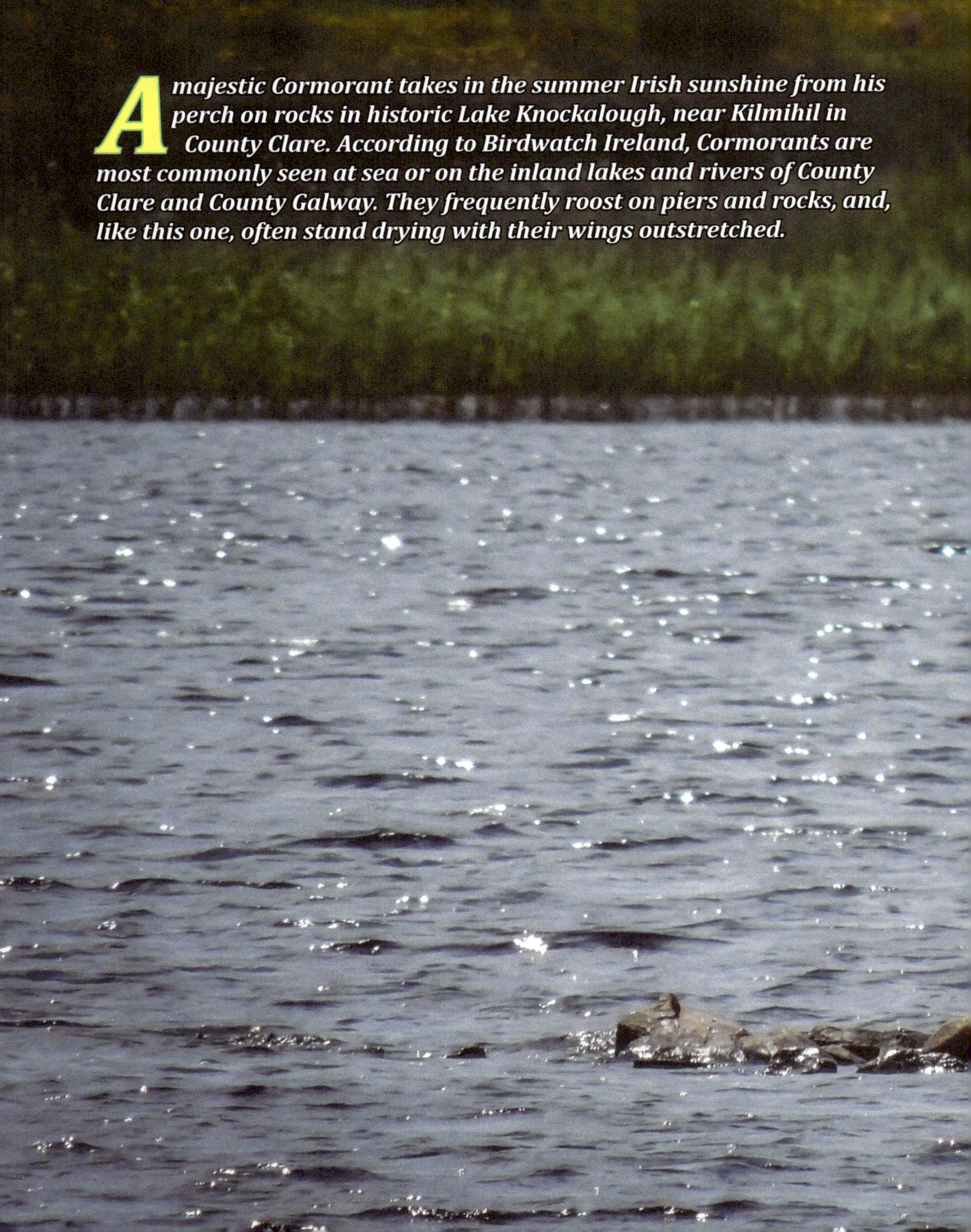

A majestic Cormorant takes in the summer Irish sunshine from his perch on rocks in historic Lake Knockalough, near Kilmihil in County Clare. According to Birdwatch Ireland, Cormorants are most commonly seen at sea or on the inland lakes and rivers of County Clare and County Galway. They frequently roost on piers and rocks, and, like this one, often stand drying with their wings outstretched.

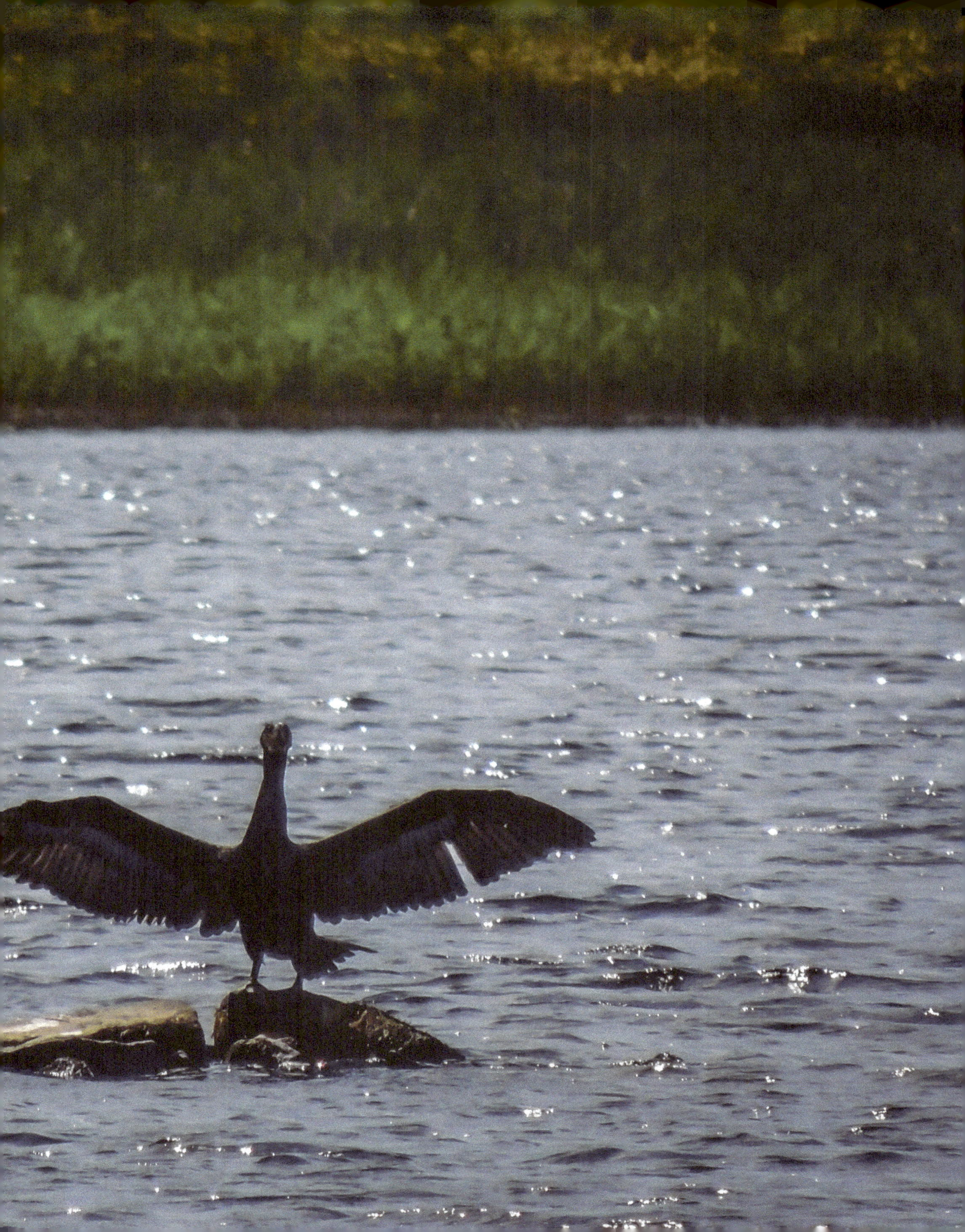

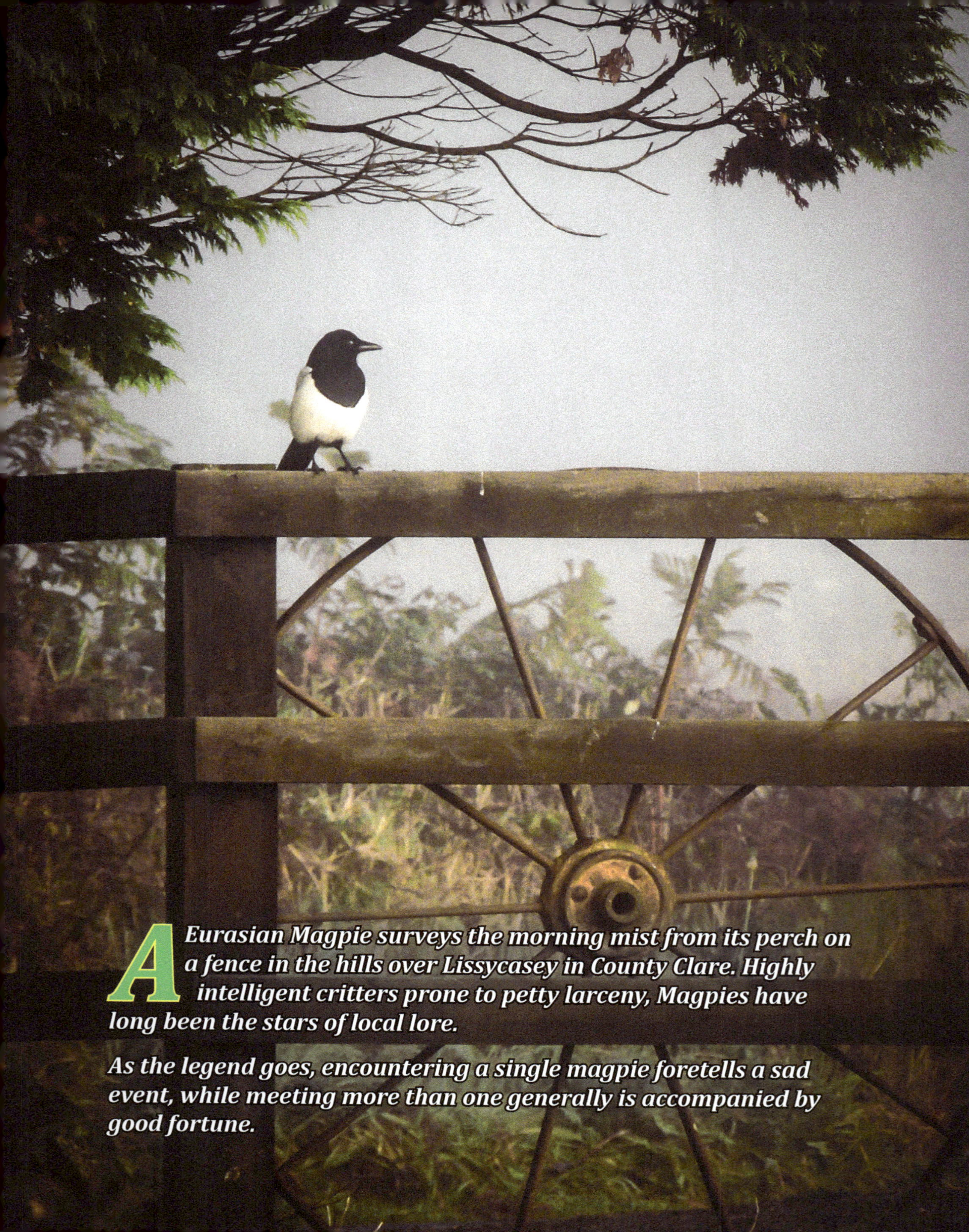

A Eurasian Magpie surveys the morning mist from its perch on a fence in the hills over Lissycasey in County Clare. Highly intelligent critters prone to petty larceny, Magpies have long been the stars of local lore.

As the legend goes, encountering a single magpie foretells a sad event, while meeting more than one generally is accompanied by good fortune.

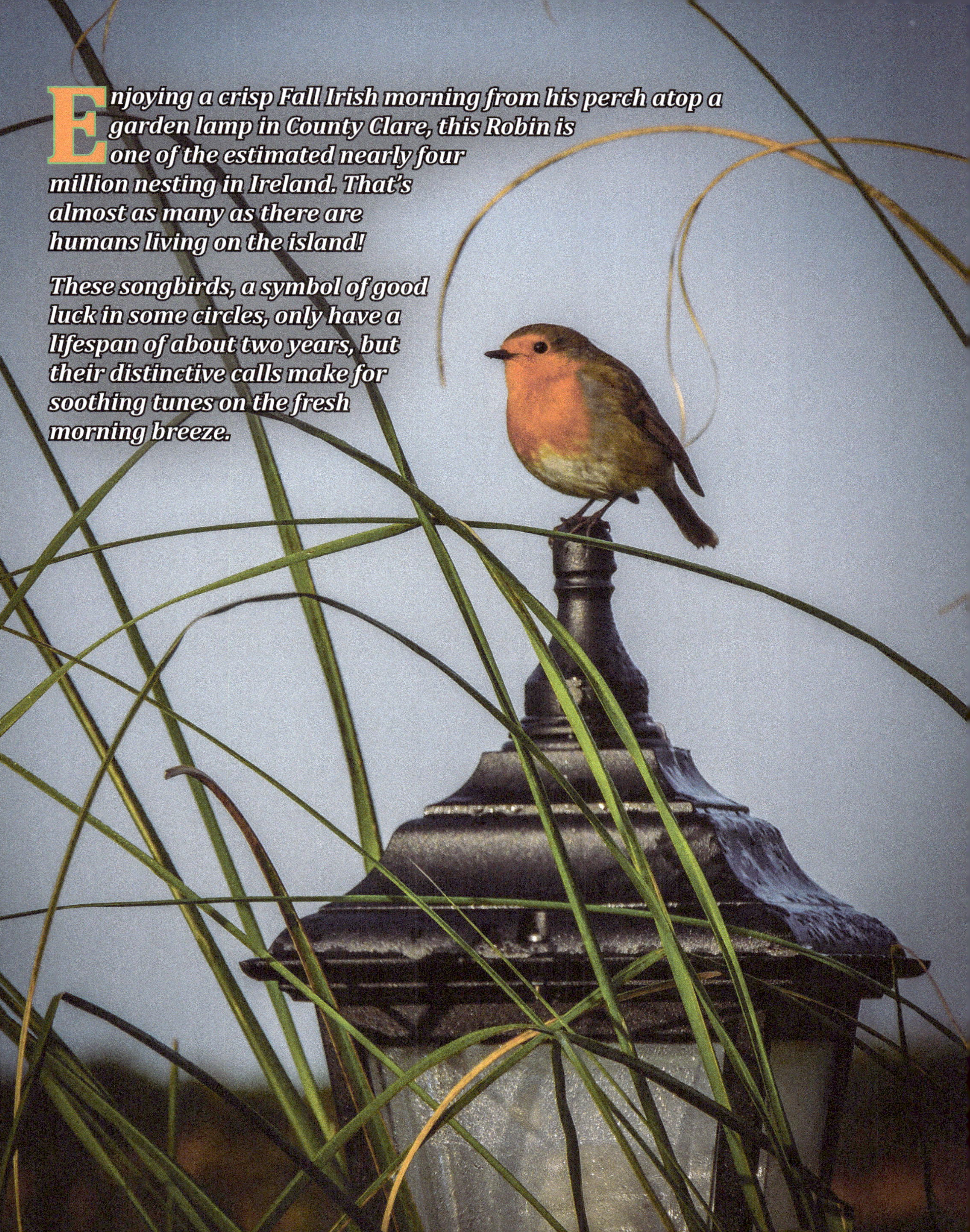

Enjoying a crisp Fall Irish morning from his perch atop a garden lamp in County Clare, this Robin is one of the estimated nearly four million nesting in Ireland. That's almost as many as there are humans living on the island!

These songbirds, a symbol of good luck in some circles, only have a lifespan of about two years, but their distinctive calls make for soothing tunes on the fresh morning breeze.

An enchanting and surreal scene over County Clare, as the morning sun shines a path through the misty Shannon River Valley for a Eurasian Magpie.

The earliest recorded sightings of Eurasian Magpies in Ireland were in 1676 in Wexford. The Magpie population grew steadily, but suffered a major setback in the 1950s, most likely due to the increased use of chemicals and pesticides in farming.

The population has enjoyed a resurgence with the banning and improved regulation of many agricultural chemicals, and the species now is the 8th most widespread bird in the country.

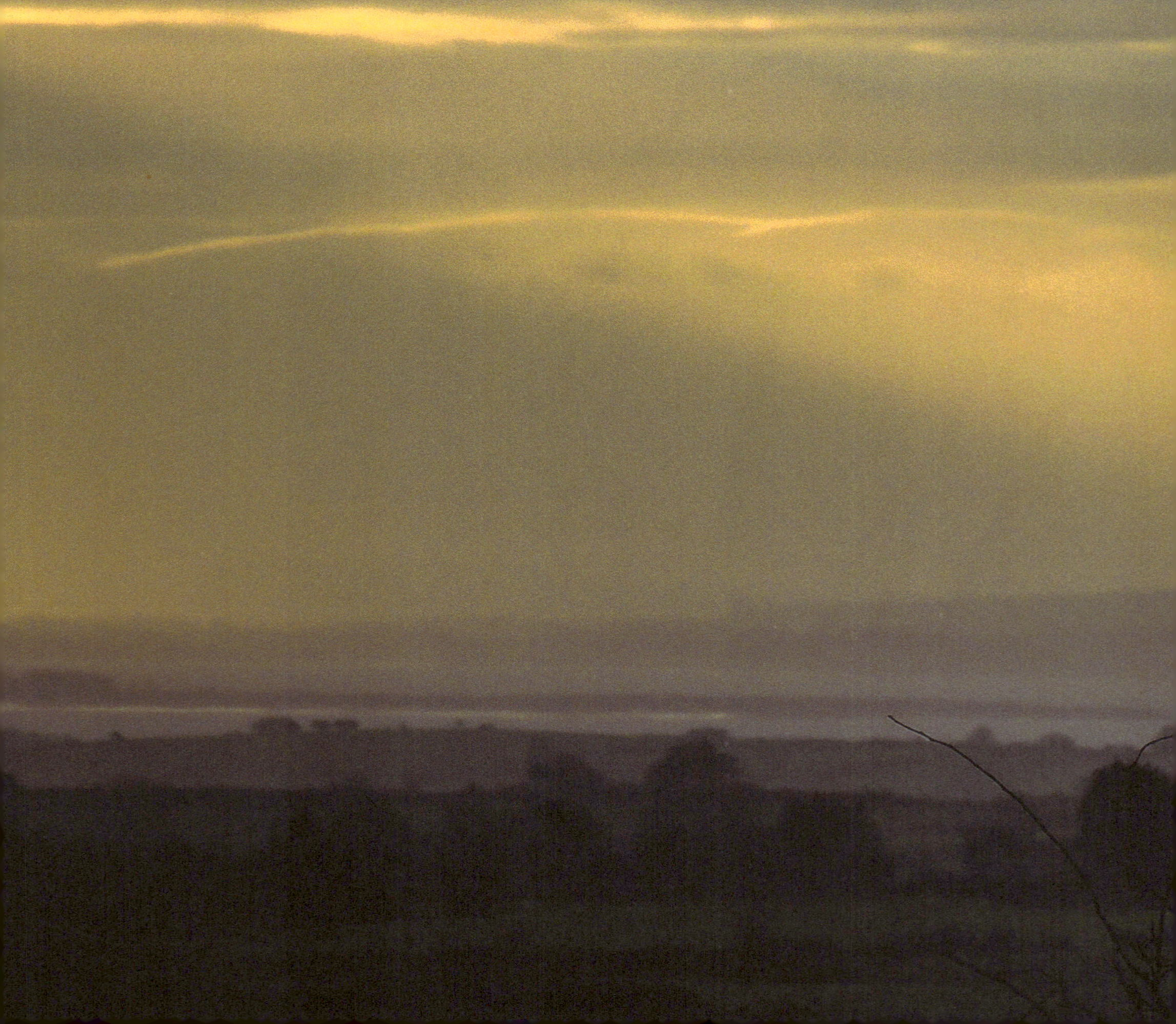

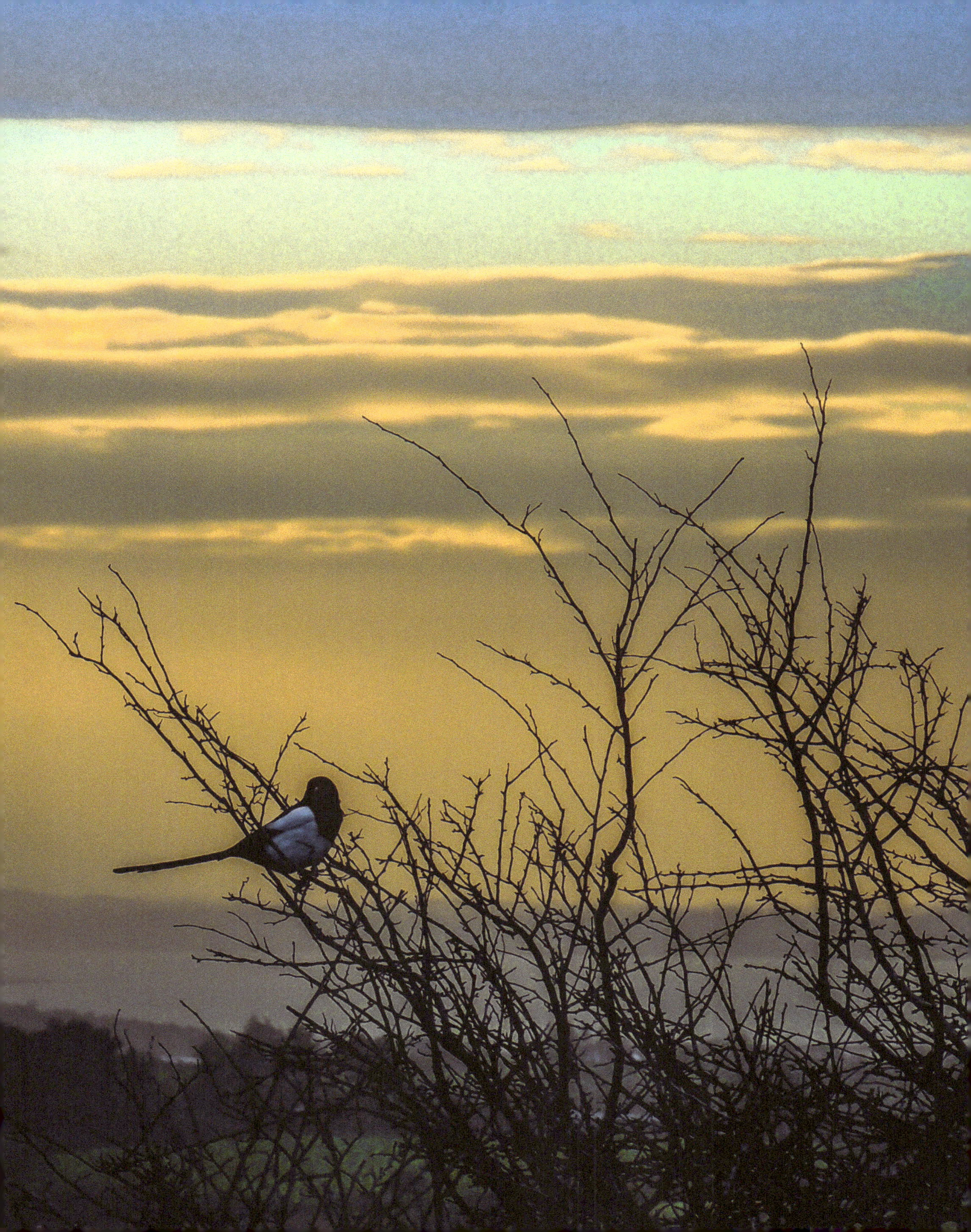

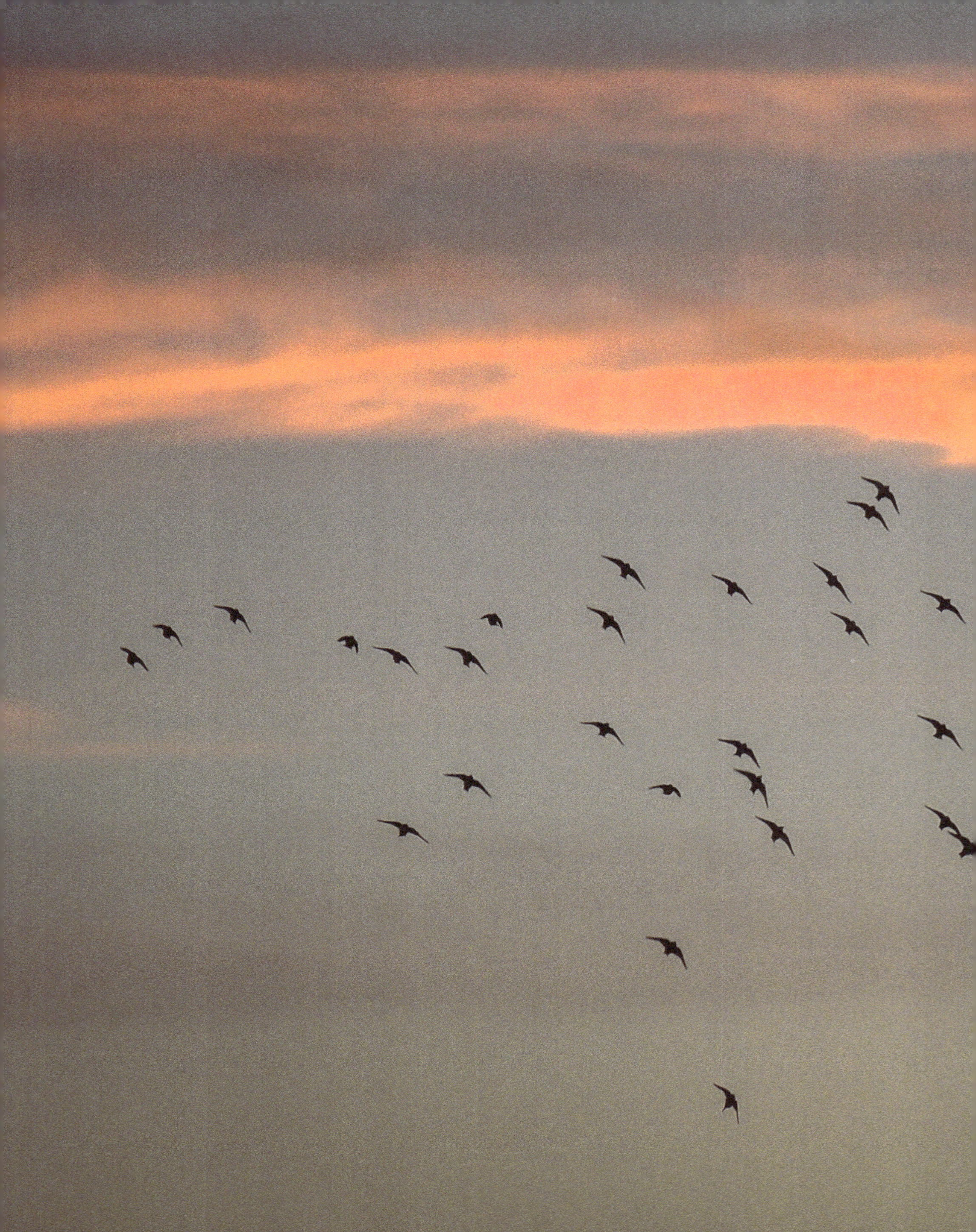

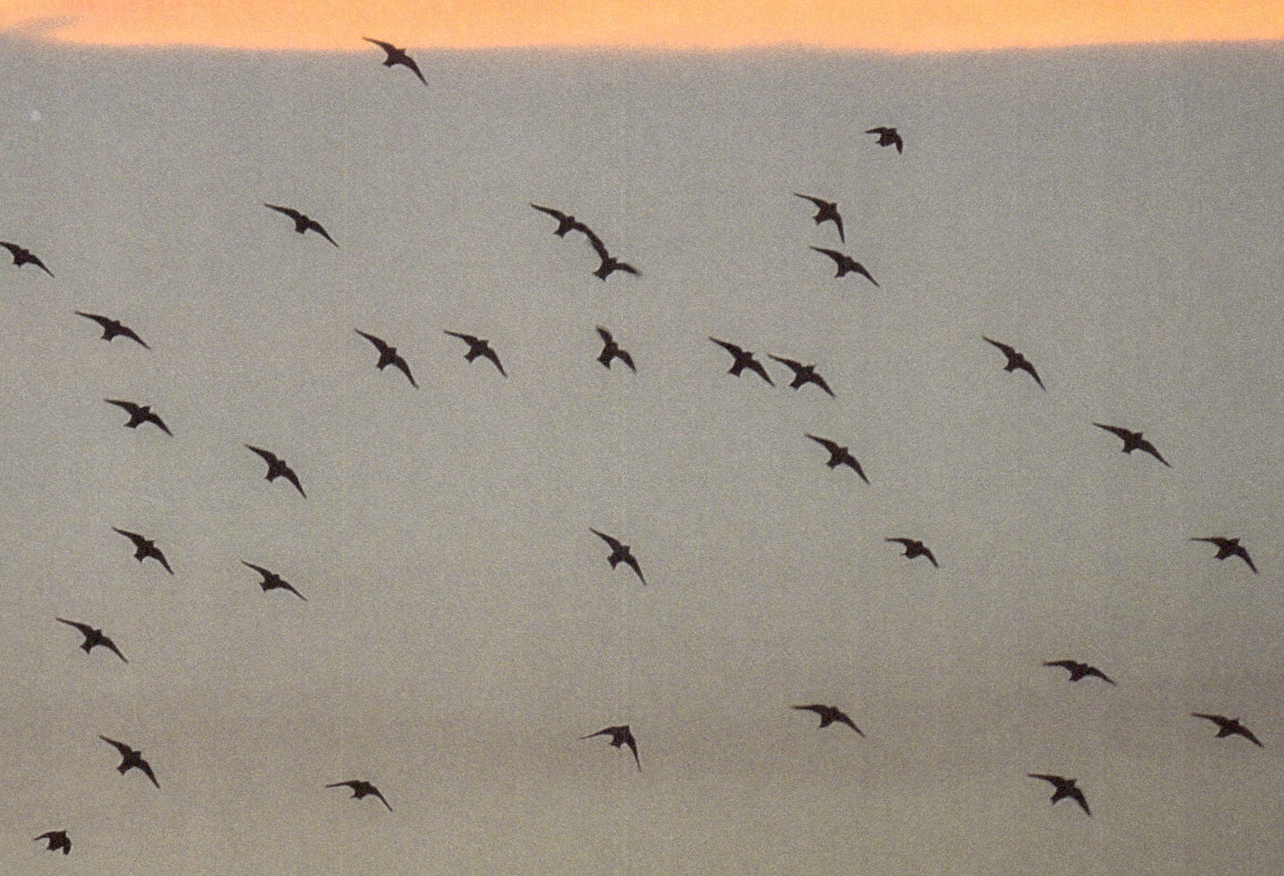

A murmuration of Starlings dances rhythmically in the winter sky to the waning light of a brilliant sunset over County Clare. Starlings are widespread throughout Ireland at all times of the year, though their population is declining in other parts of Europe.

They typically form huge flocks during winter in Ireland, joined by cousins visiting from the European continent. Flocks as large as 500,000 have been reported, and they can provide some spectacular aerobatic displays, usually at dusk.

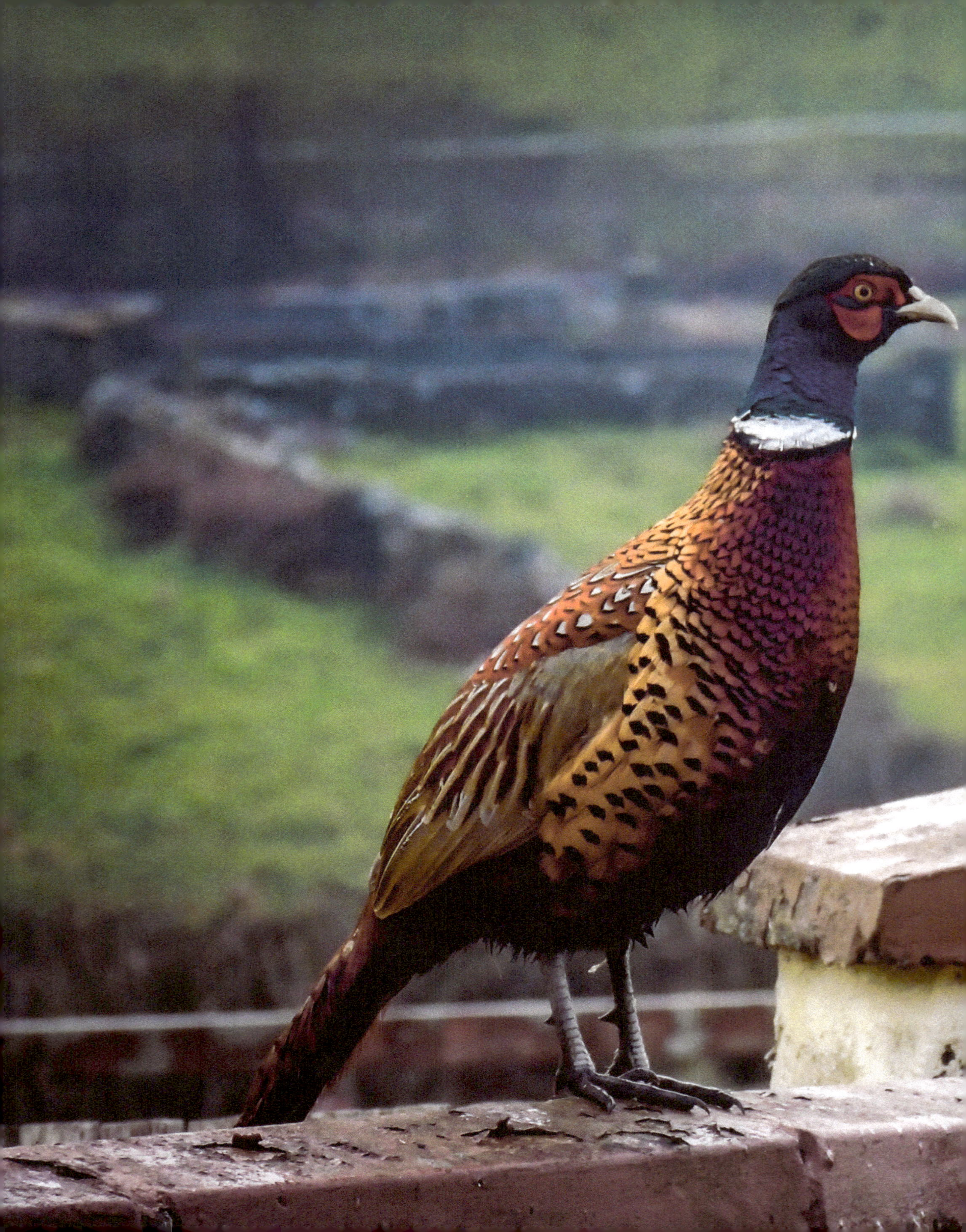

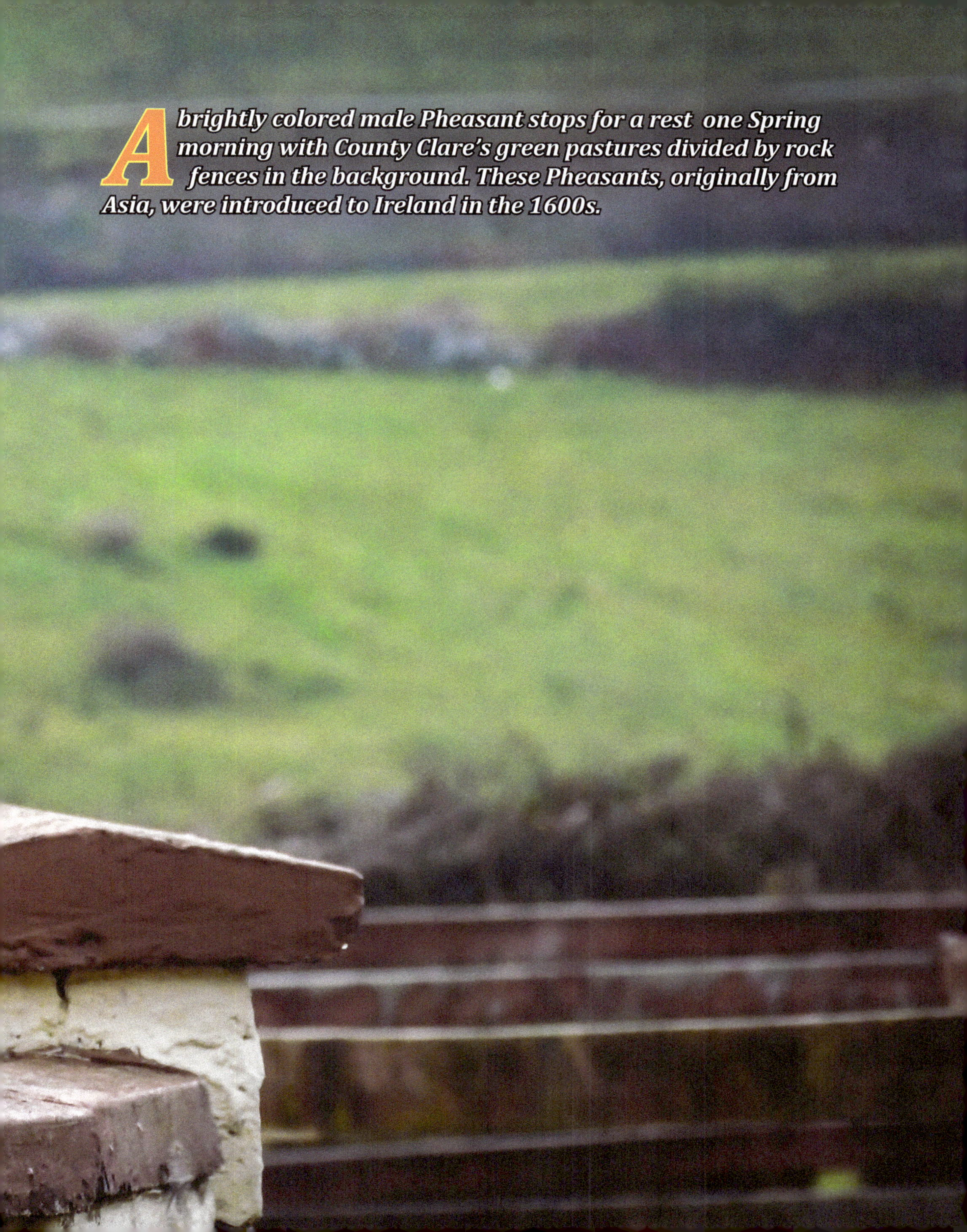

A brightly colored male Pheasant stops for a rest one Spring morning with County Clare's green pastures divided by rock fences in the background. These Pheasants, originally from Asia, were introduced to Ireland in the 1600s.

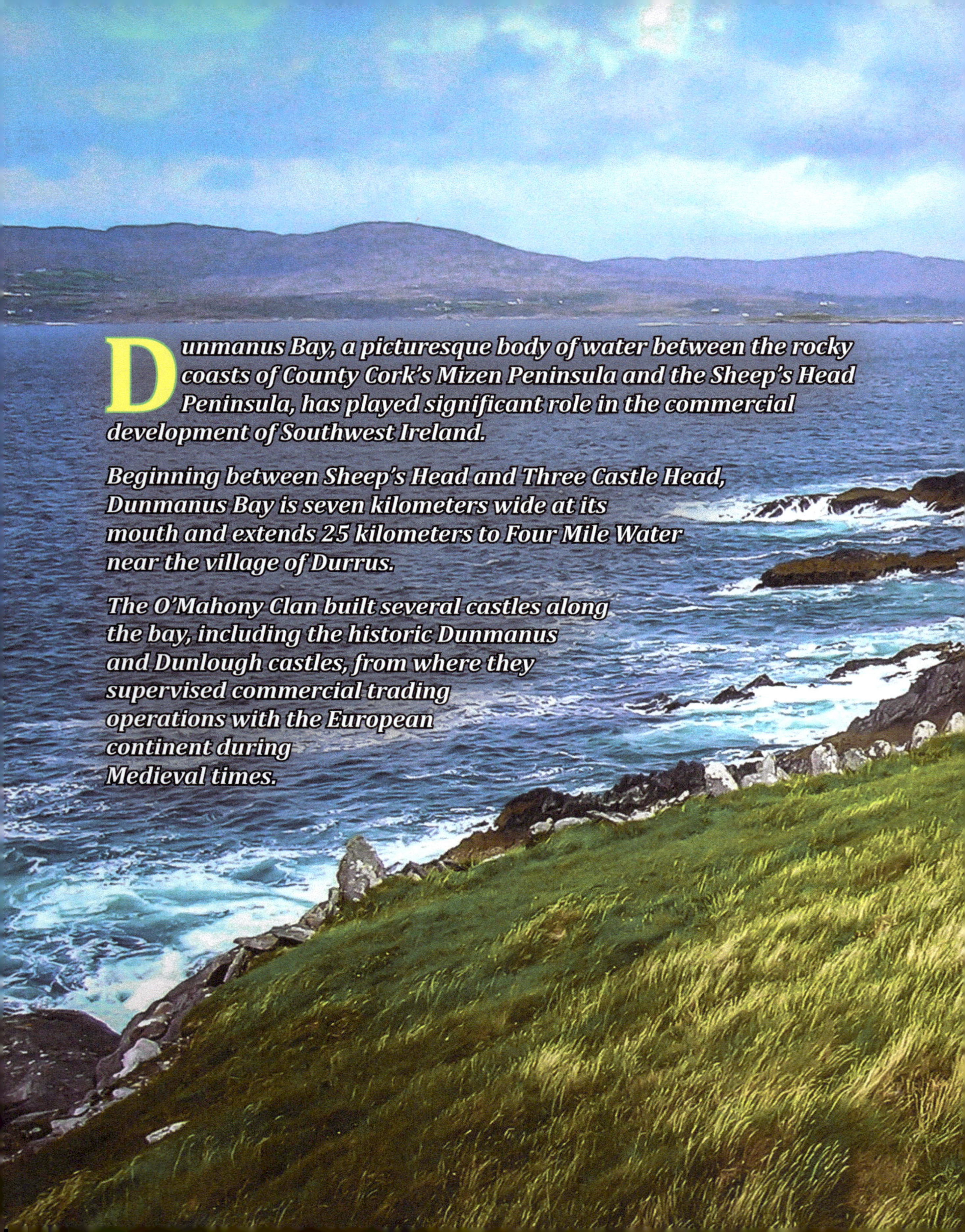

Dunmanus Bay, a picturesque body of water between the rocky coasts of County Cork's Mizen Peninsula and the Sheep's Head Peninsula, has played significant role in the commercial development of Southwest Ireland.

Beginning between Sheep's Head and Three Castle Head, Dunmanus Bay is seven kilometers wide at its mouth and extends 25 kilometers to Four Mile Water near the village of Durrus.

The O'Mahony Clan built several castles along the bay, including the historic Dunmanus and Dunlough castles, from where they supervised commercial trading operations with the European continent during Medieval times.

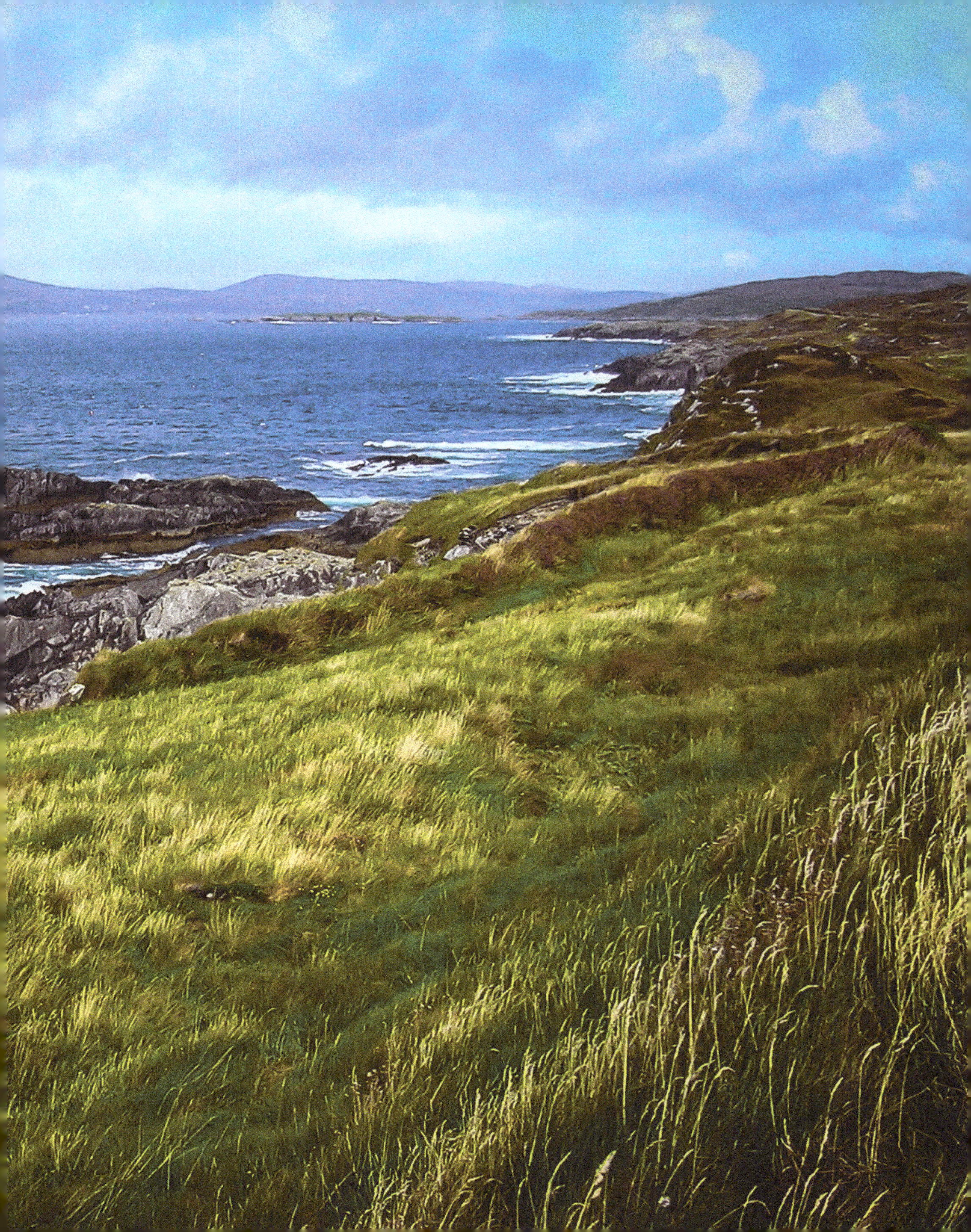

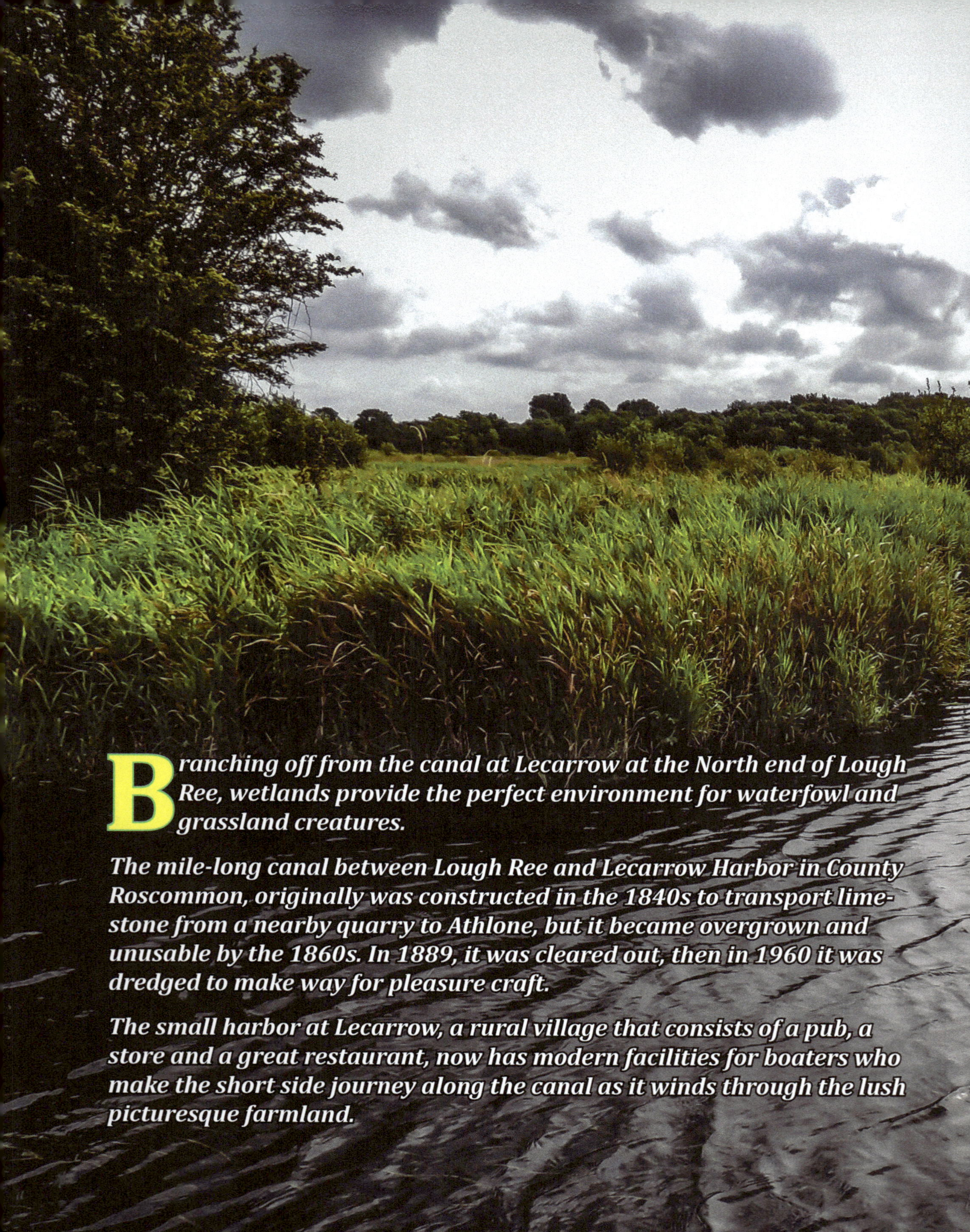

Branching off from the canal at Lecarrow at the North end of Lough Ree, wetlands provide the perfect environment for waterfowl and grassland creatures.

The mile-long canal between Lough Ree and Lecarrow Harbor in County Roscommon, originally was constructed in the 1840s to transport limestone from a nearby quarry to Athlone, but it became overgrown and unusable by the 1860s. In 1889, it was cleared out, then in 1960 it was dredged to make way for pleasure craft.

The small harbor at Lecarrow, a rural village that consists of a pub, a store and a great restaurant, now has modern facilities for boaters who make the short side journey along the canal as it winds through the lush picturesque farmland.

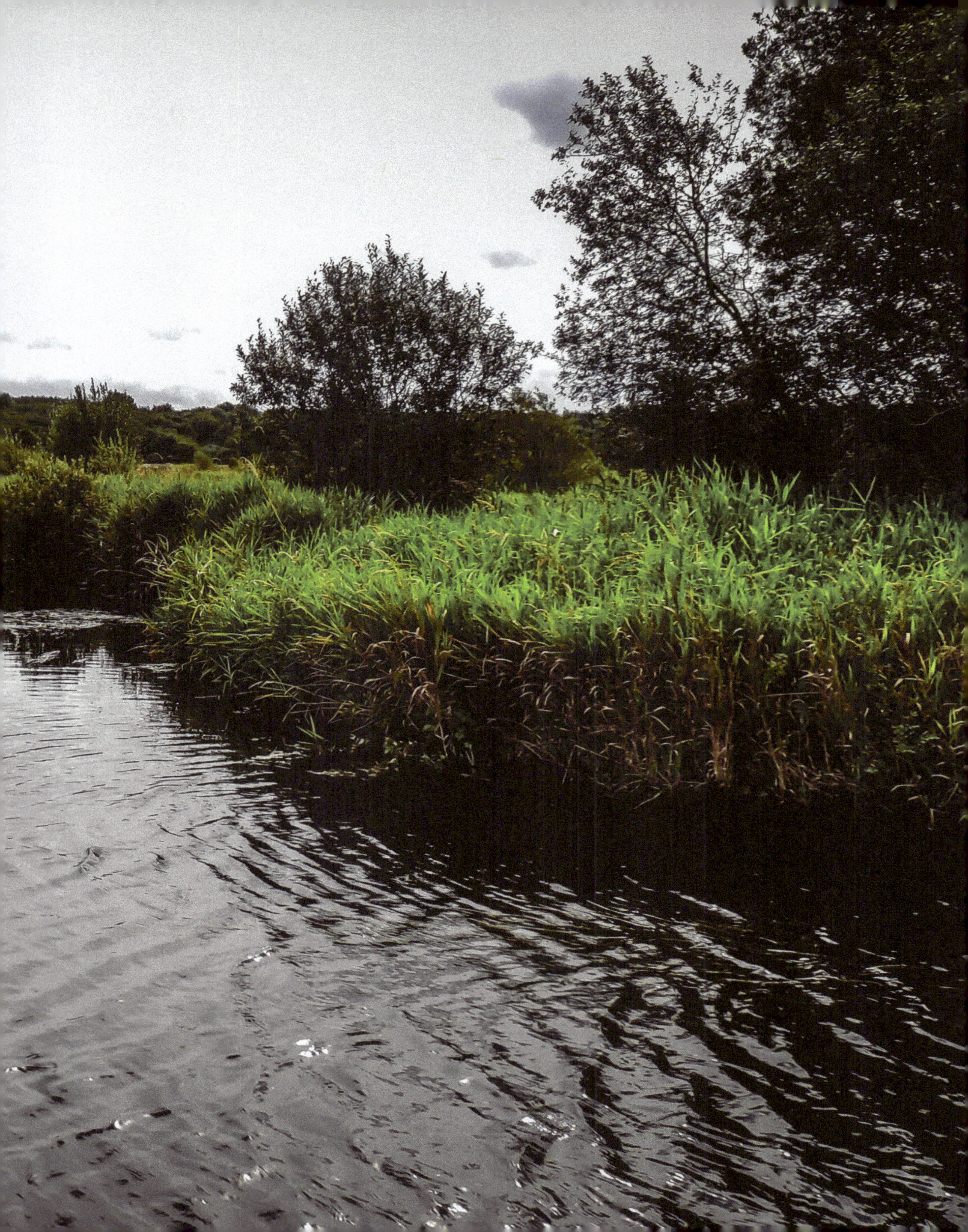

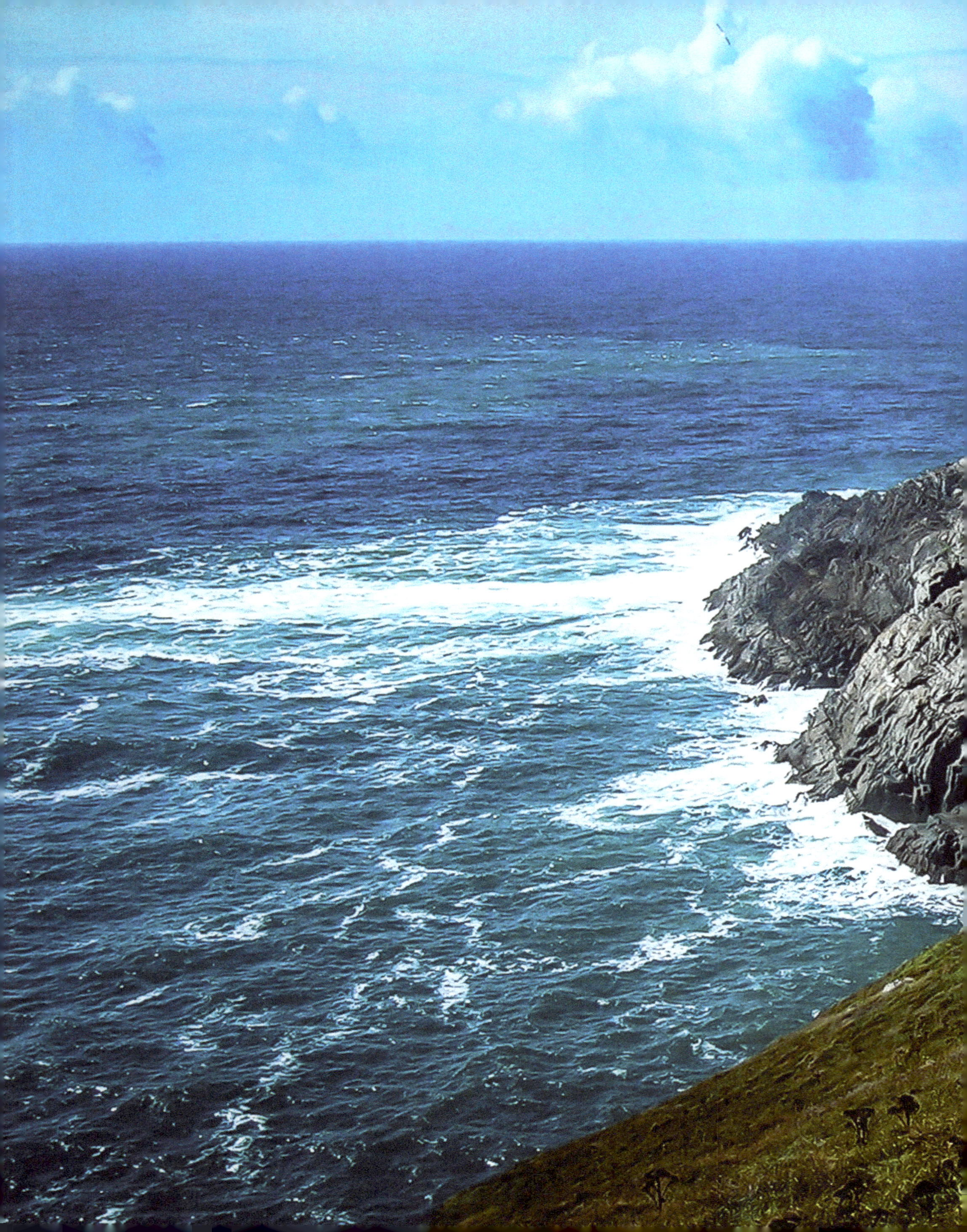

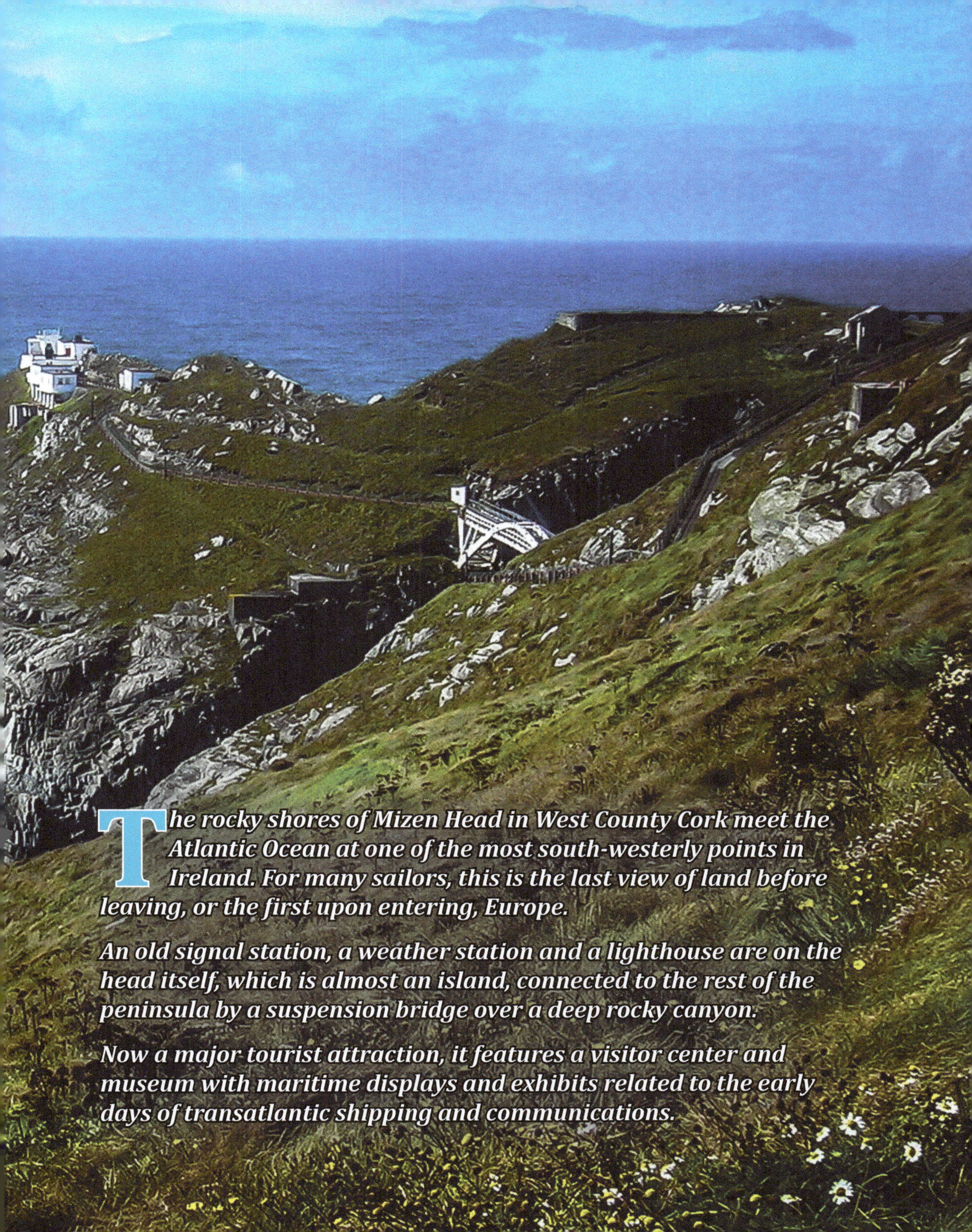

The rocky shores of Mizen Head in West County Cork meet the Atlantic Ocean at one of the most south-westerly points in Ireland. For many sailors, this is the last view of land before leaving, or the first upon entering, Europe.

An old signal station, a weather station and a lighthouse are on the head itself, which is almost an island, connected to the rest of the peninsula by a suspension bridge over a deep rocky canyon.

Now a major tourist attraction, it features a visitor center and museum with maritime displays and exhibits related to the early days of transatlantic shipping and communications.

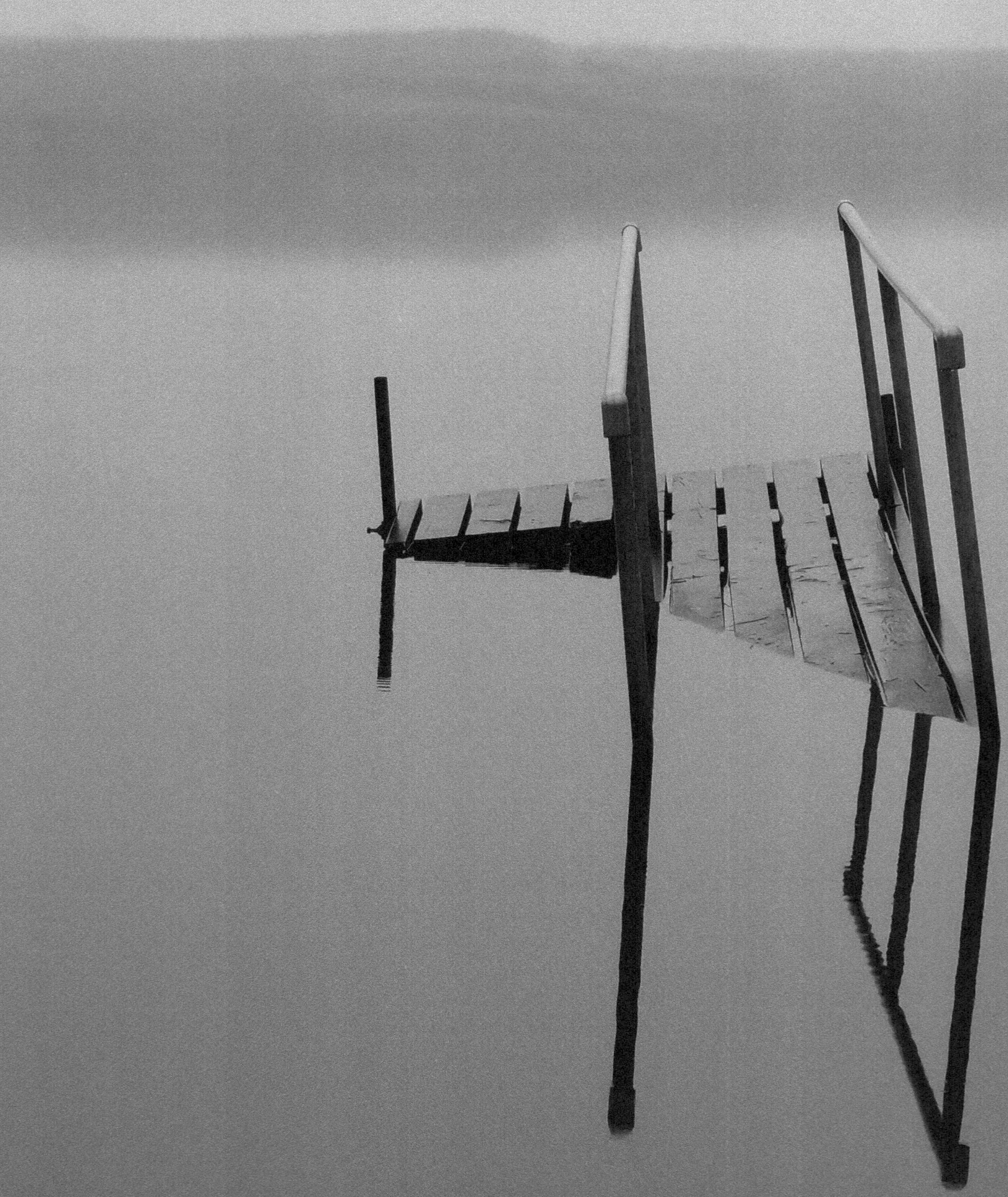

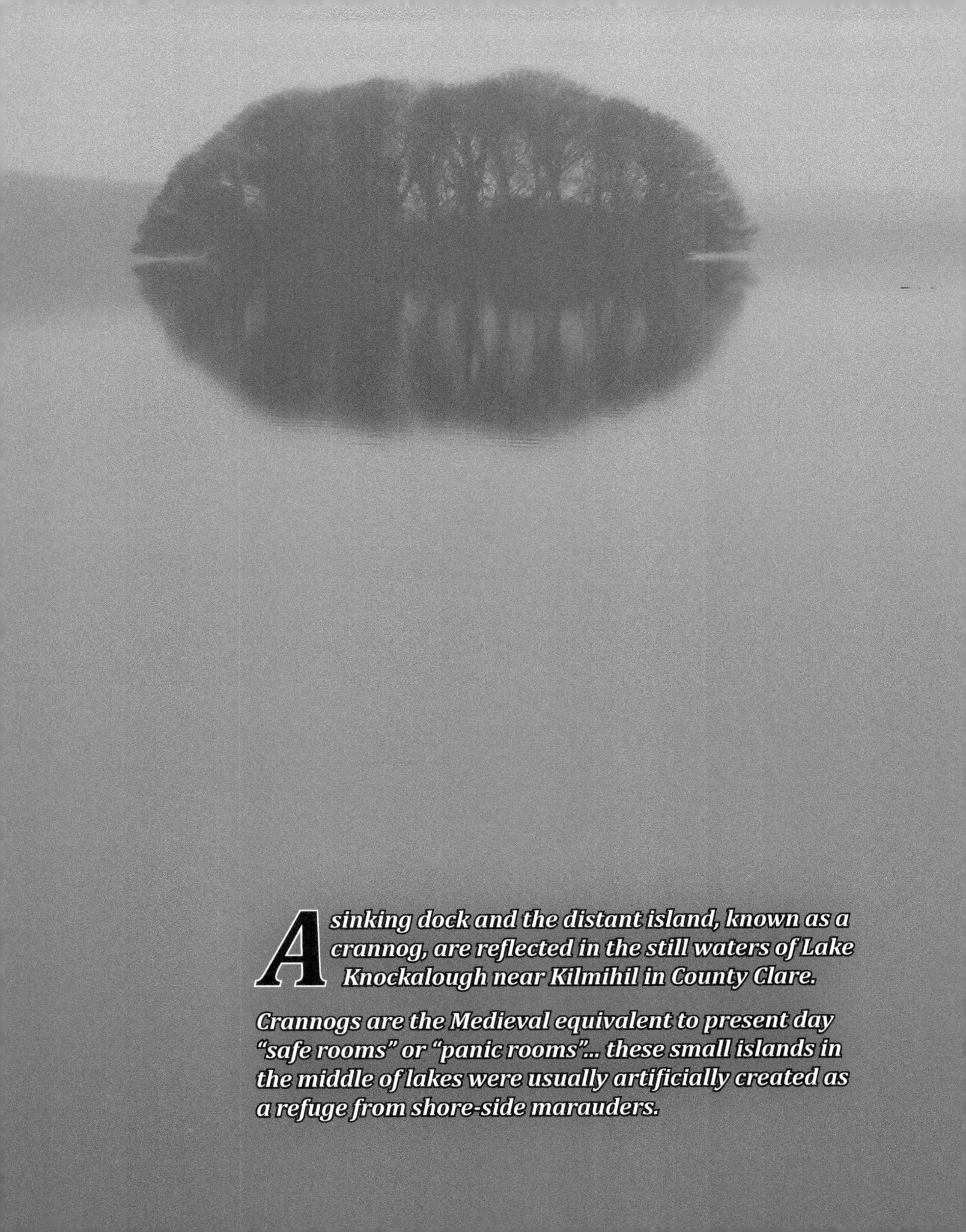

A sinking dock and the distant island, known as a crannog, are reflected in the still waters of Lake Knockalough near Kilmihil in County Clare.

Crannogs are the Medieval equivalent to present day "safe rooms" or "panic rooms"... these small islands in the middle of lakes were usually artificially created as a refuge from shore-side marauders.

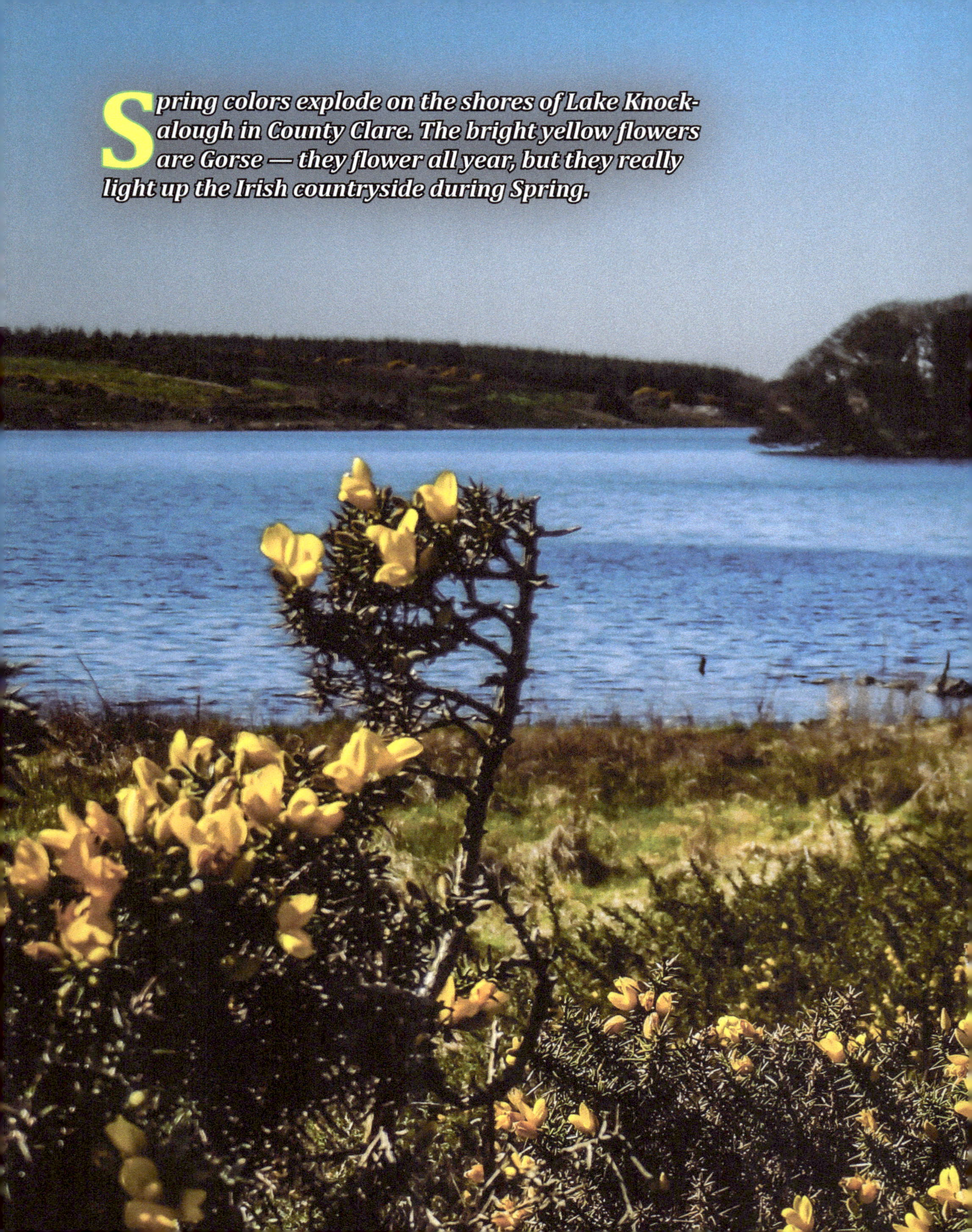

Spring colors explode on the shores of Lake Knock-alough in County Clare. The bright yellow flowers are Gorse — they flower all year, but they really light up the Irish countryside during Spring.

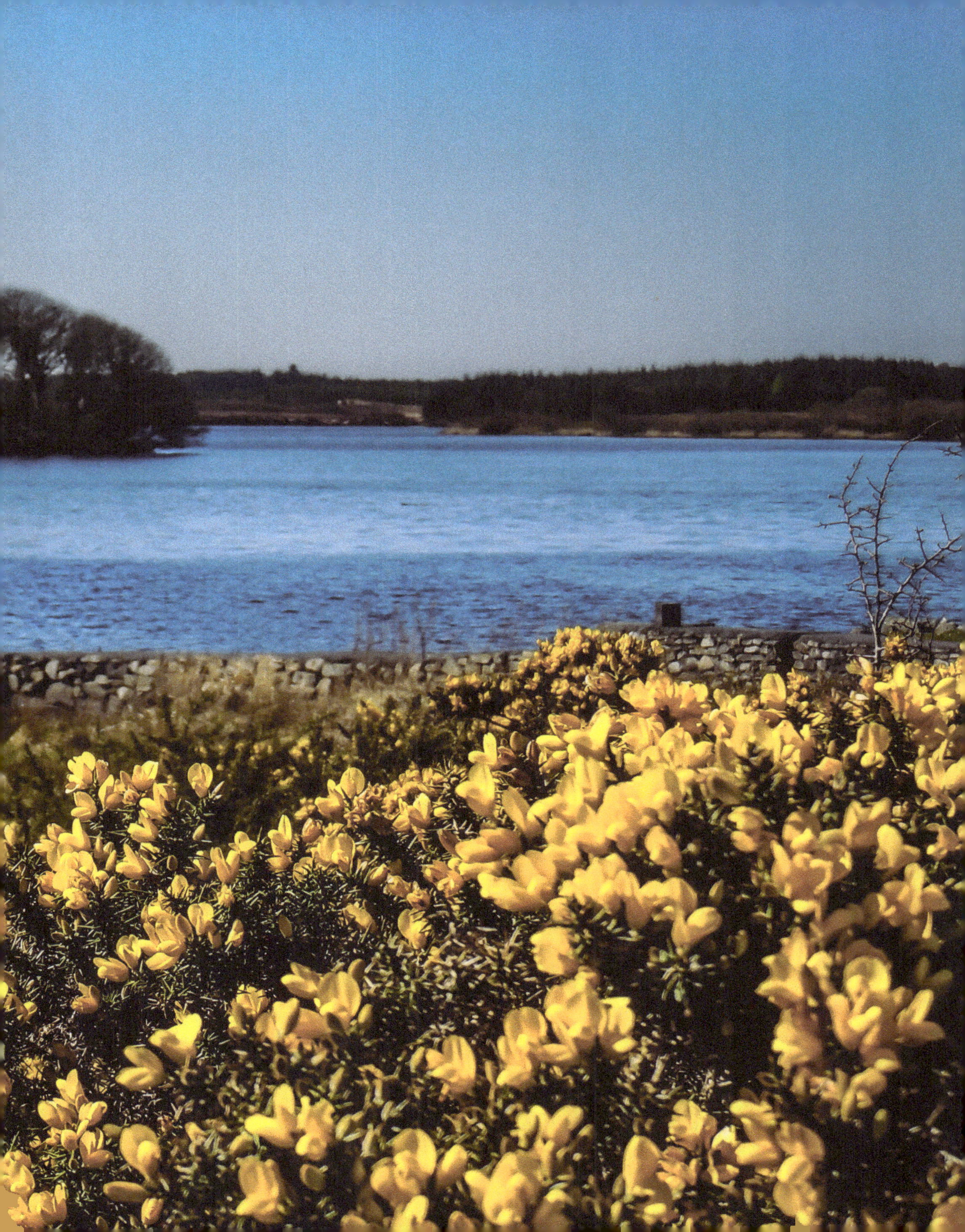

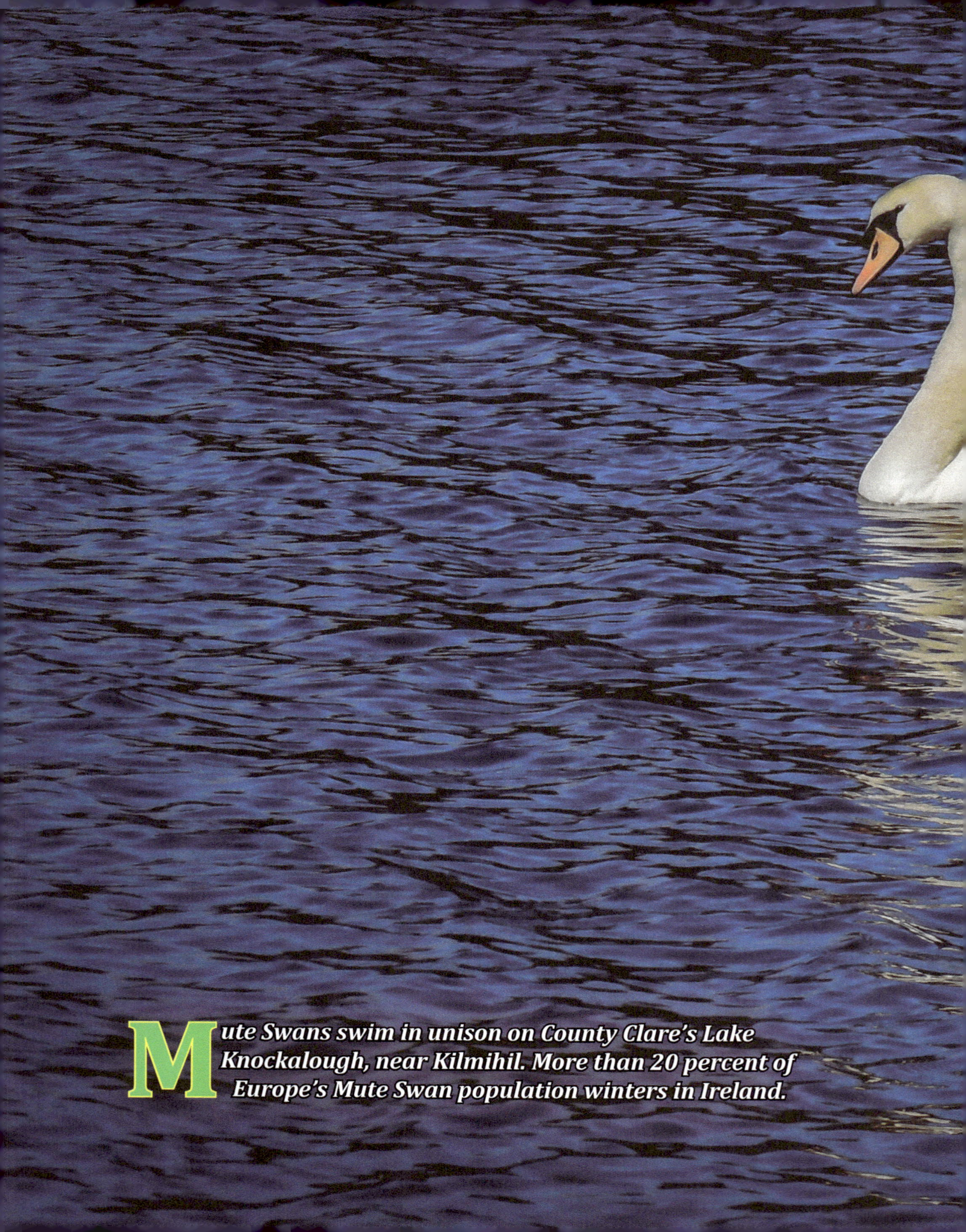

Mute Swans swim in unison on County Clare's Lake Knockalough, near Kilmihil. More than 20 percent of Europe's Mute Swan population winters in Ireland.

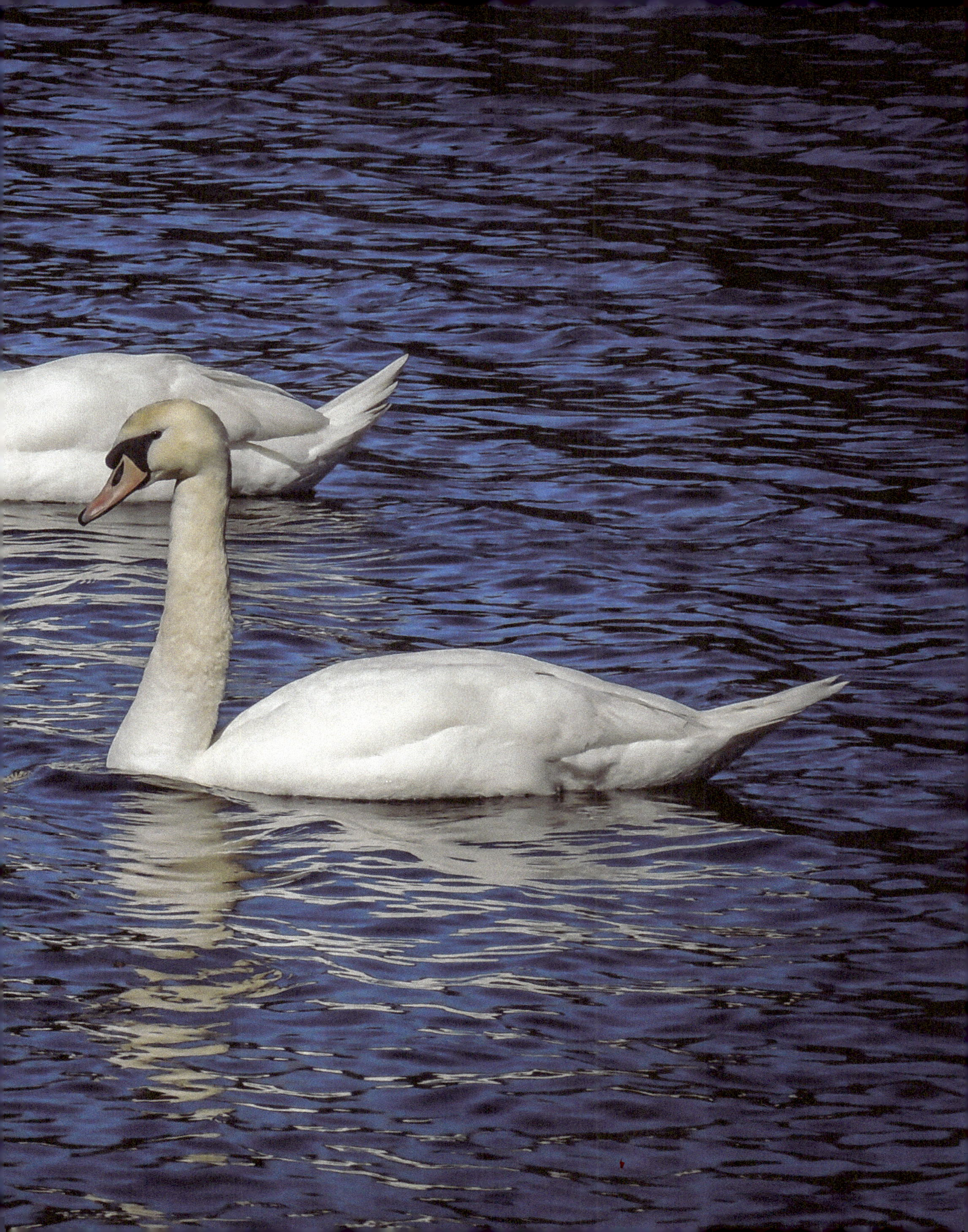

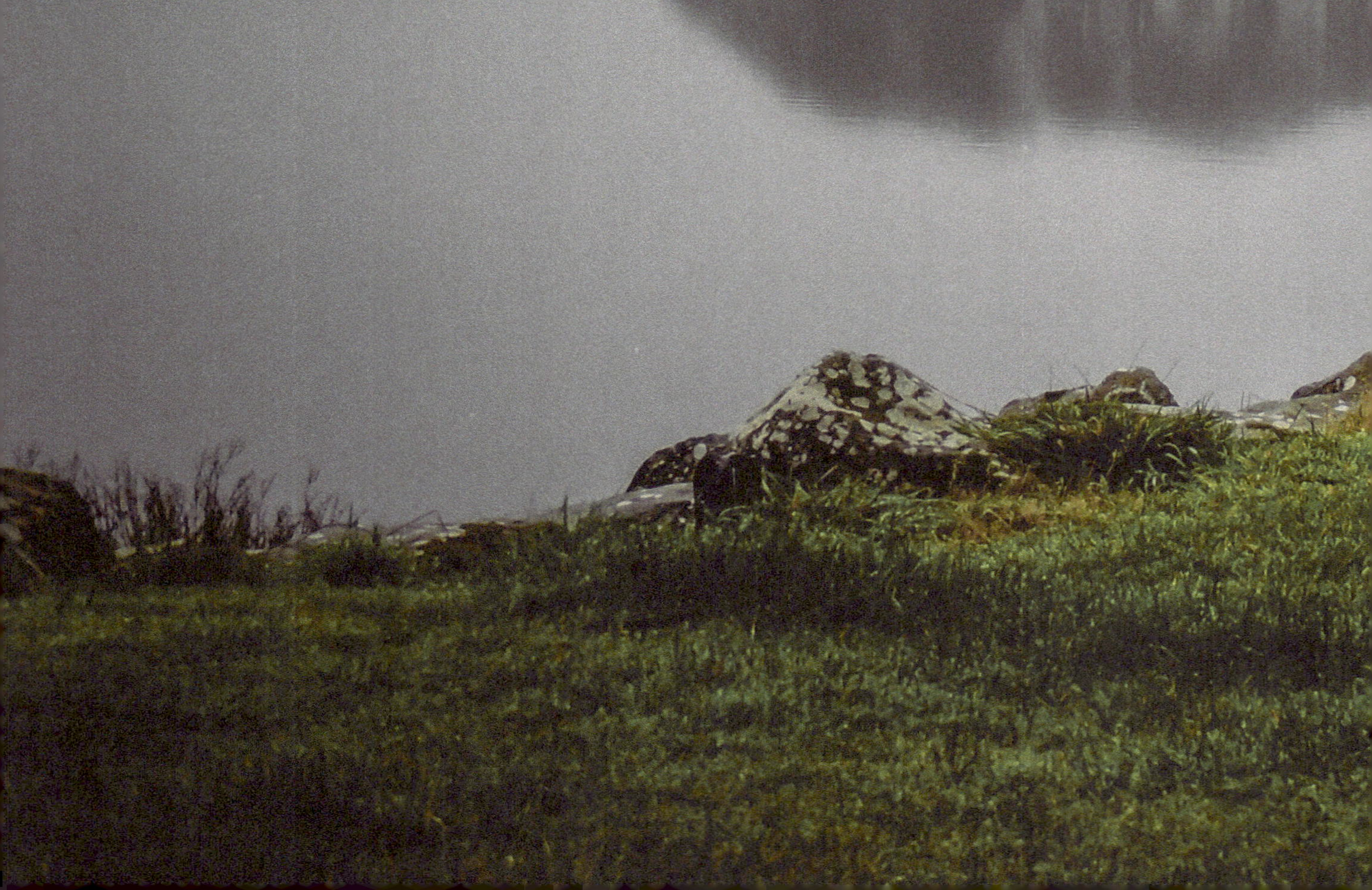

A morning Irish mist rises on Lake Knockalough, near Kilmihil in County Clare. This tranquil spot, partially developed as a recreational and picnic area, has a rich history dating back hundreds of years.

Ruins of an old castle are located on the crannog, the Medieval artificial island in the center of the lake.

In addition to its history, Lake Knockalough is recognized as a popular fishing hole for brown and rainbow trout.

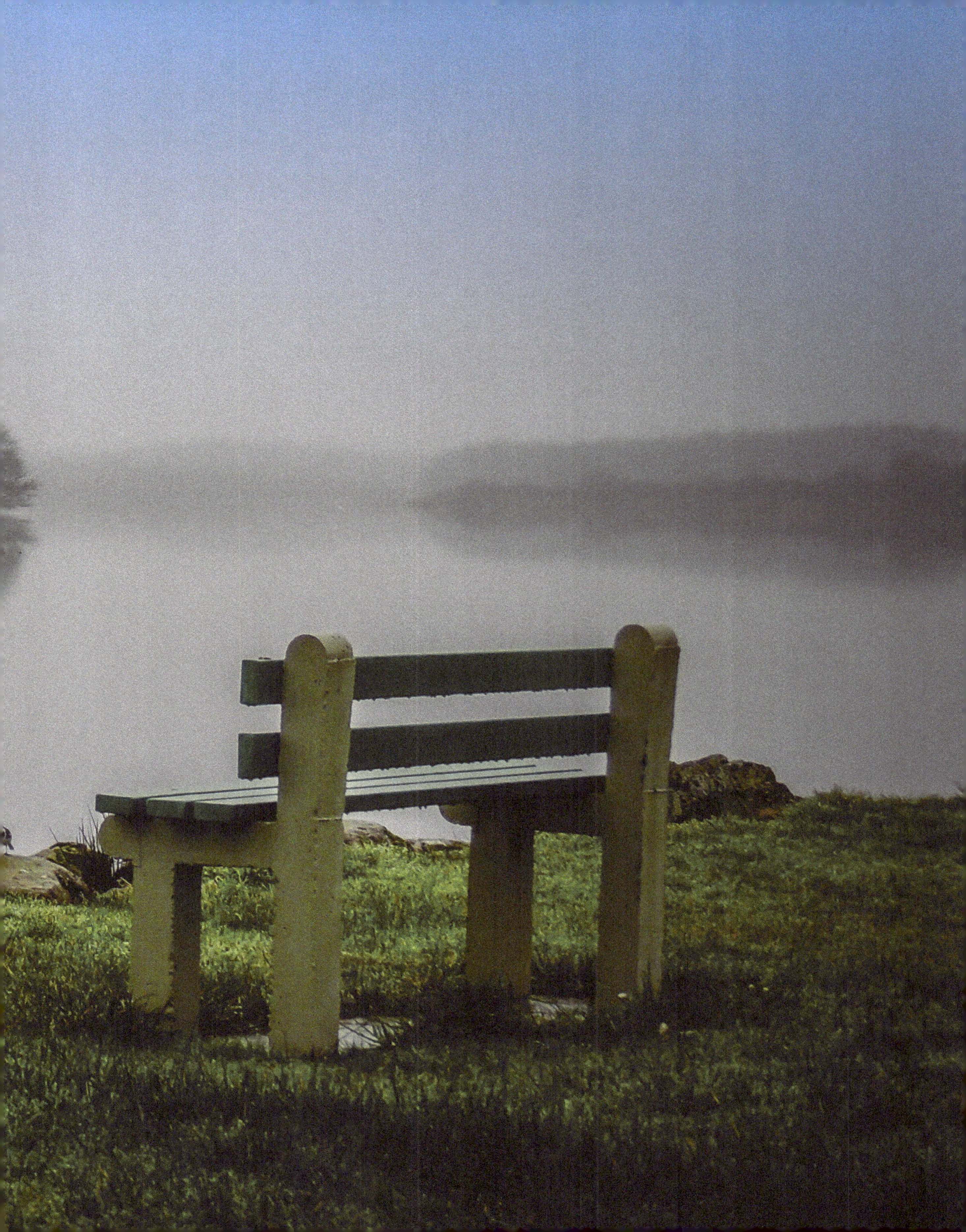

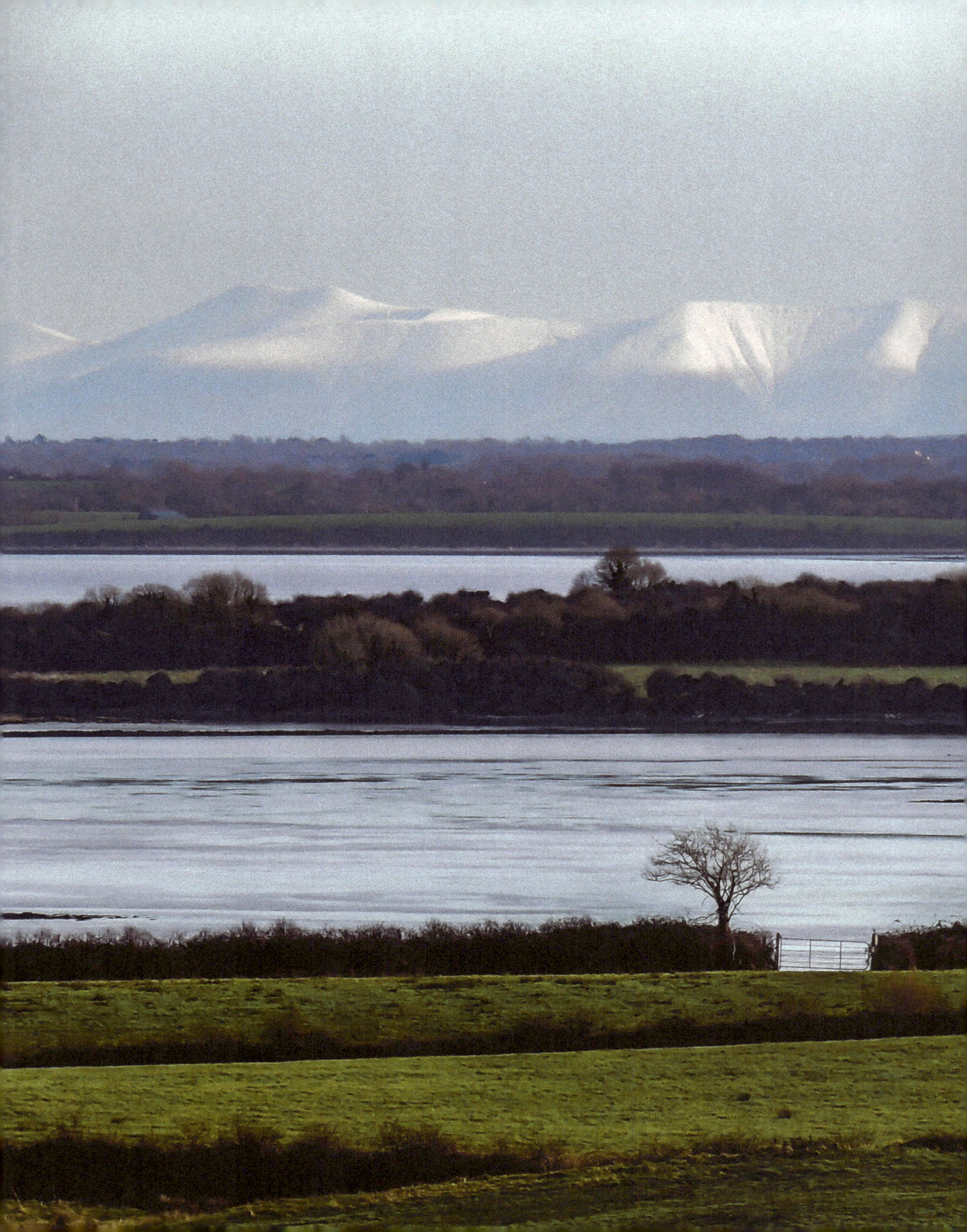

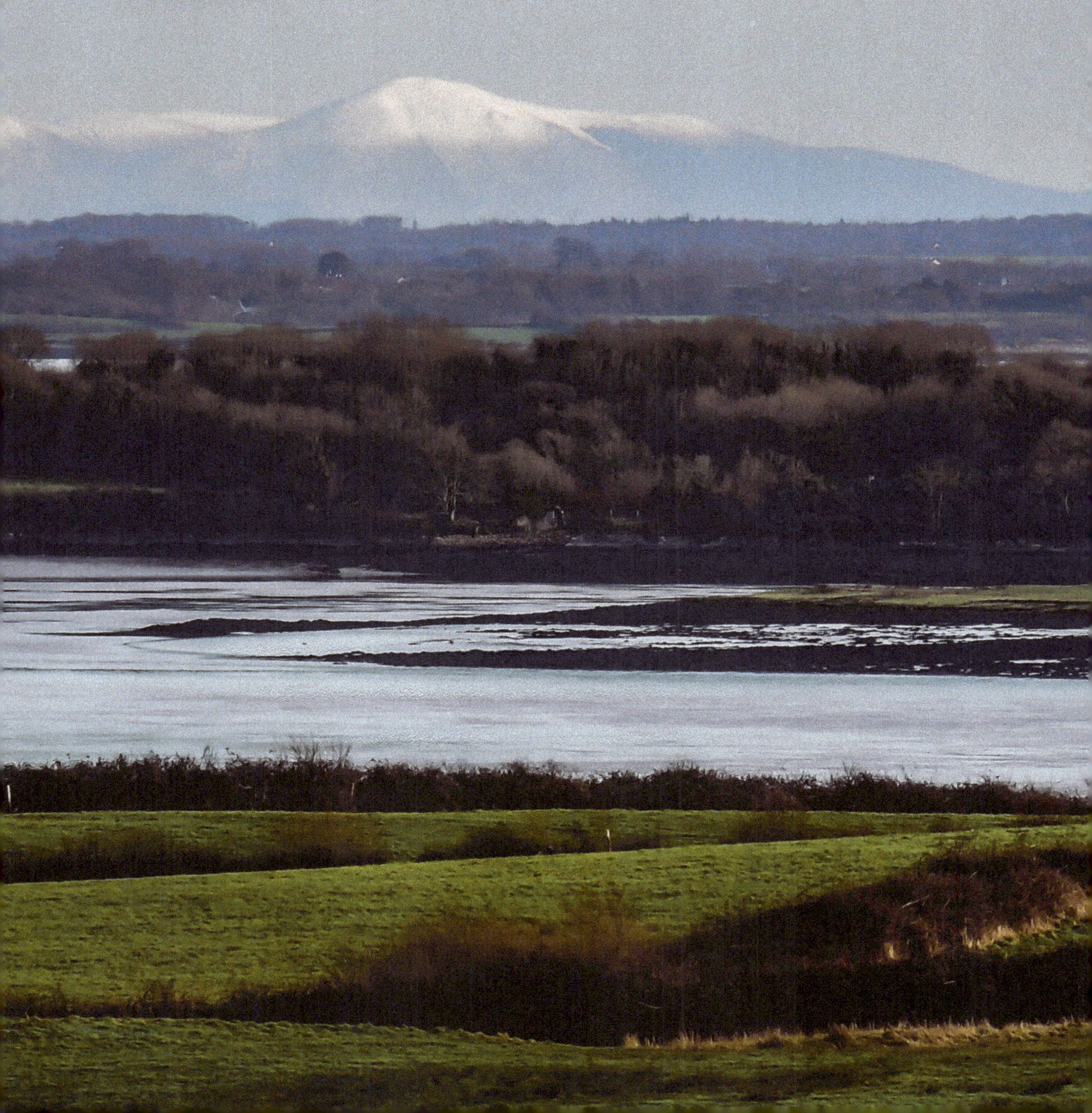

Snow-capped peaks of Ireland's Galtee Mountains, stretching across counties Tipperary and Limerick, hover in the distance with the Shannon Estuary and fields of County Clare in the foreground.

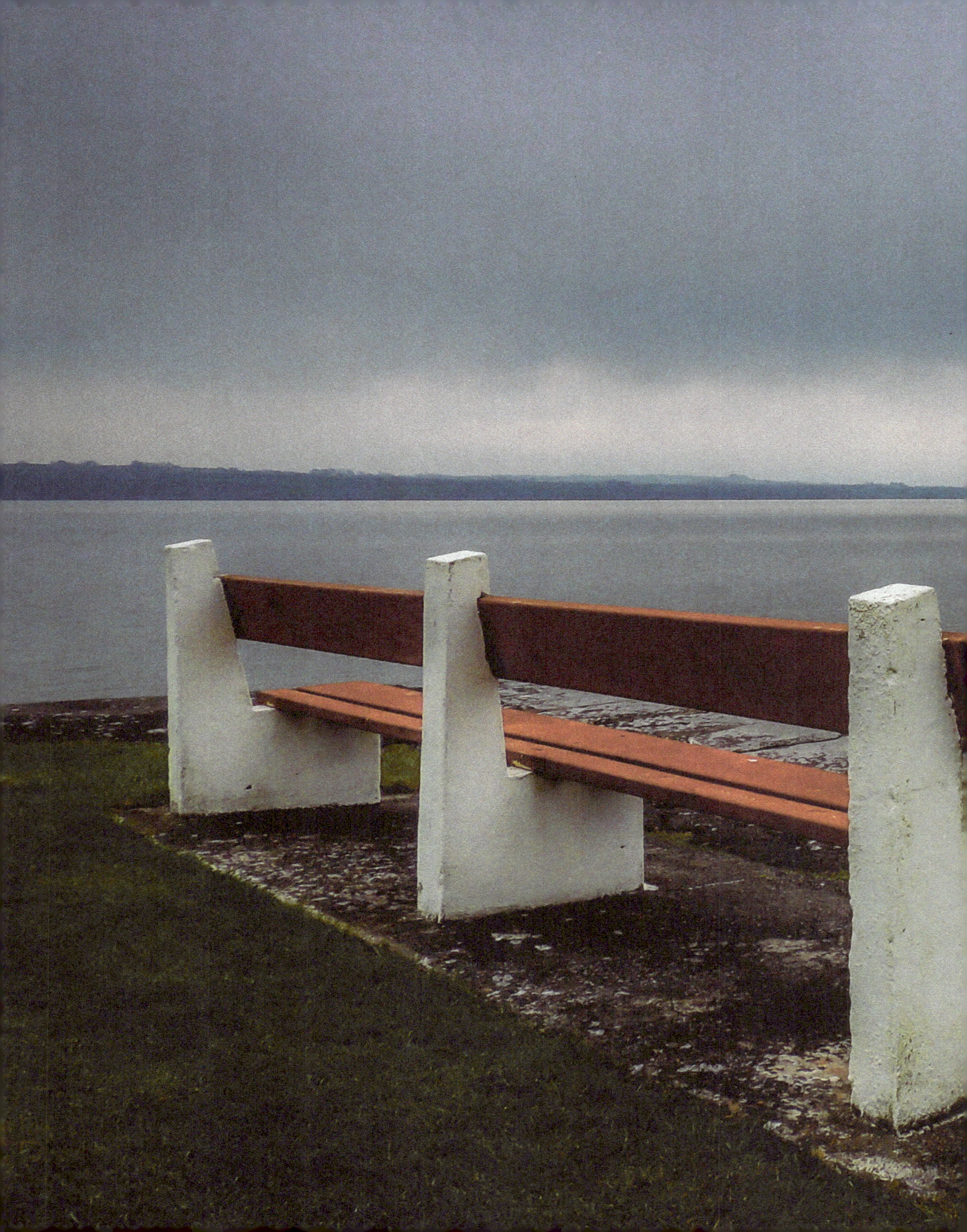

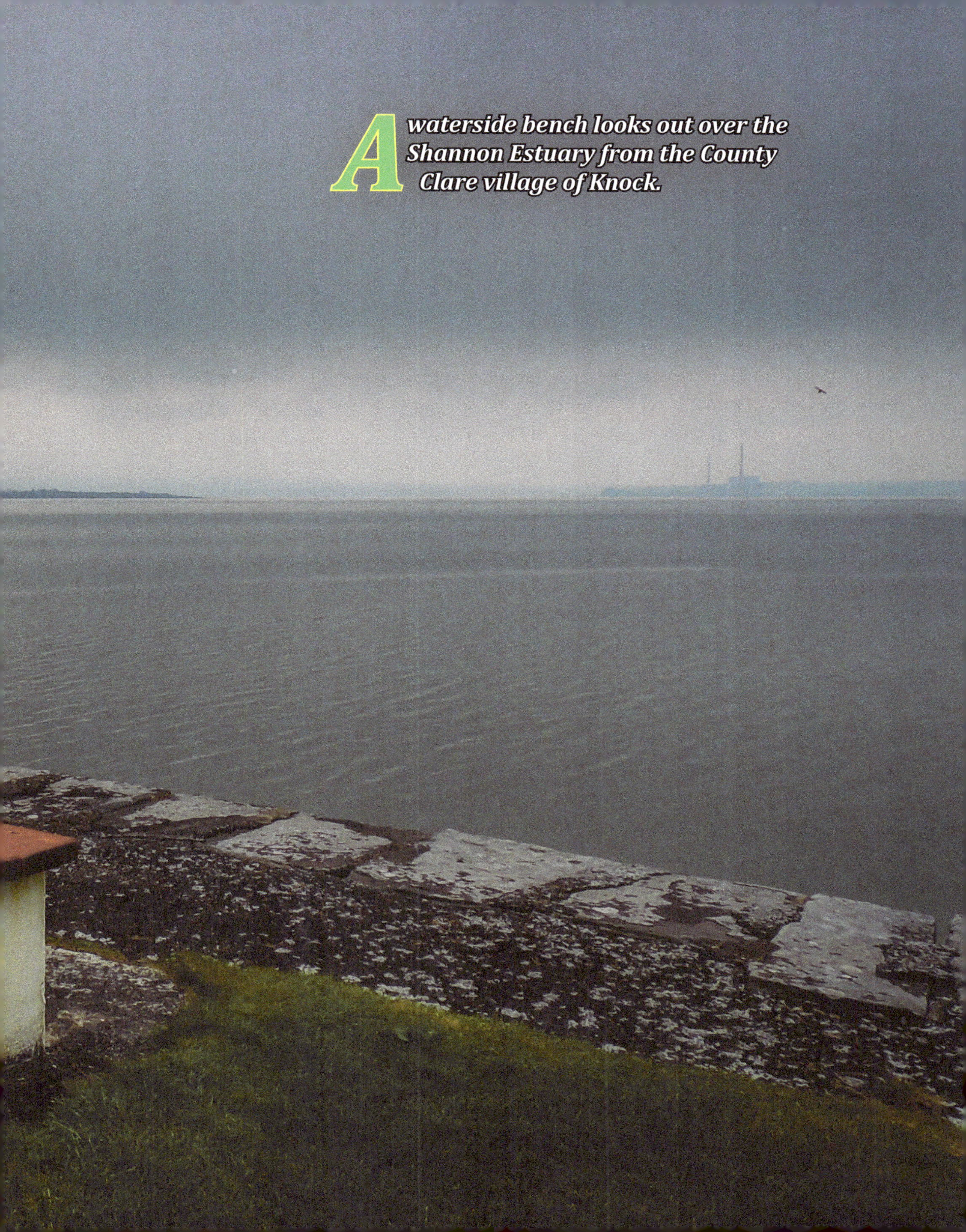

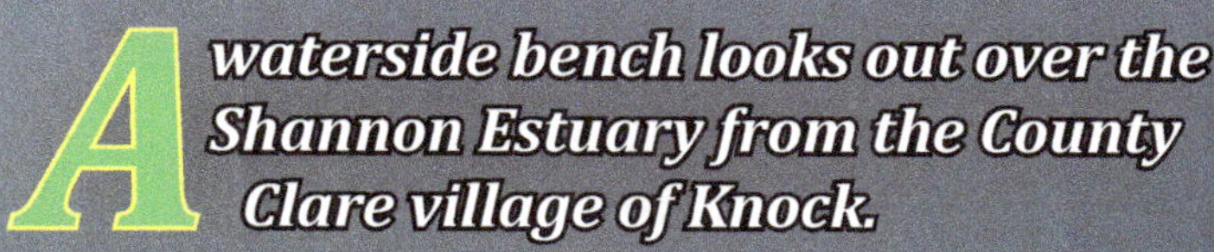

A waterside bench looks out over the Shannon Estuary from the County Clare village of Knock.

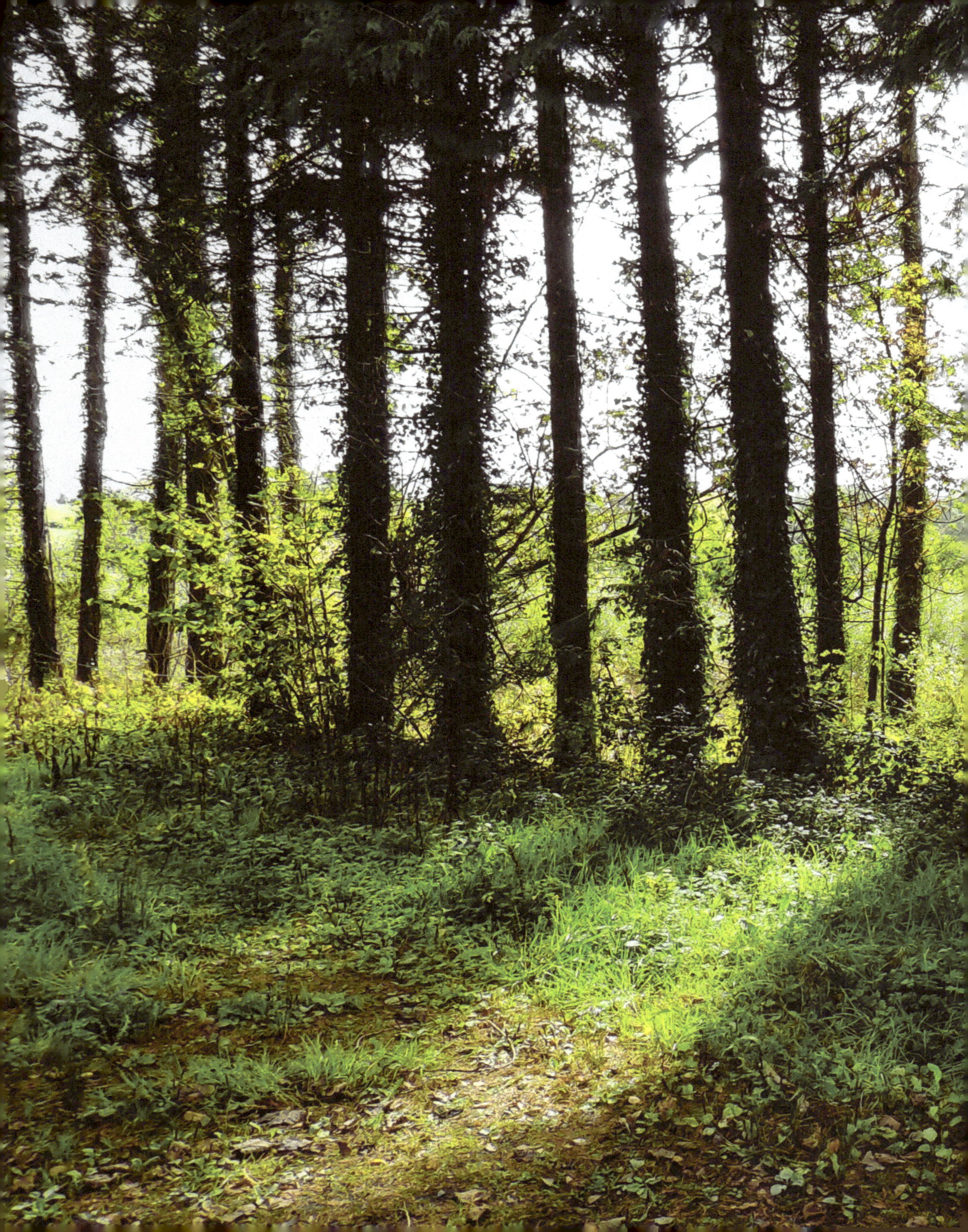

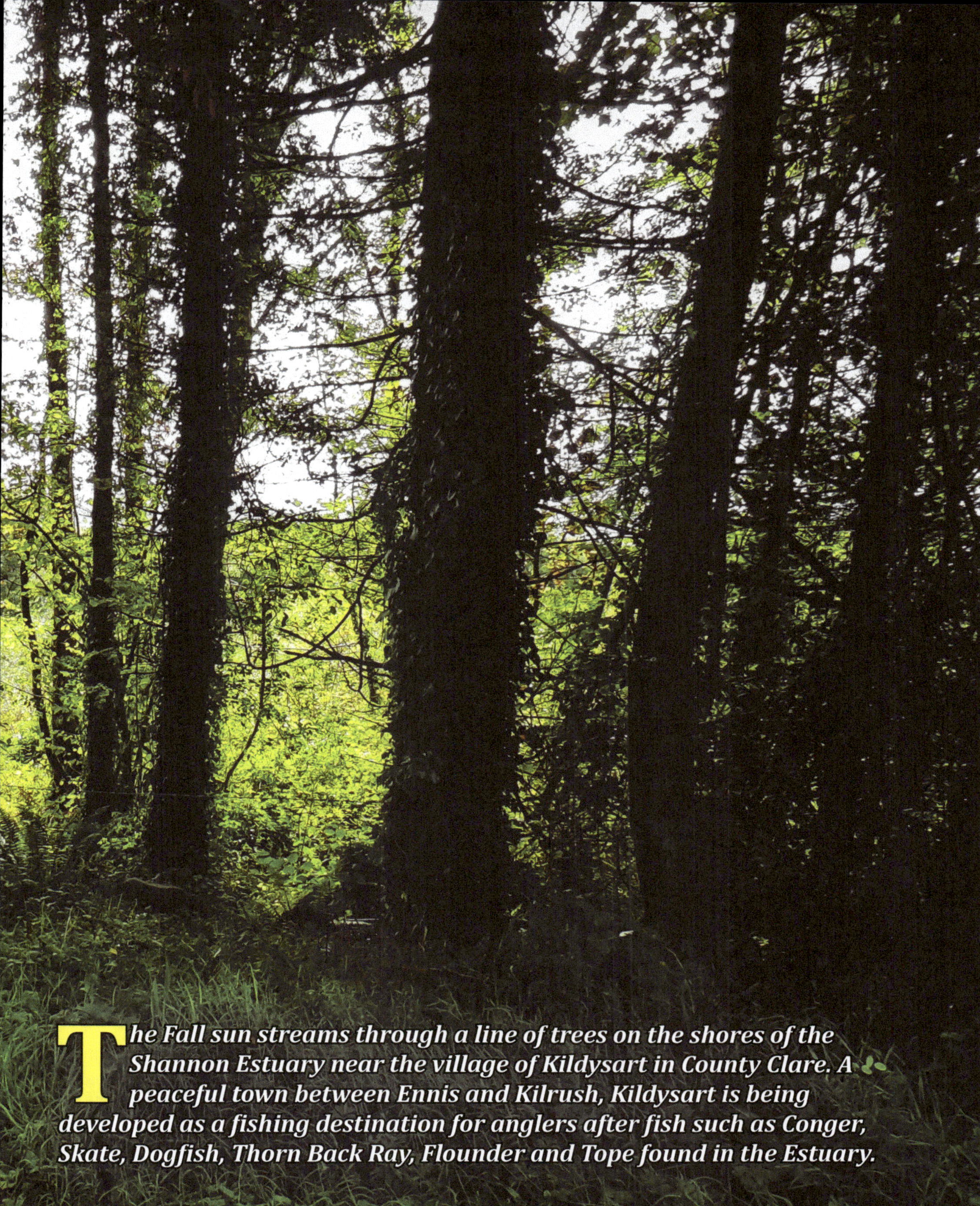

The Fall sun streams through a line of trees on the shores of the Shannon Estuary near the village of Kildysart in County Clare. A peaceful town between Ennis and Kilrush, Kildysart is being developed as a fishing destination for anglers after fish such as Conger, Skate, Dogfish, Thorn Back Ray, Flounder and Tope found in the Estuary.

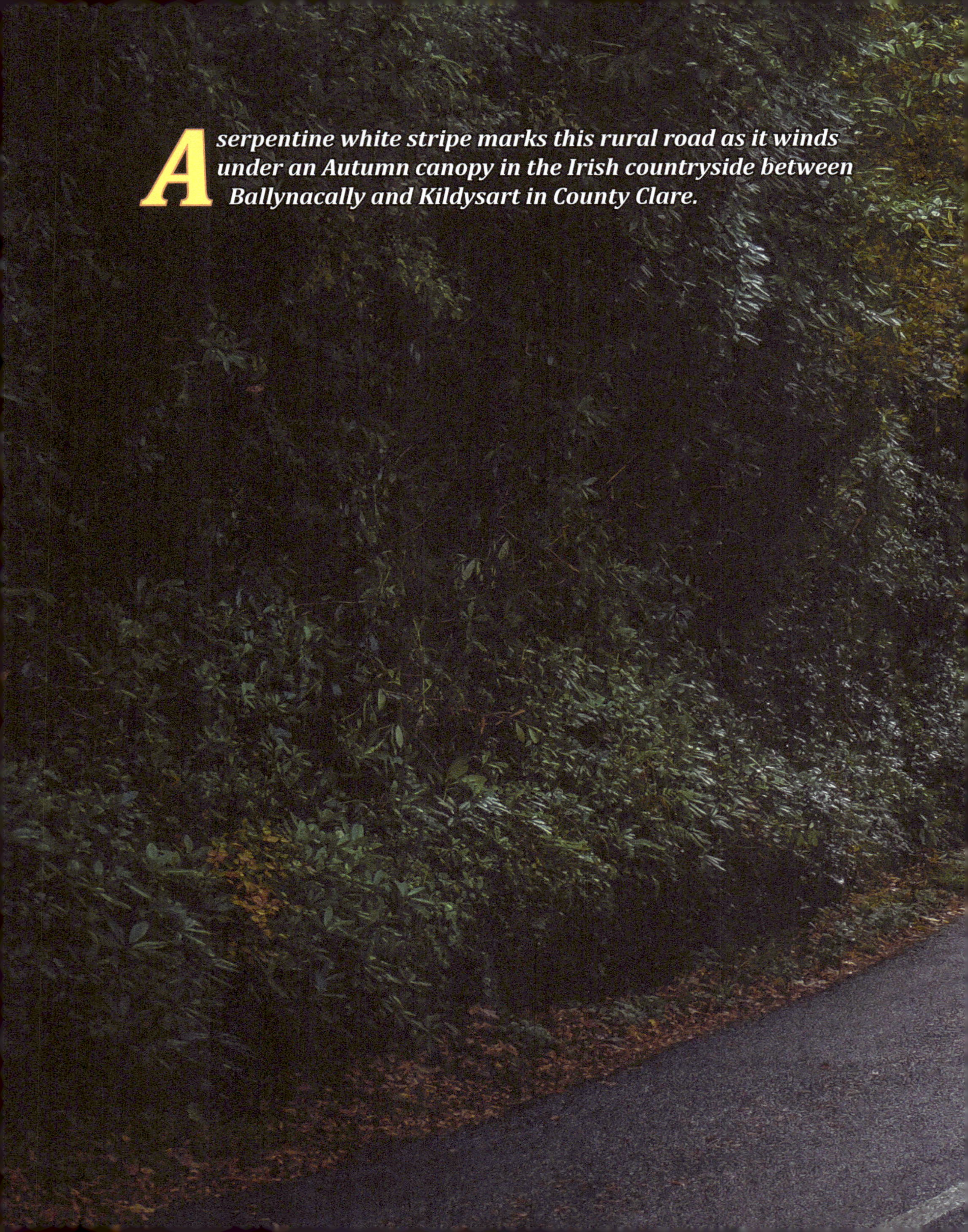

A serpentine white stripe marks this rural road as it winds under an Autumn canopy in the Irish countryside between Ballynacally and Kildysart in County Clare.

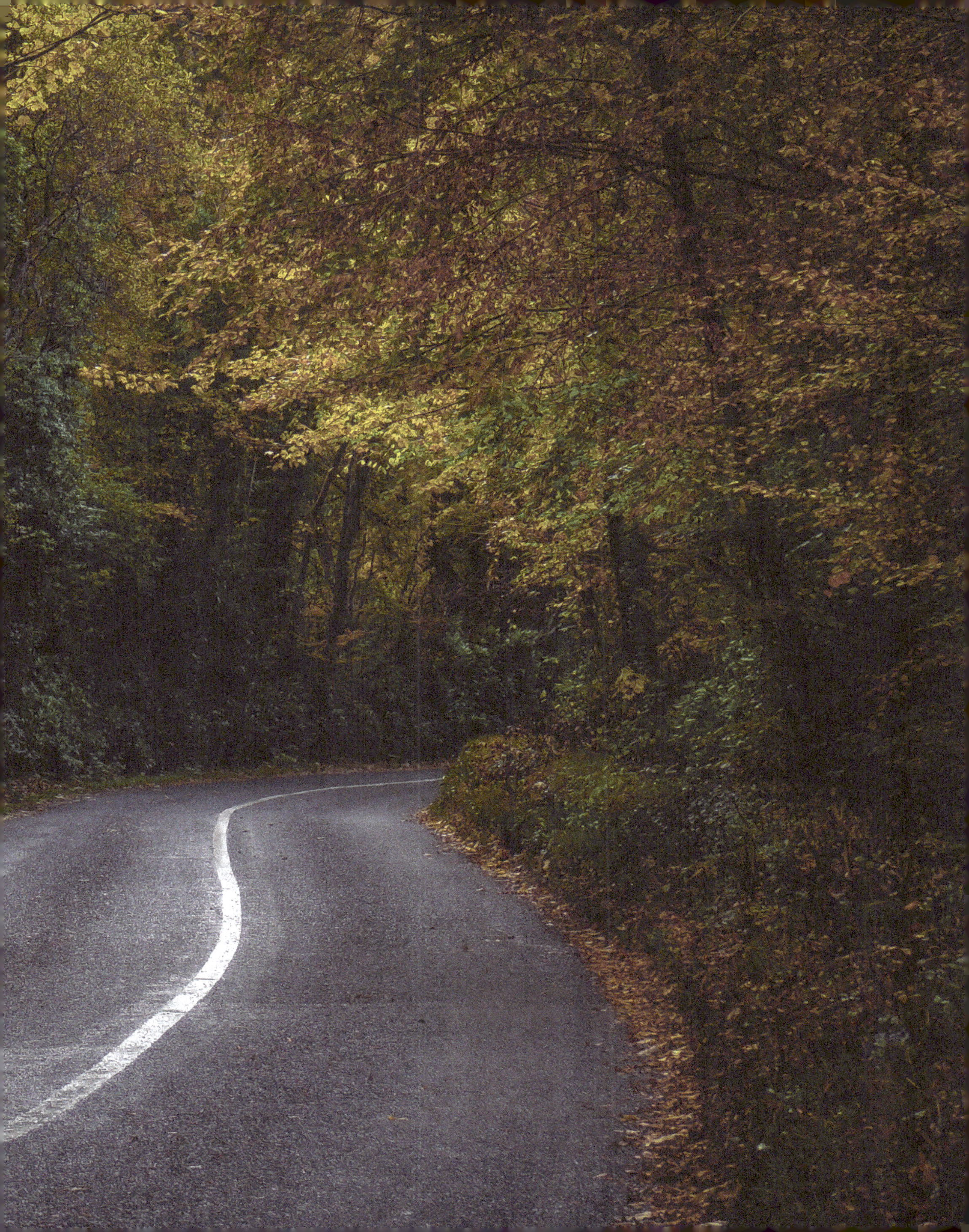

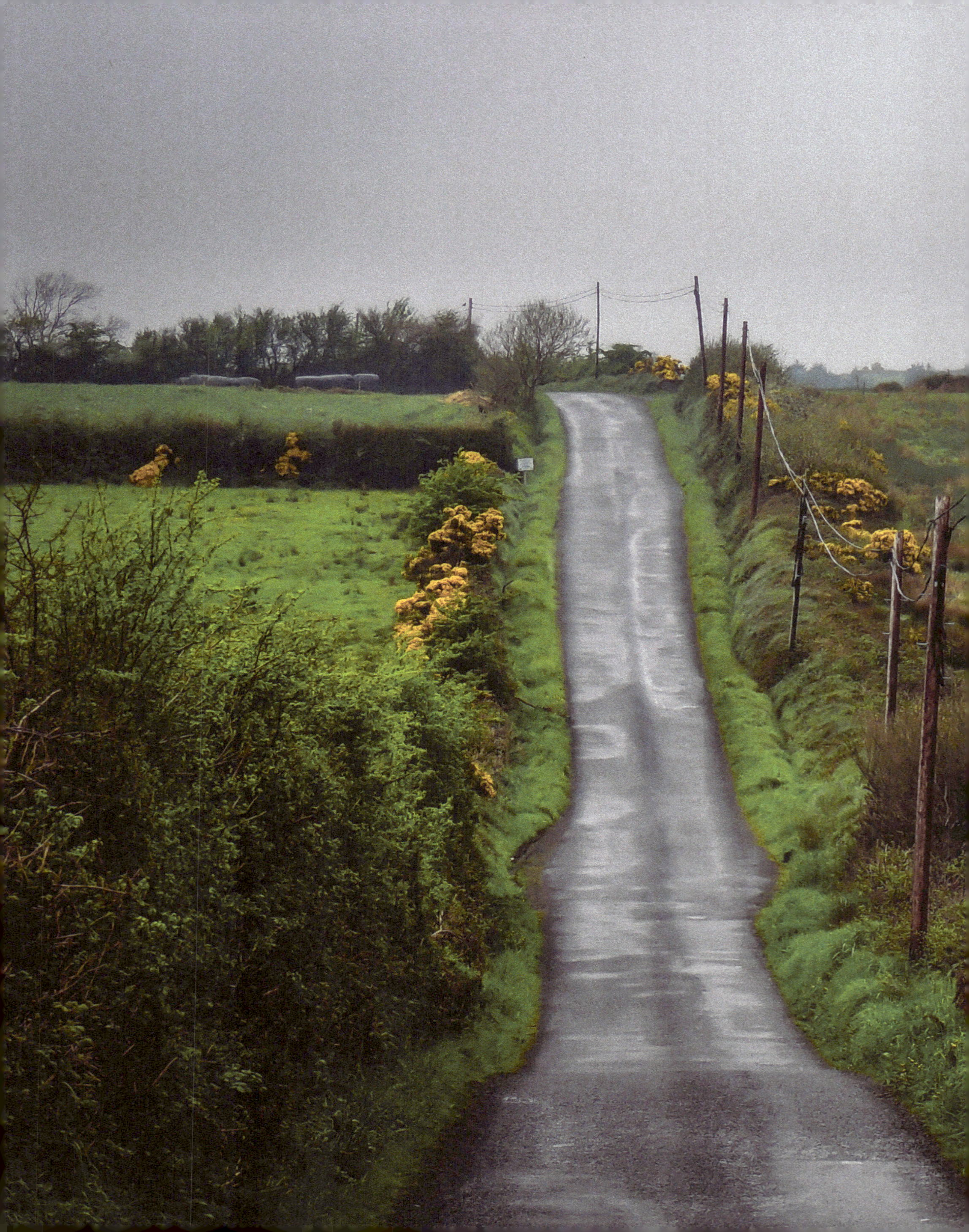

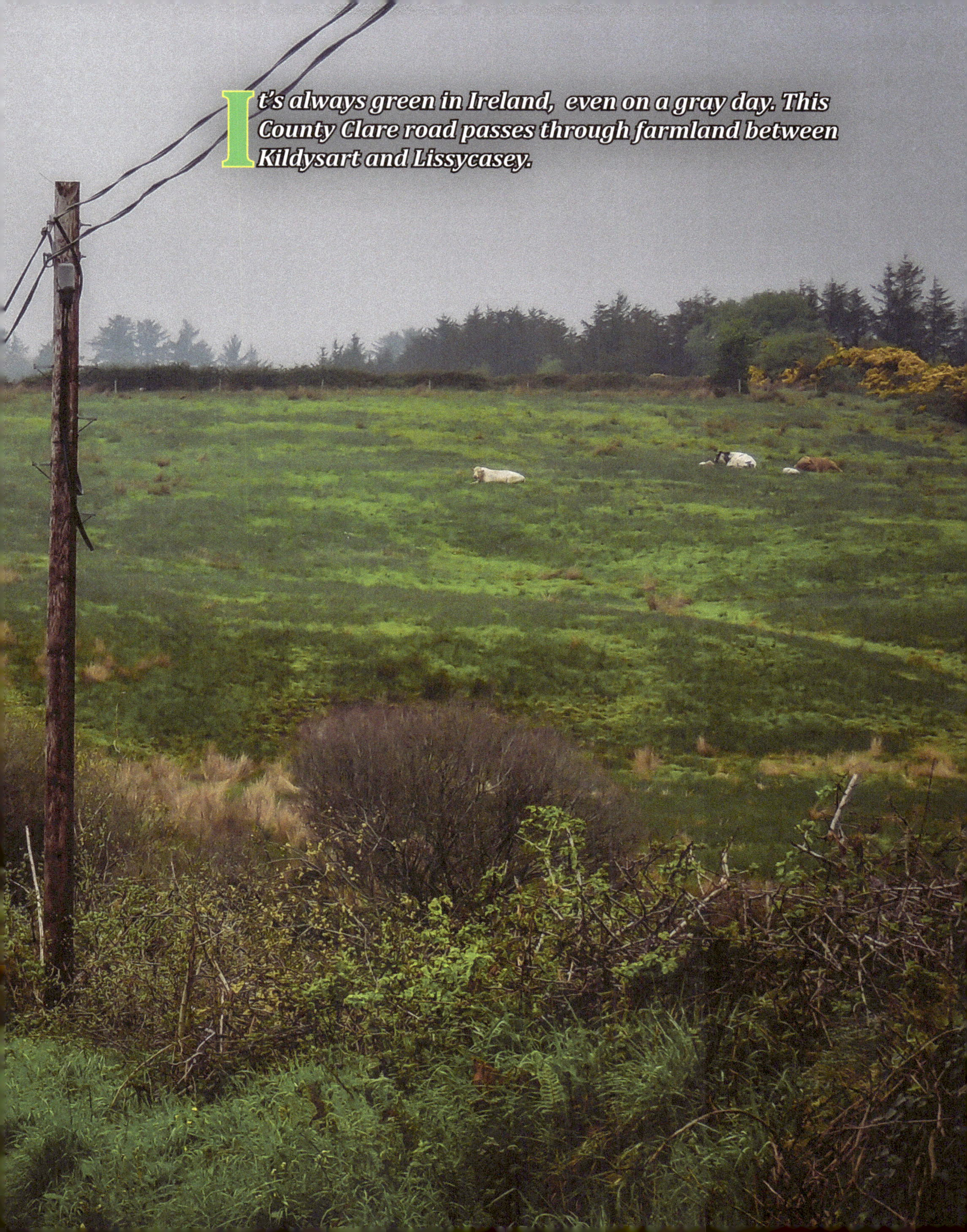

It's always green in Ireland, even on a gray day. This County Clare road passes through farmland between Kildysart and Lissycasey.

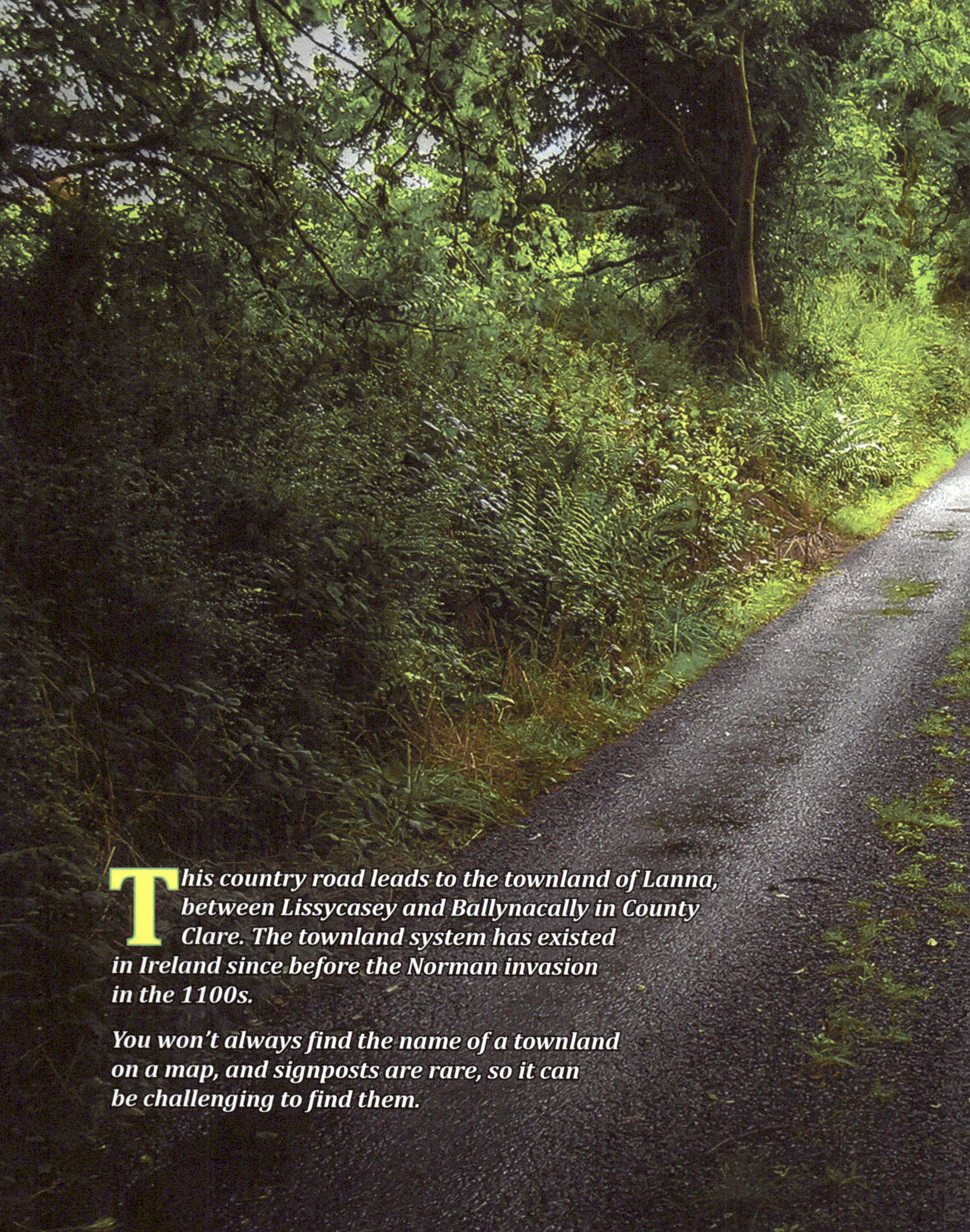

This country road leads to the townland of Lanna, between Lissycasey and Ballynacally in County Clare. The townland system has existed in Ireland since before the Norman invasion in the 1100s.

You won't always find the name of a townland on a map, and signposts are rare, so it can be challenging to find them.

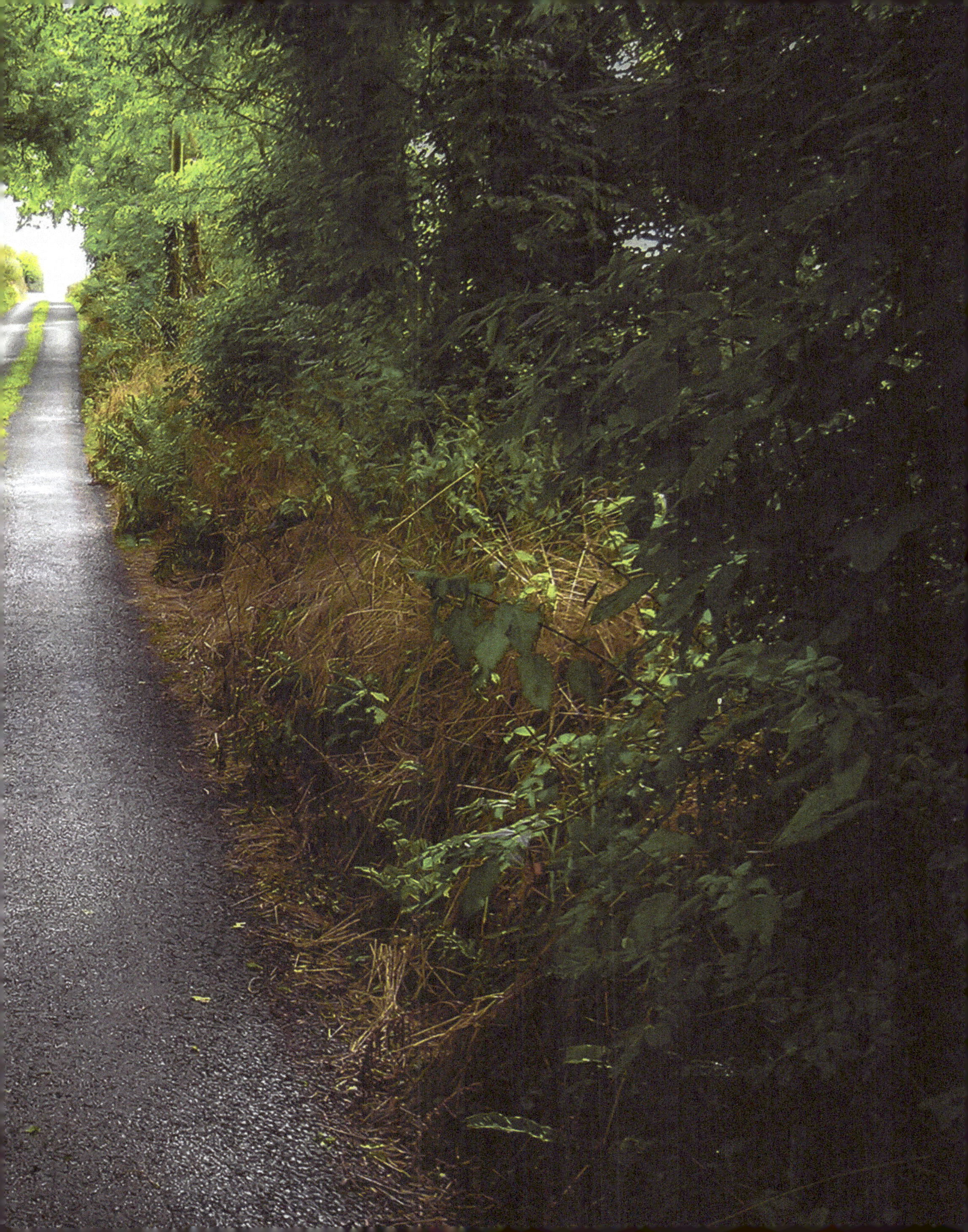

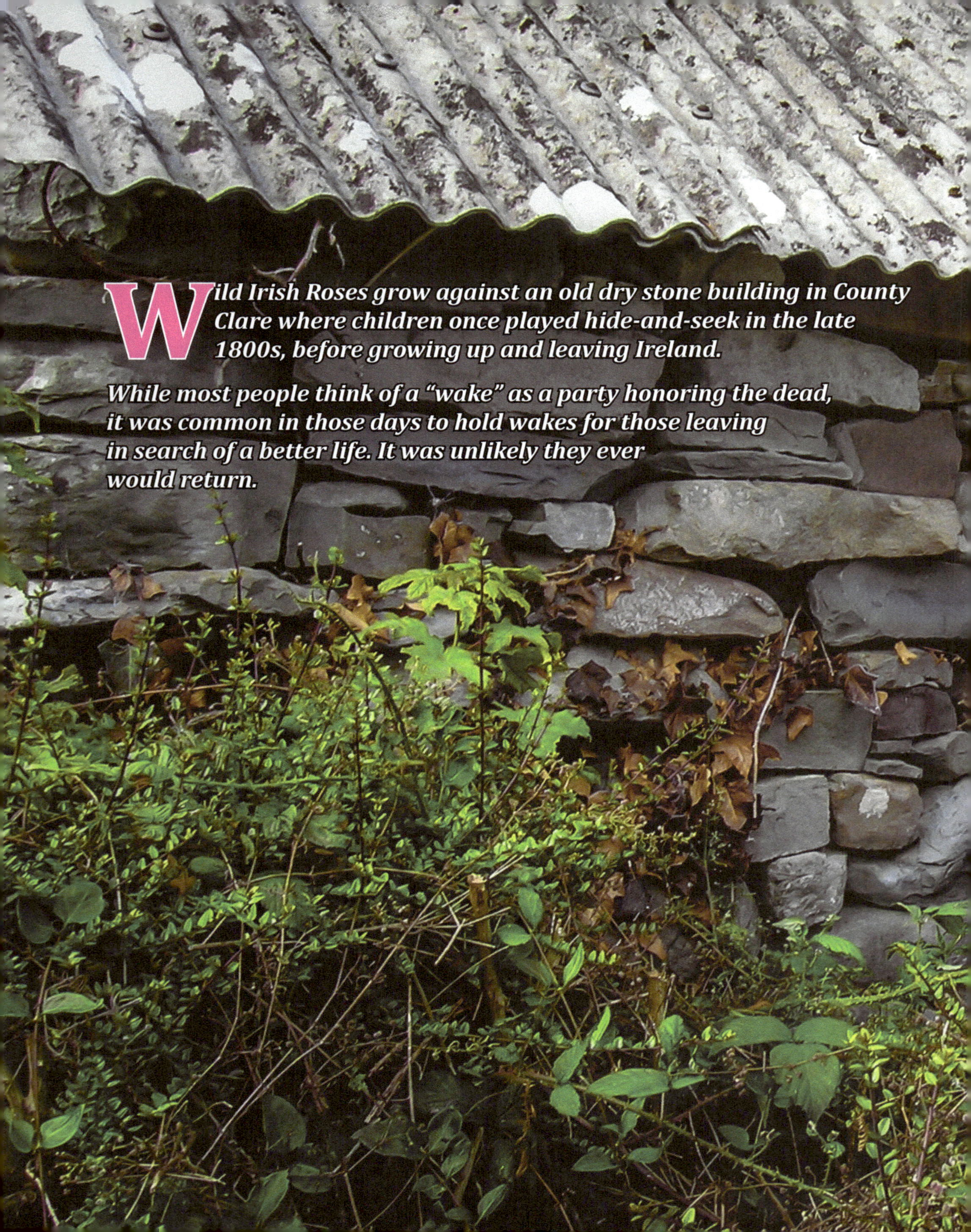

Wild Irish Roses grow against an old dry stone building in County Clare where children once played hide-and-seek in the late 1800s, before growing up and leaving Ireland.

While most people think of a "wake" as a party honoring the dead, it was common in those days to hold wakes for those leaving in search of a better life. It was unlikely they ever would return.

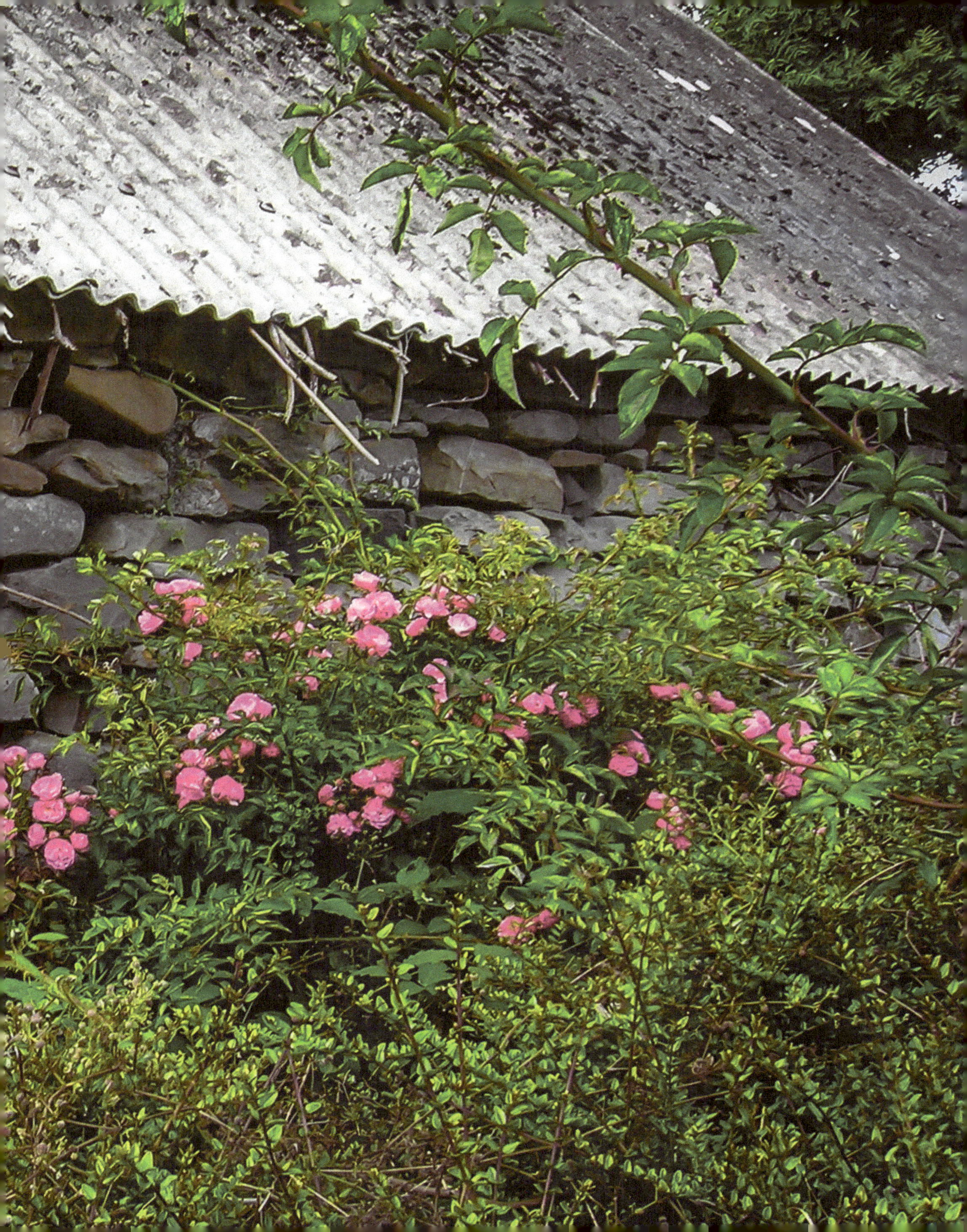

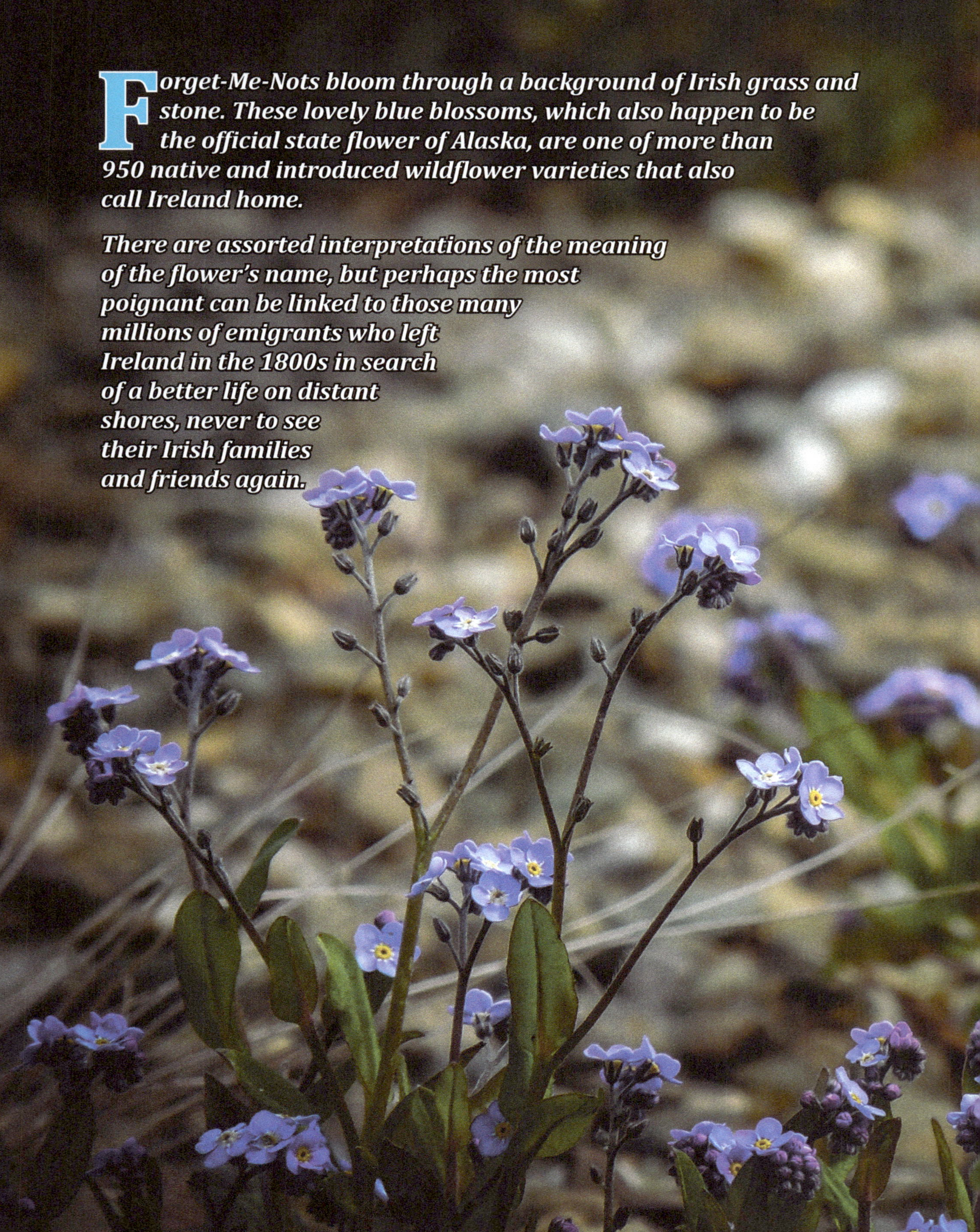
Forget-Me-Nots bloom through a background of Irish grass and stone. These lovely blue blossoms, which also happen to be the official state flower of Alaska, are one of more than 950 native and introduced wildflower varieties that also call Ireland home.

There are assorted interpretations of the meaning of the flower's name, but perhaps the most poignant can be linked to those many millions of emigrants who left Ireland in the 1800s in search of a better life on distant shores, never to see their Irish families and friends again.

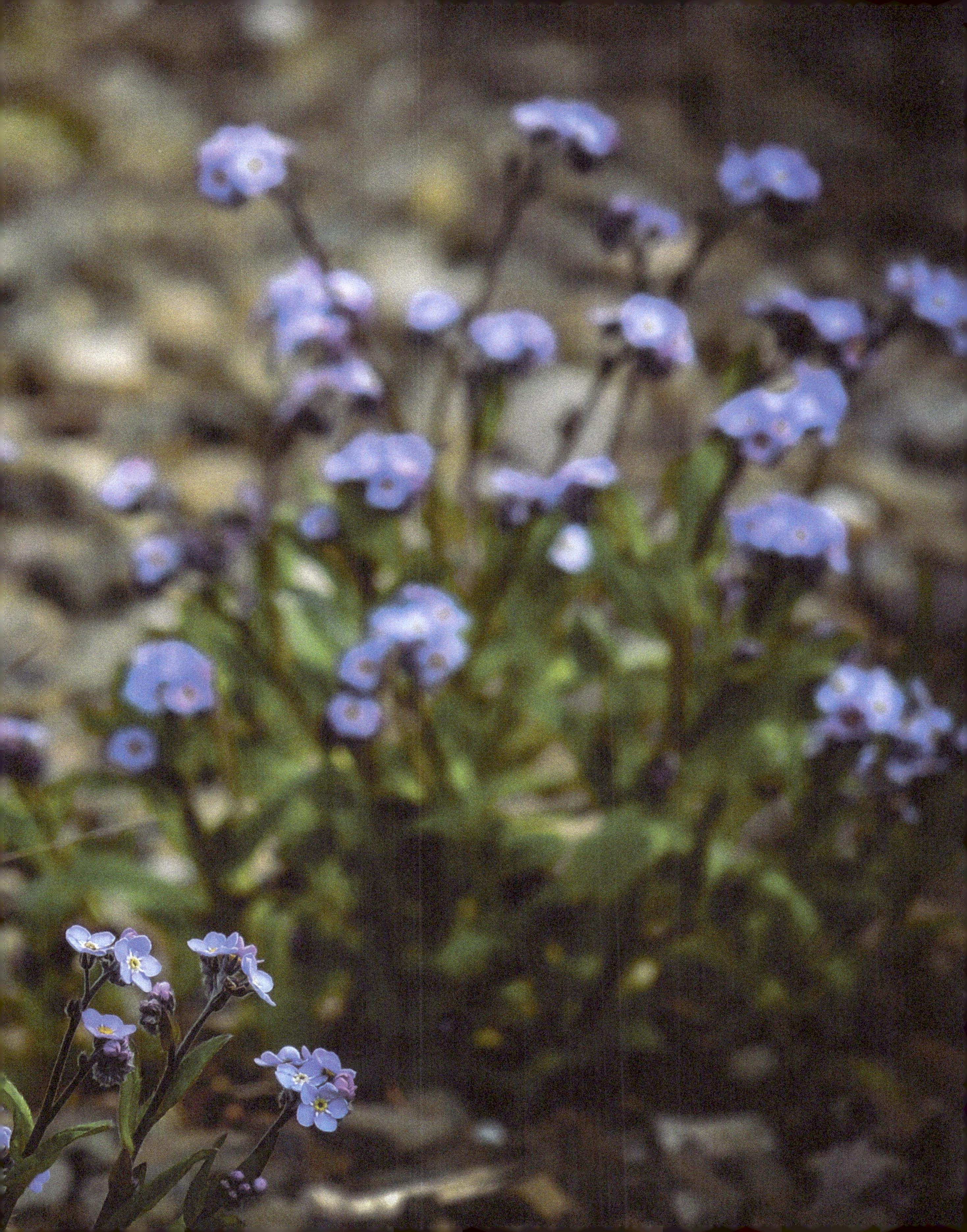

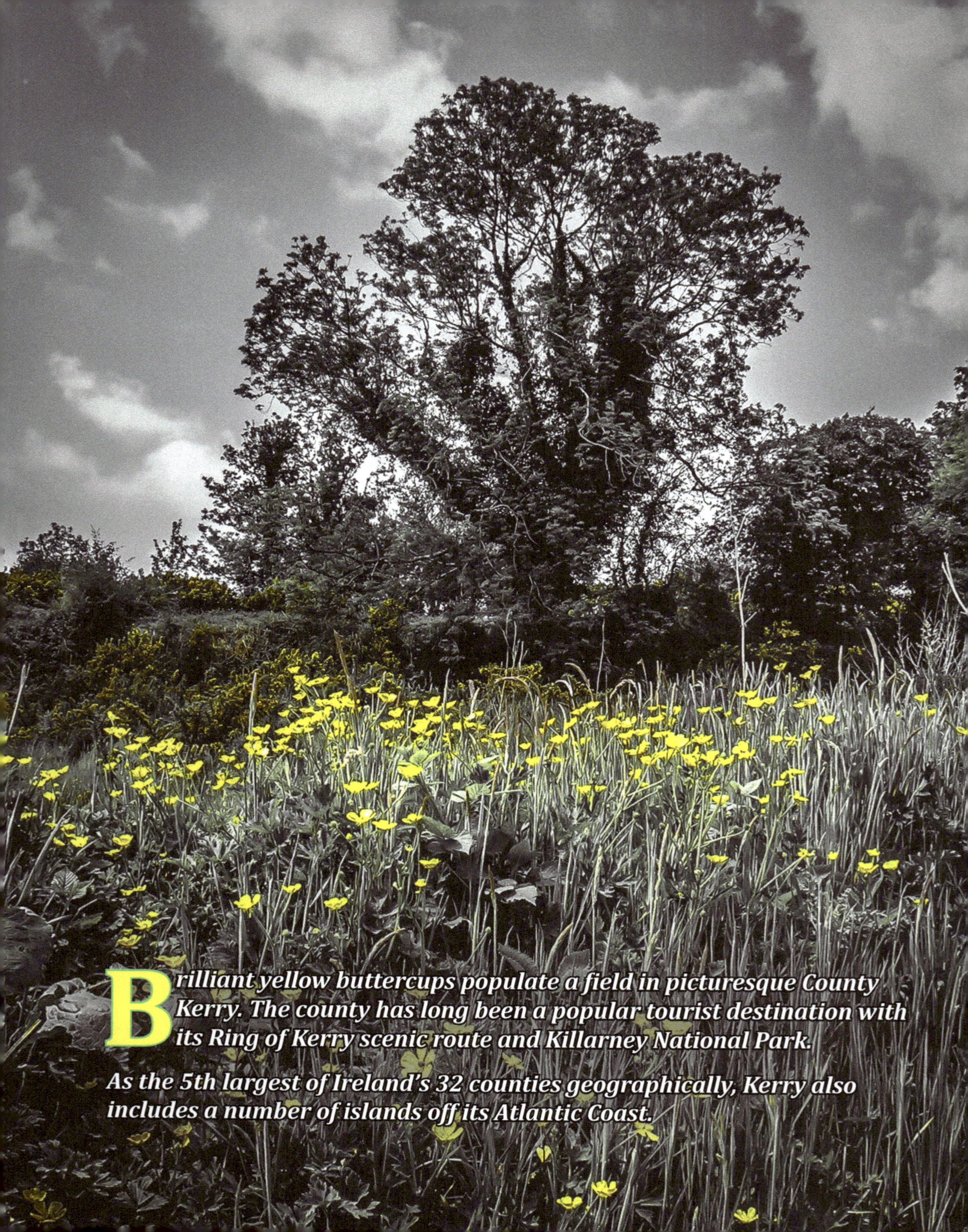
Brilliant yellow buttercups populate a field in picturesque County Kerry. The county has long been a popular tourist destination with its Ring of Kerry scenic route and Killarney National Park.

As the 5th largest of Ireland's 32 counties geographically, Kerry also includes a number of islands off its Atlantic Coast.

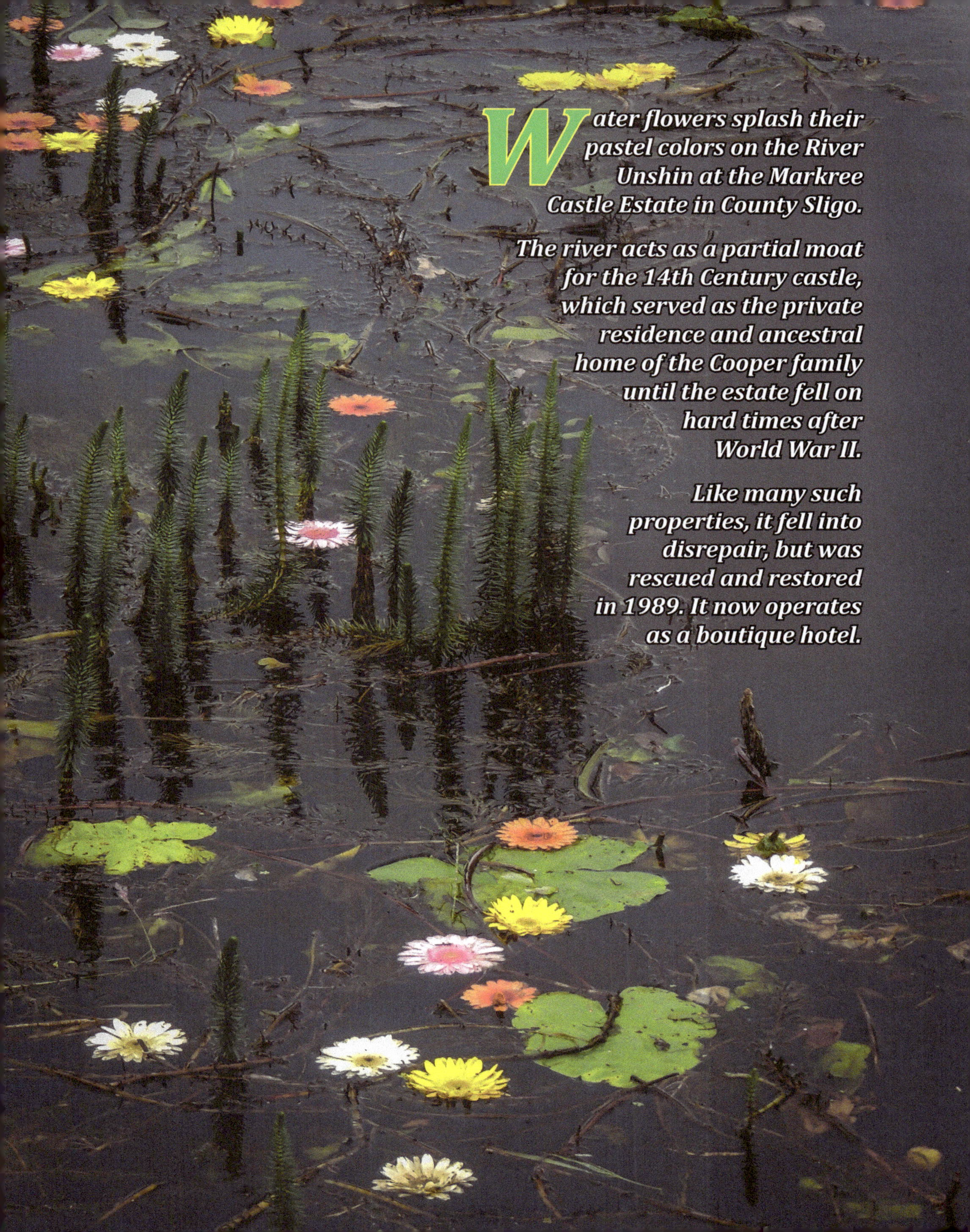

Water flowers splash their pastel colors on the River Unshin at the Markree Castle Estate in County Sligo.

The river acts as a partial moat for the 14th Century castle, which served as the private residence and ancestral home of the Cooper family until the estate fell on hard times after World War II.

Like many such properties, it fell into disrepair, but was rescued and restored in 1989. It now operates as a boutique hotel.

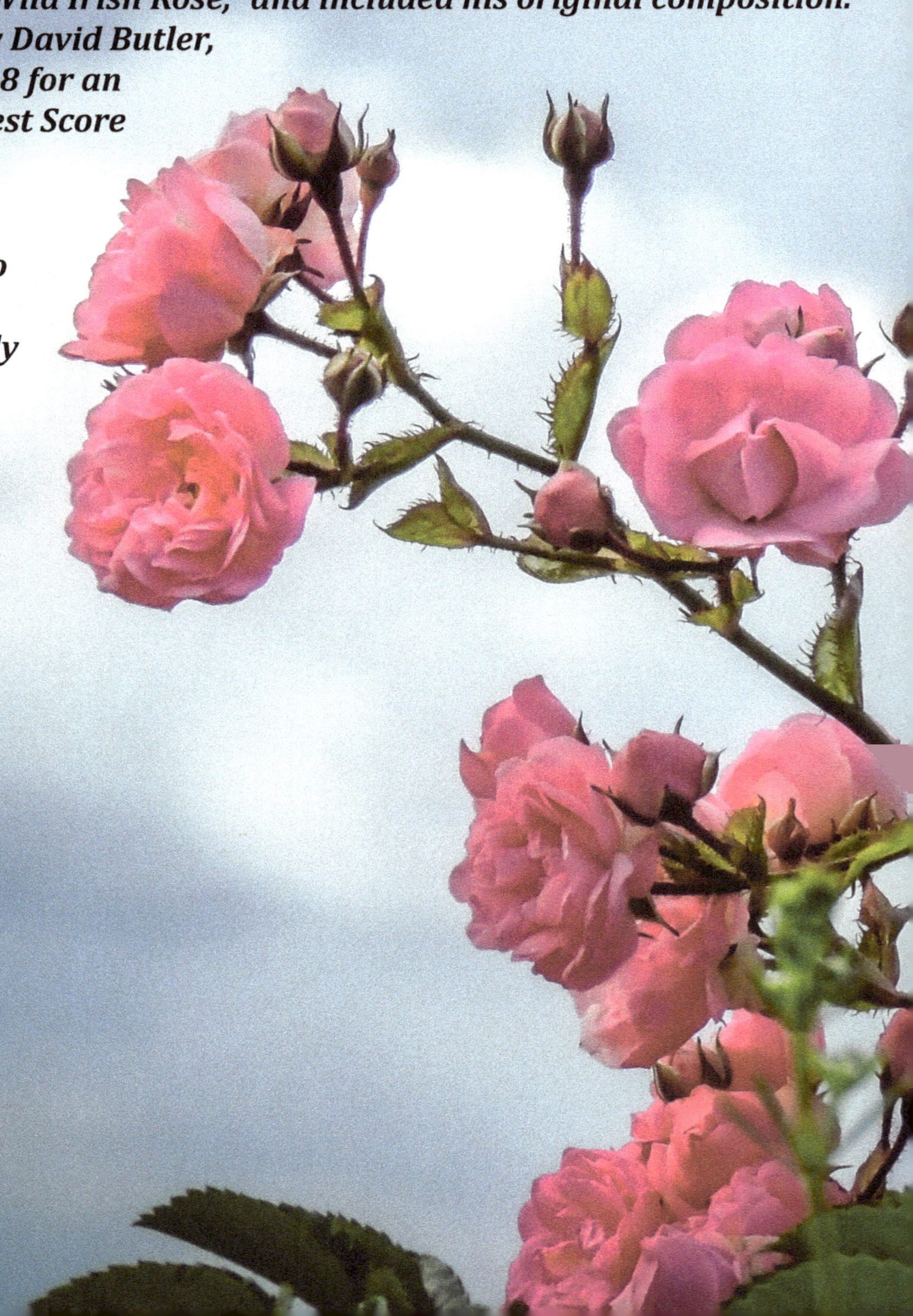

Wild Irish Roses burst into color in the enchanting Irish countryside over Lissycasey, County Clare. These brilliant pink blossoms inspired the popular song, "My Wild Irish Rose."

The iconic tune, which has been covered by numerous musicians over the years, was written by Irish-American actor, songwriter and singer Chancellor "Chauncey" Olcott in 1899 for his production of "A Romance in Athlone."

In 1947, Warner Brothers released a film based Chauncey's life — it was called, of course, "My Wild Irish Rose," and included his original composition. The movie, directed by David Butler, was nominated in 1948 for an Academy Award for Best Score in a Musical Picture.

Chauncey, who died in 1932 in Monte Carlo at the age of 74, was inducted posthumously into the Songwriters Hall of Fame in 1970.

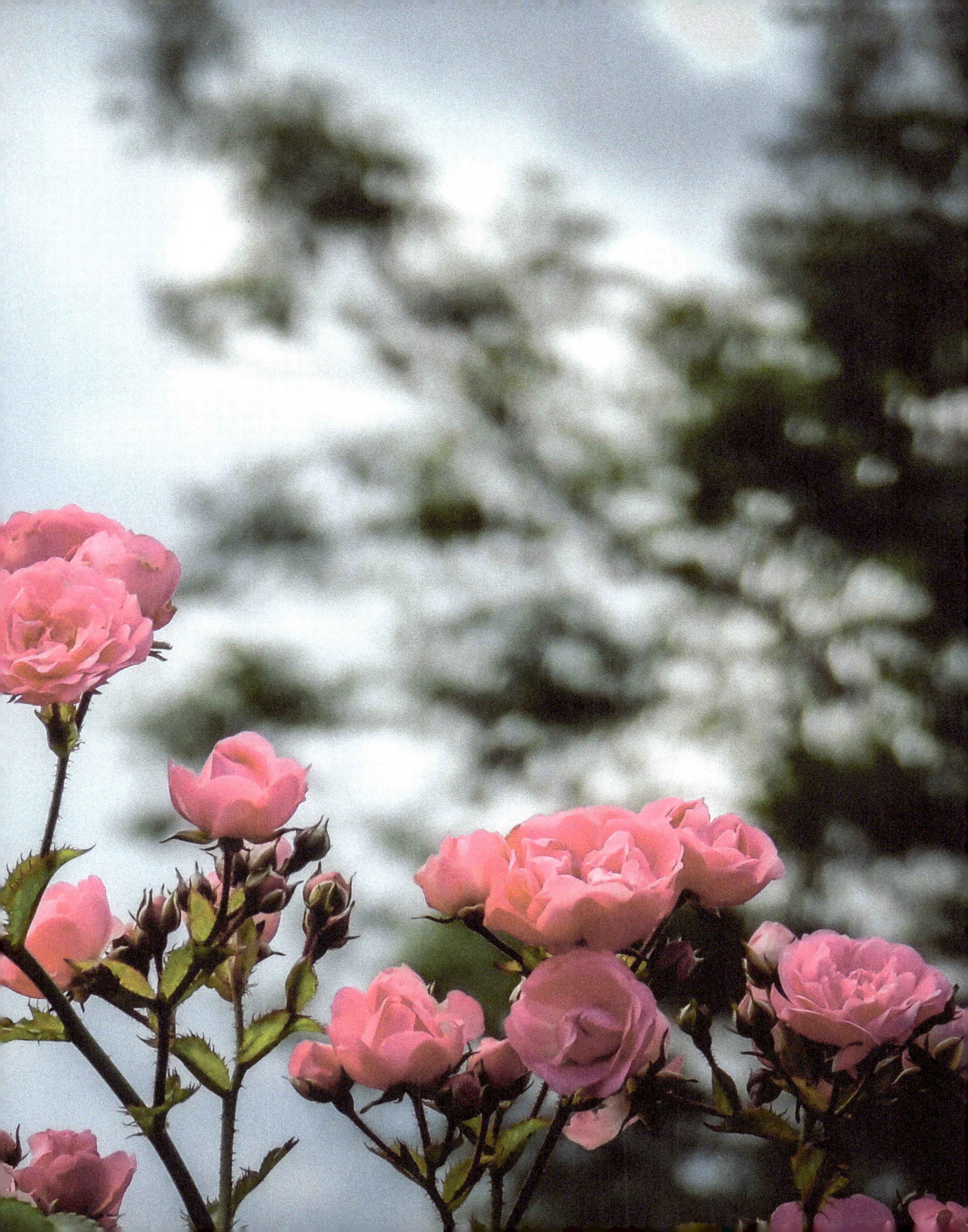

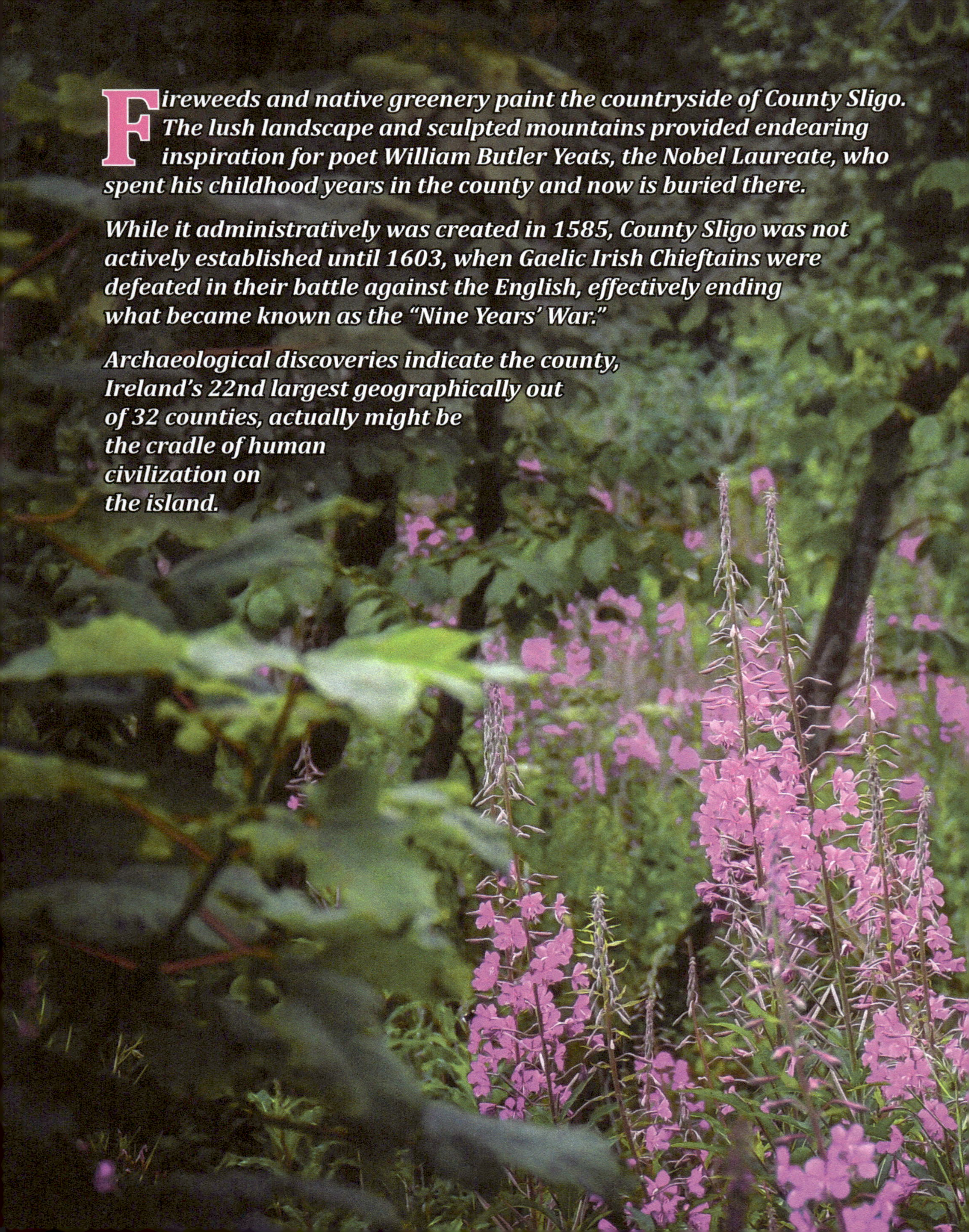

Fireweeds and native greenery paint the countryside of County Sligo. The lush landscape and sculpted mountains provided endearing inspiration for poet William Butler Yeats, the Nobel Laureate, who spent his childhood years in the county and now is buried there.

While it administratively was created in 1585, County Sligo was not actively established until 1603, when Gaelic Irish Chieftains were defeated in their battle against the English, effectively ending what became known as the "Nine Years' War."

Archaeological discoveries indicate the county, Ireland's 22nd largest geographically out of 32 counties, actually might be the cradle of human civilization on the island.

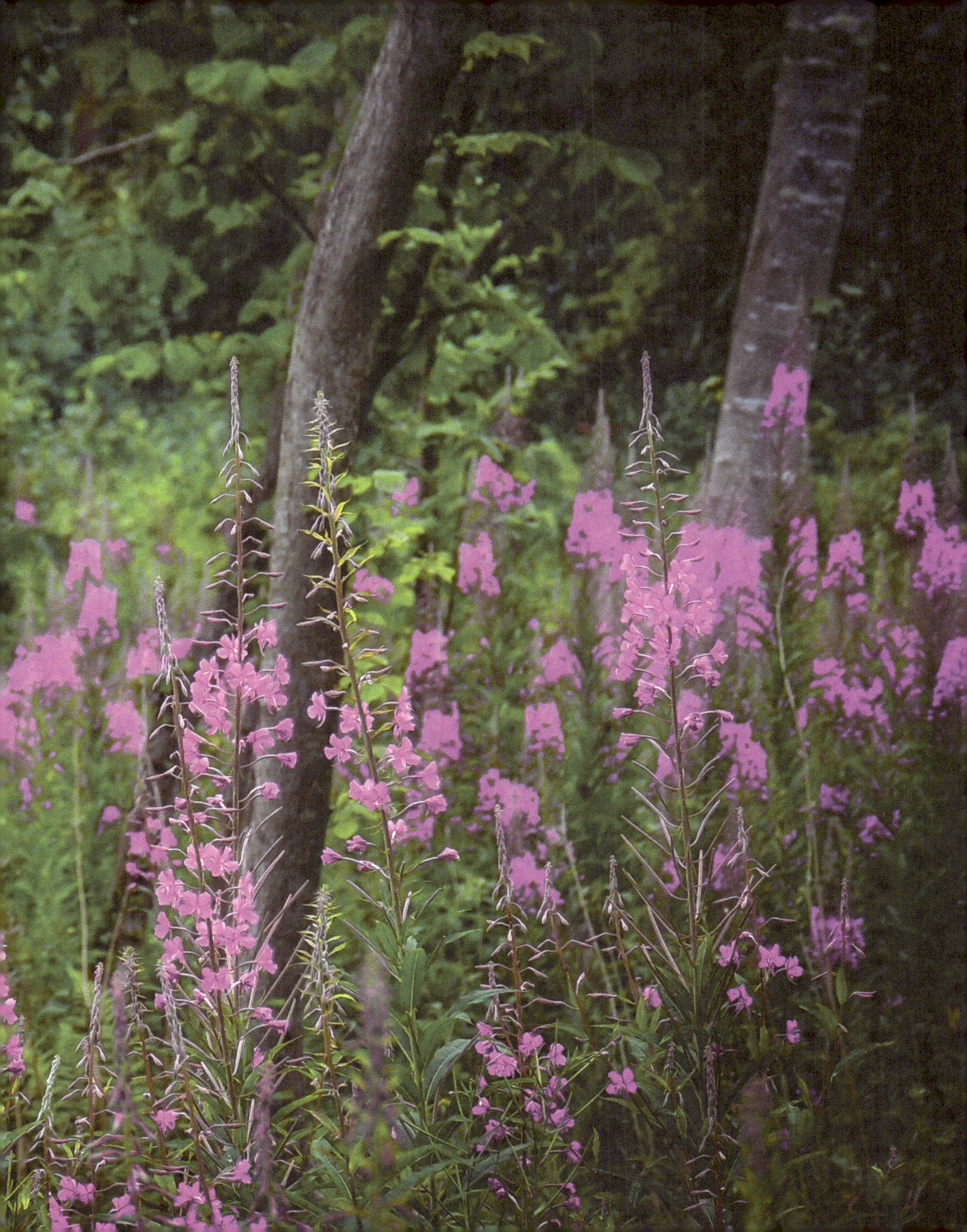

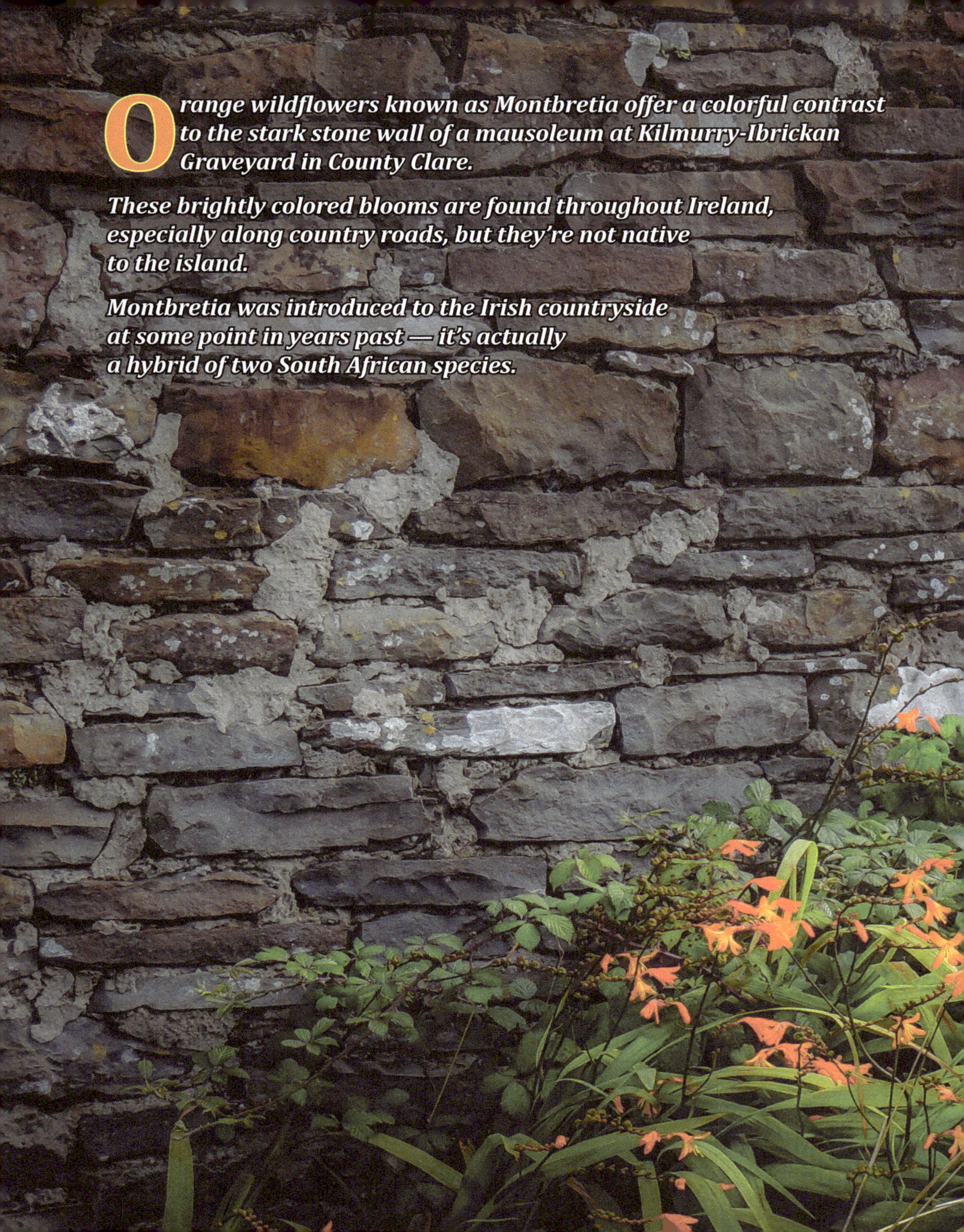

Orange wildflowers known as Montbretia offer a colorful contrast to the stark stone wall of a mausoleum at Kilmurry-Ibrickan Graveyard in County Clare.

These brightly colored blooms are found throughout Ireland, especially along country roads, but they're not native to the island.

Montbretia was introduced to the Irish countryside at some point in years past — it's actually a hybrid of two South African species.

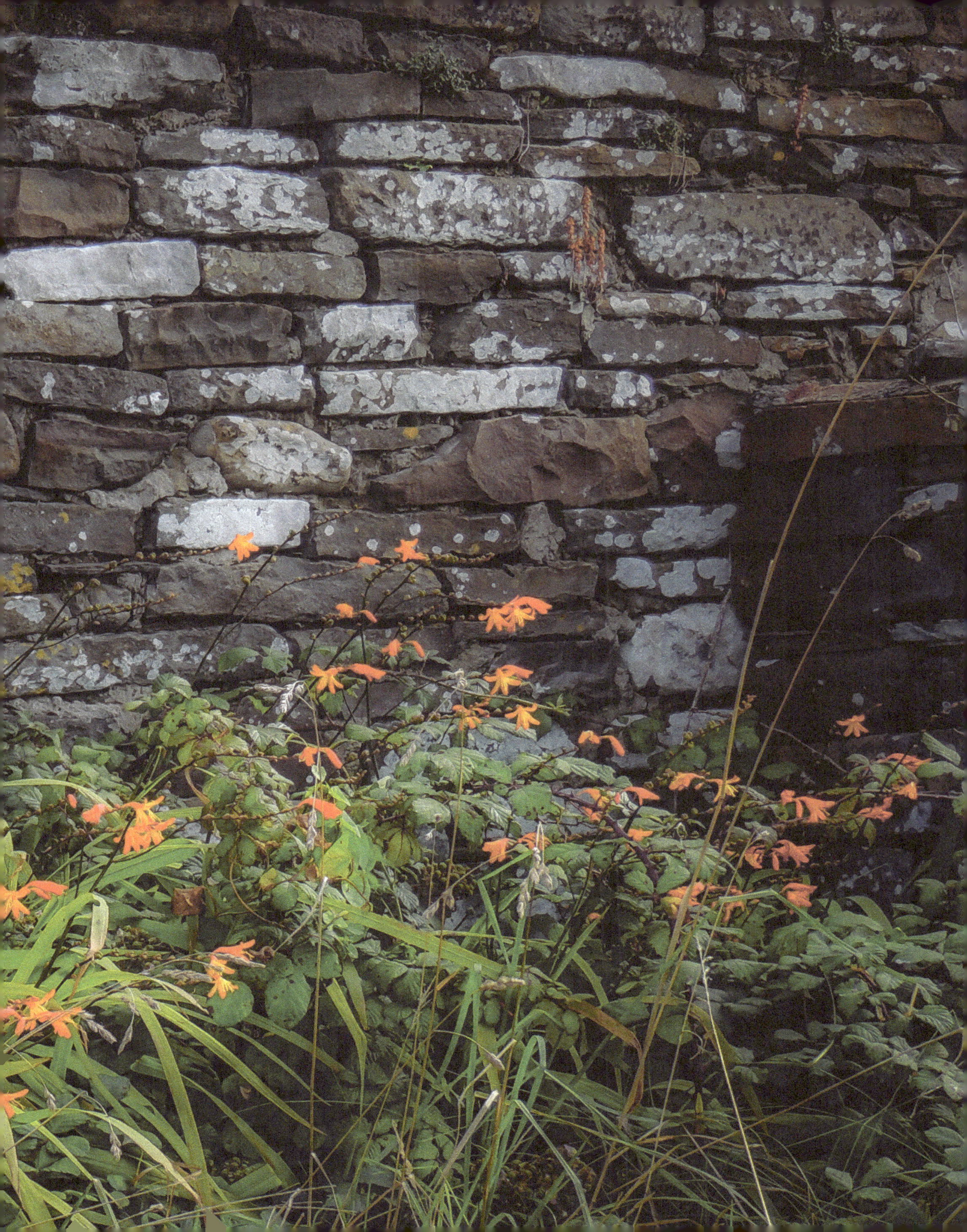

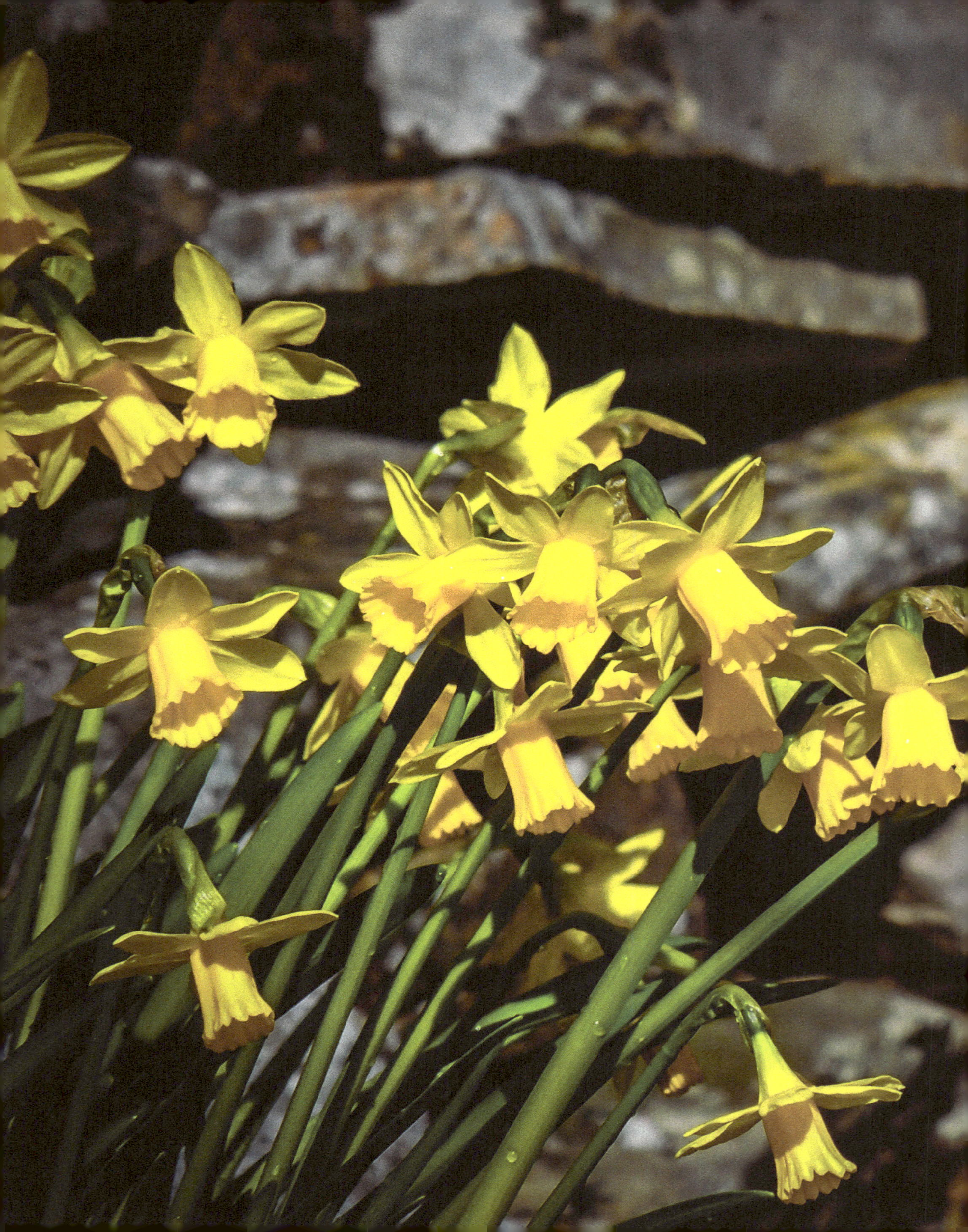

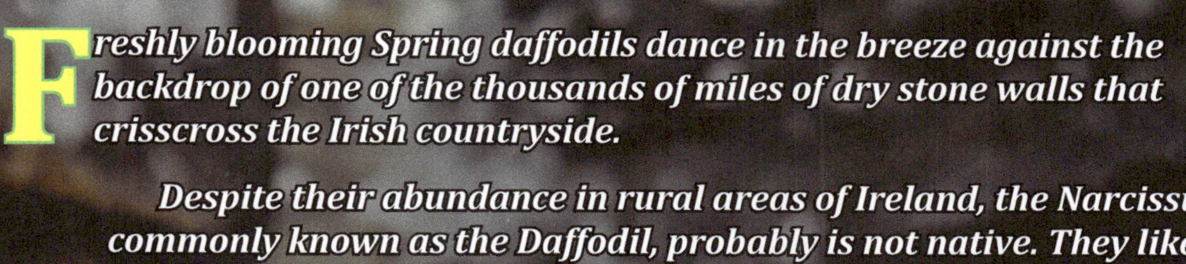

Freshly blooming Spring daffodils dance in the breeze against the backdrop of one of the thousands of miles of dry stone walls that crisscross the Irish countryside.

Despite their abundance in rural areas of Ireland, the Narcissus, commonly known as the Daffodil, probably is not native. They likely were introduced to the Irish countryside by British estate owners to add some color to large woodland areas.

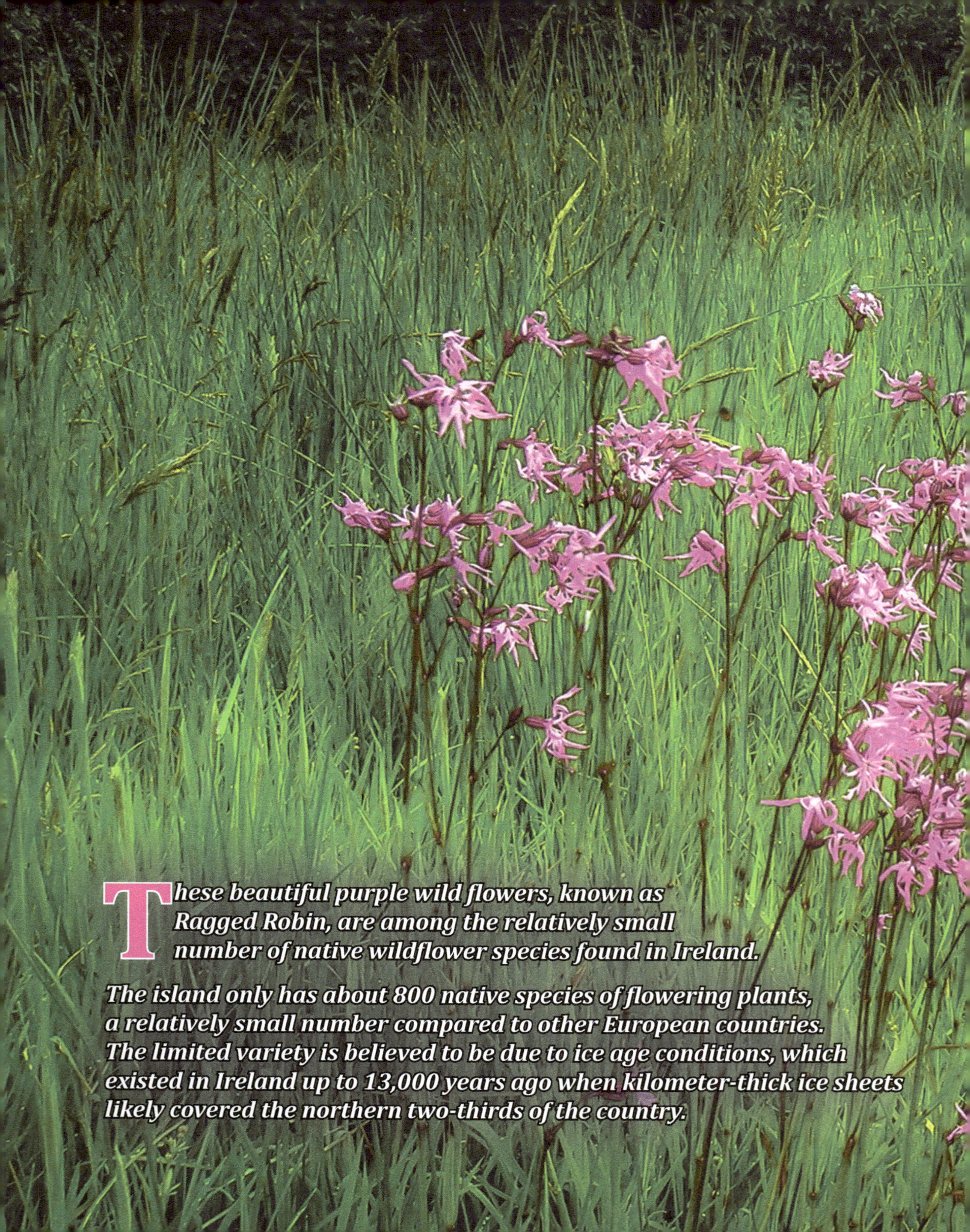

These beautiful purple wild flowers, known as Ragged Robin, are among the relatively small number of native wildflower species found in Ireland.

The island only has about 800 native species of flowering plants, a relatively small number compared to other European countries. The limited variety is believed to be due to ice age conditions, which existed in Ireland up to 13,000 years ago when kilometer-thick ice sheets likely covered the northern two-thirds of the country.

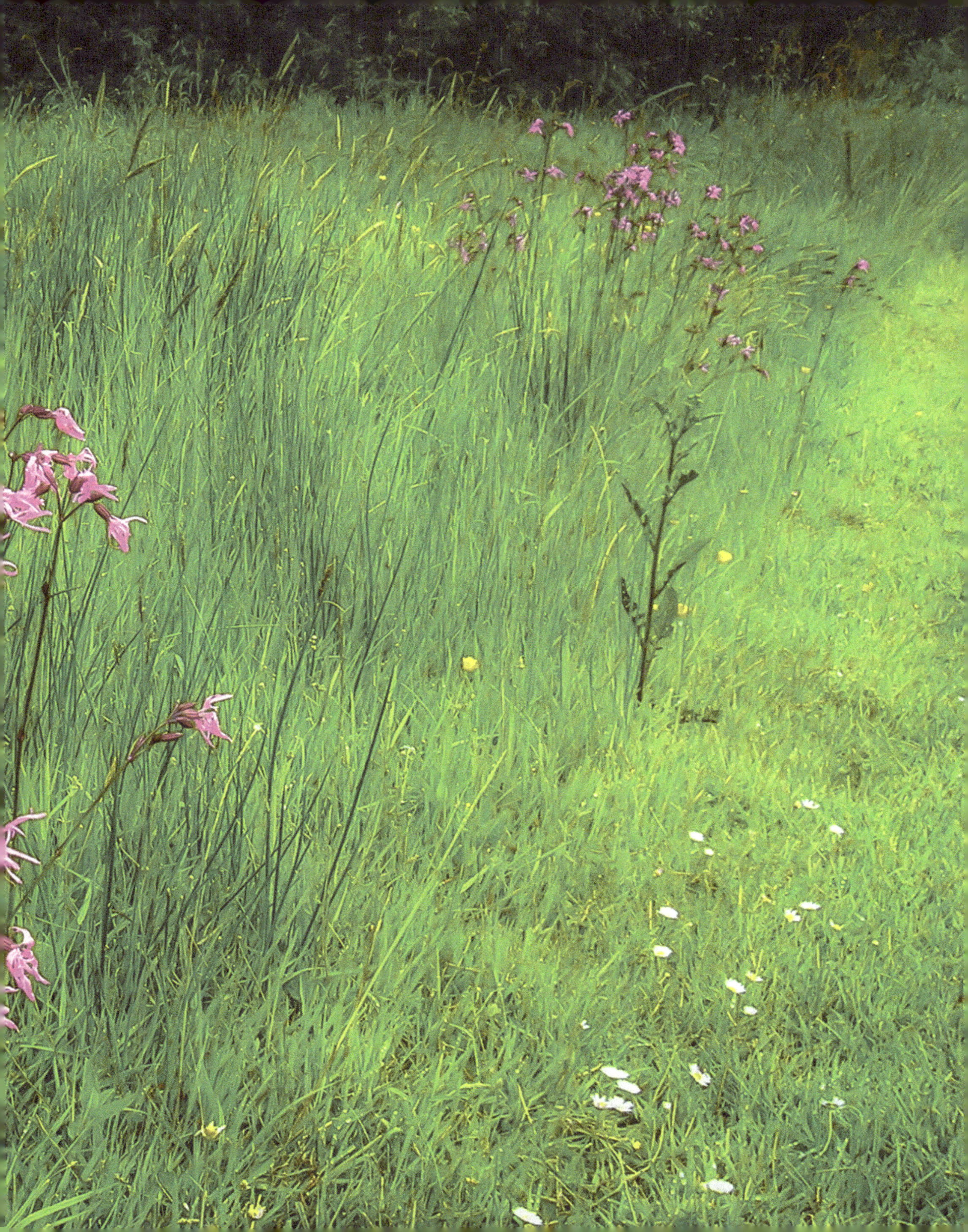

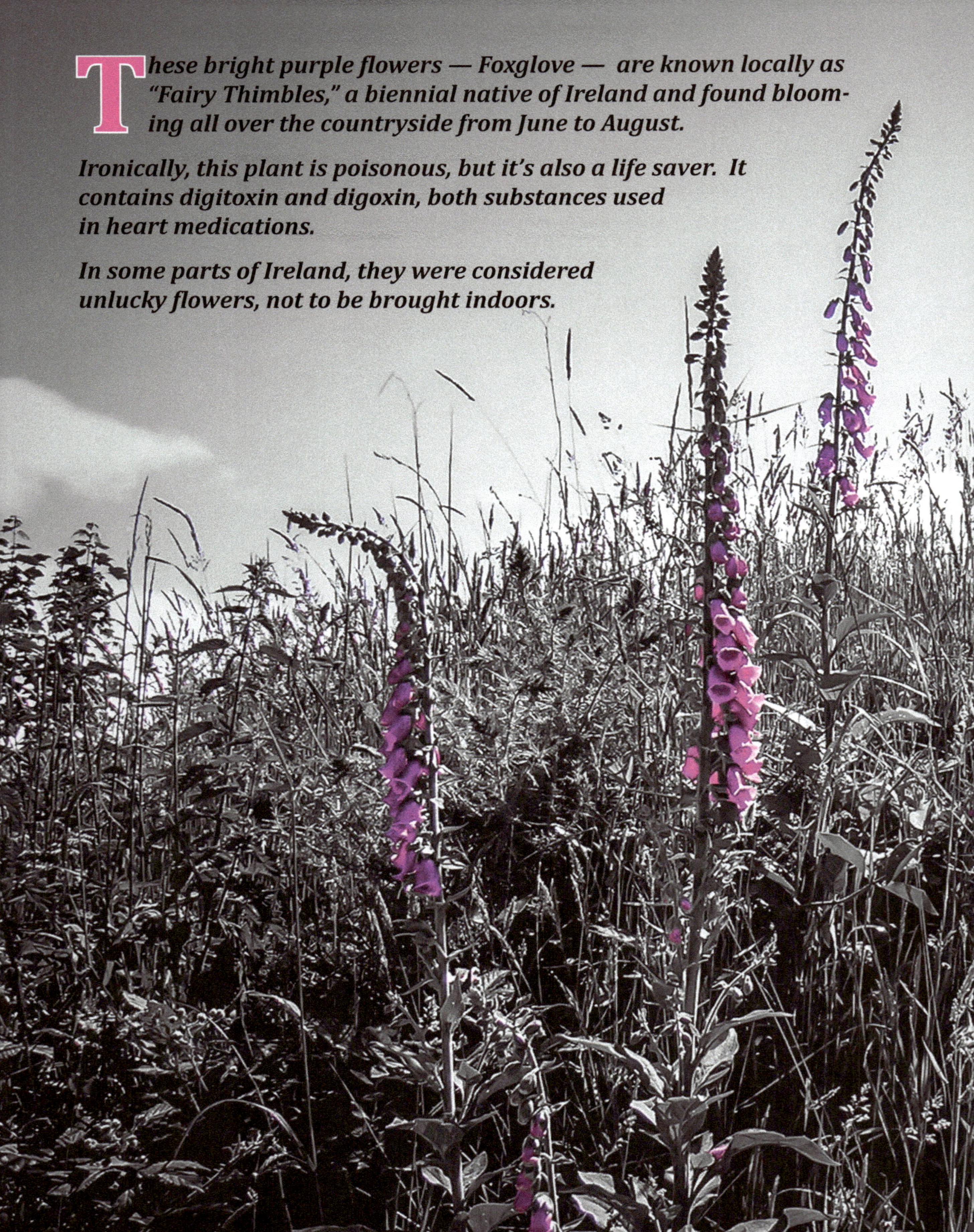

These bright purple flowers — Foxglove — are known locally as "Fairy Thimbles," a biennial native of Ireland and found blooming all over the countryside from June to August.

Ironically, this plant is poisonous, but it's also a life saver. It contains digitoxin and digoxin, both substances used in heart medications.

In some parts of Ireland, they were considered unlucky flowers, not to be brought indoors.

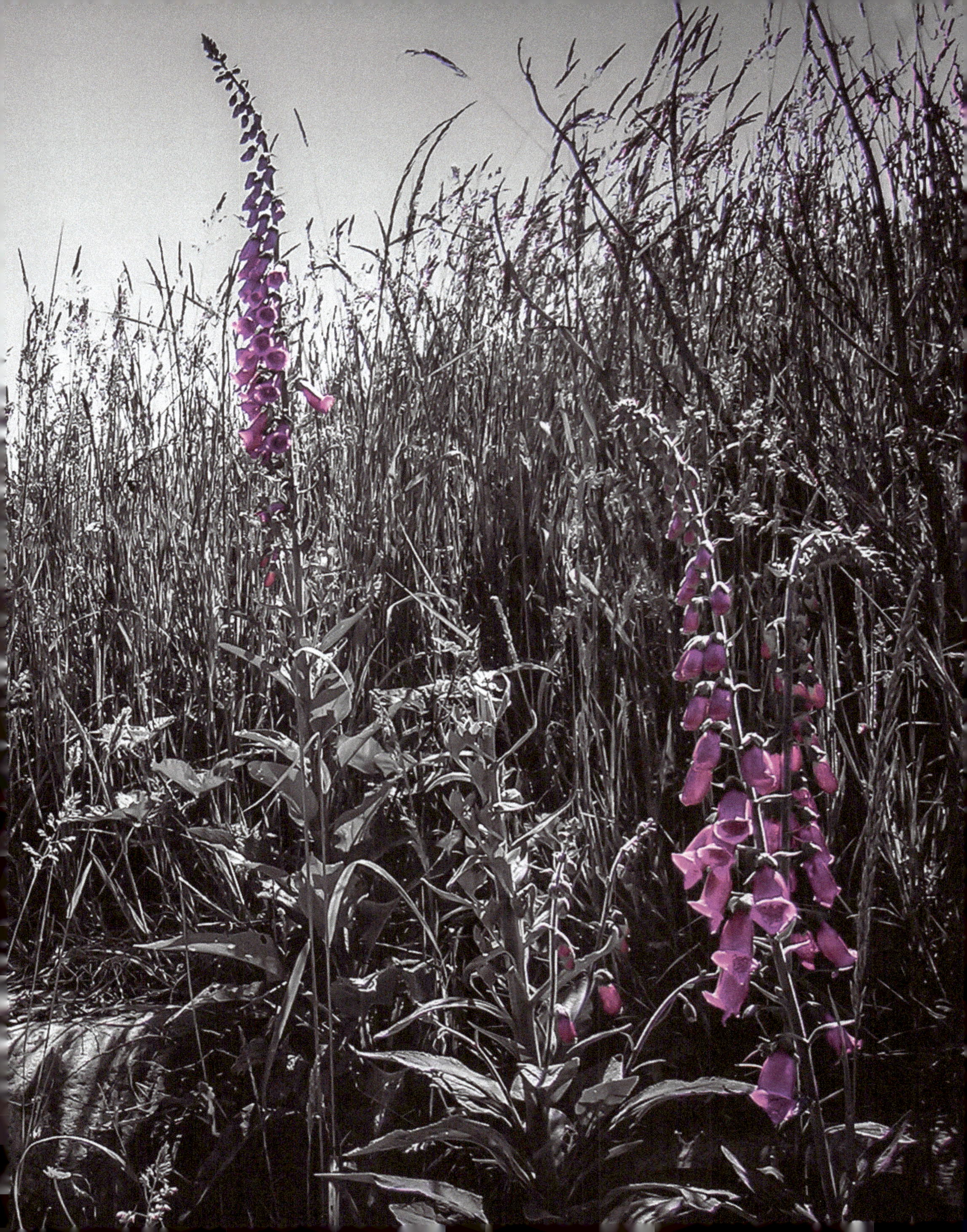

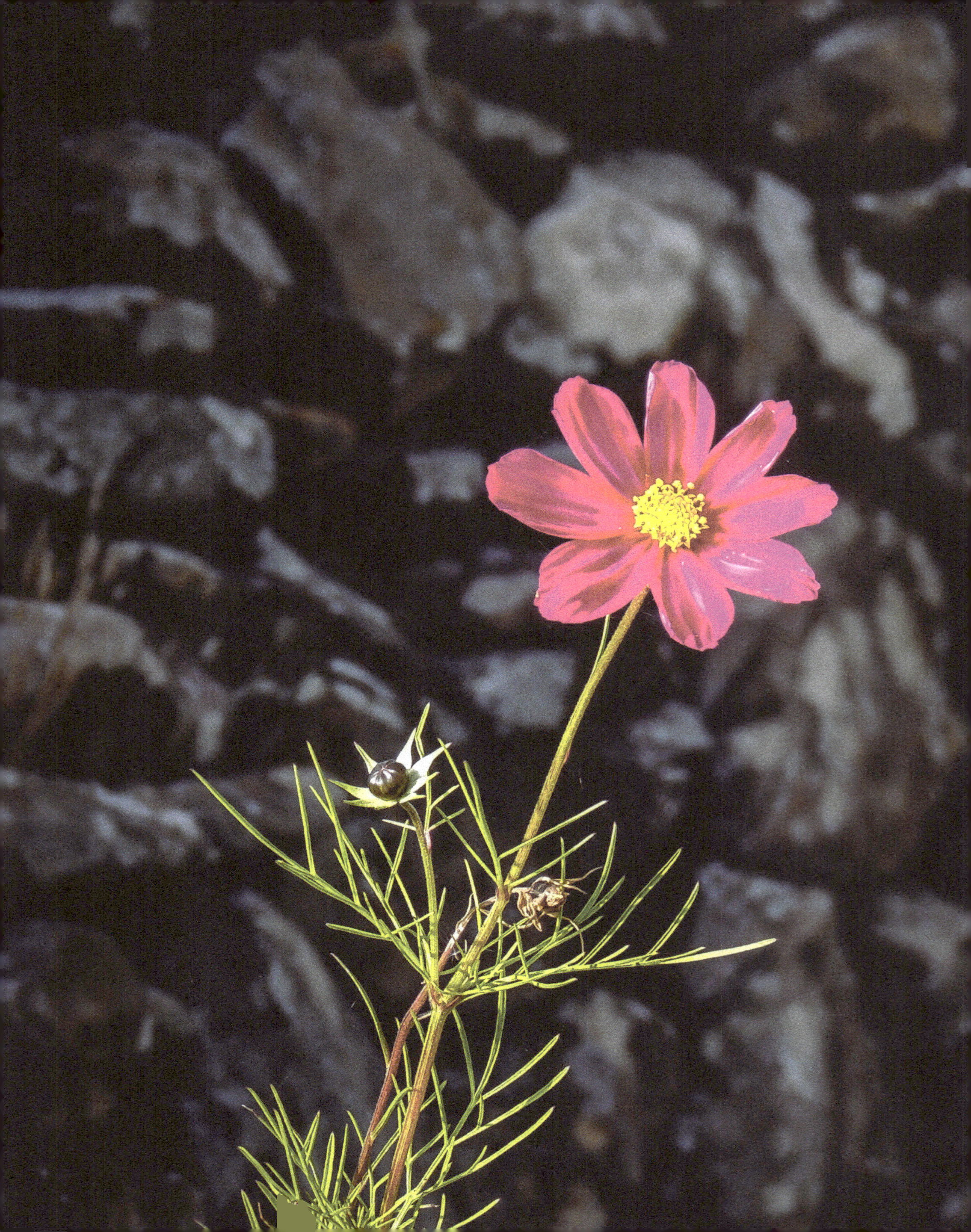

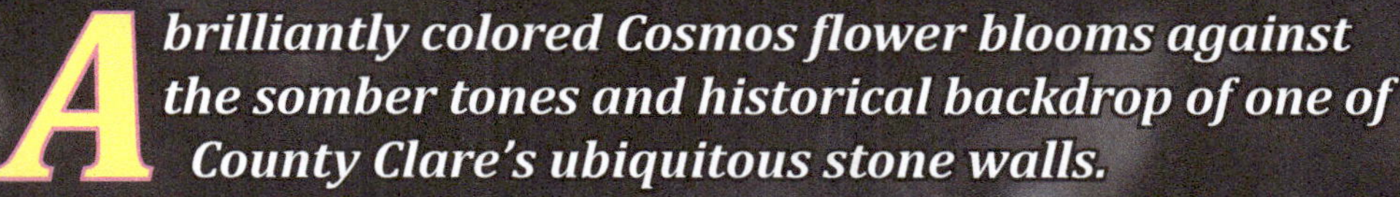

A brilliantly colored Cosmos flower blooms against the somber tones and historical backdrop of one of County Clare's ubiquitous stone walls.

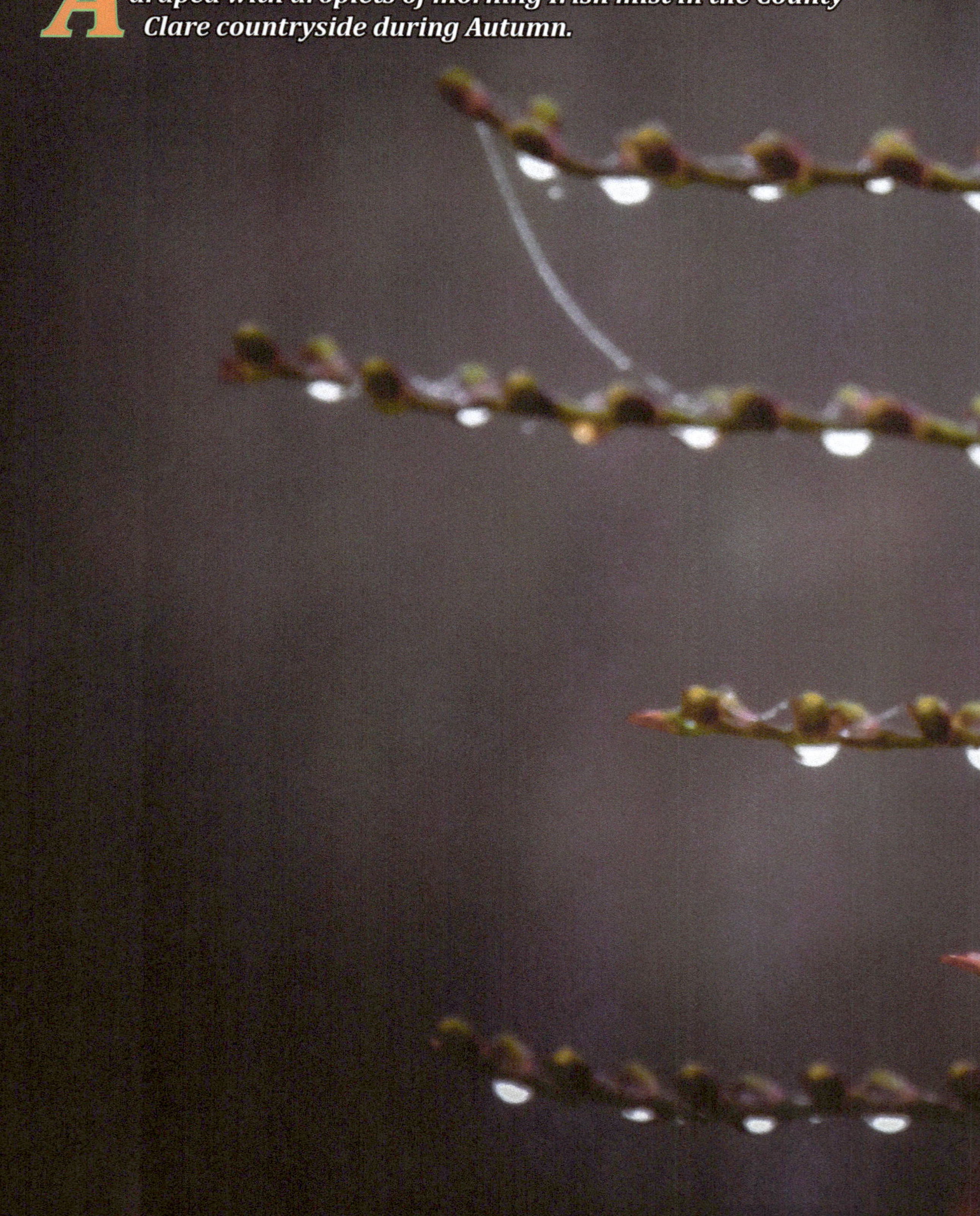

A lingering Montbretia bloom is surrounded by branches draped with droplets of morning Irish mist in the County Clare countryside during Autumn.

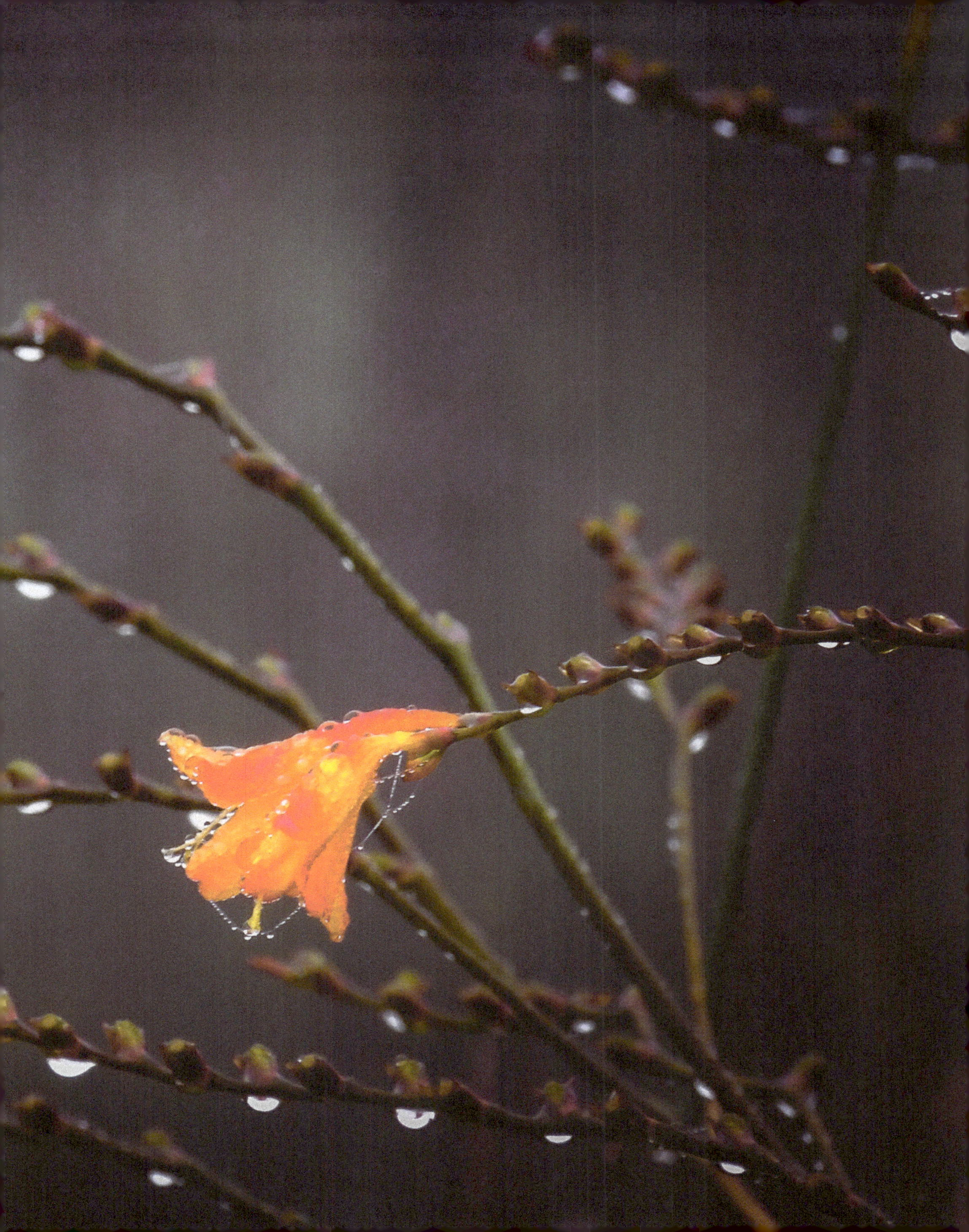

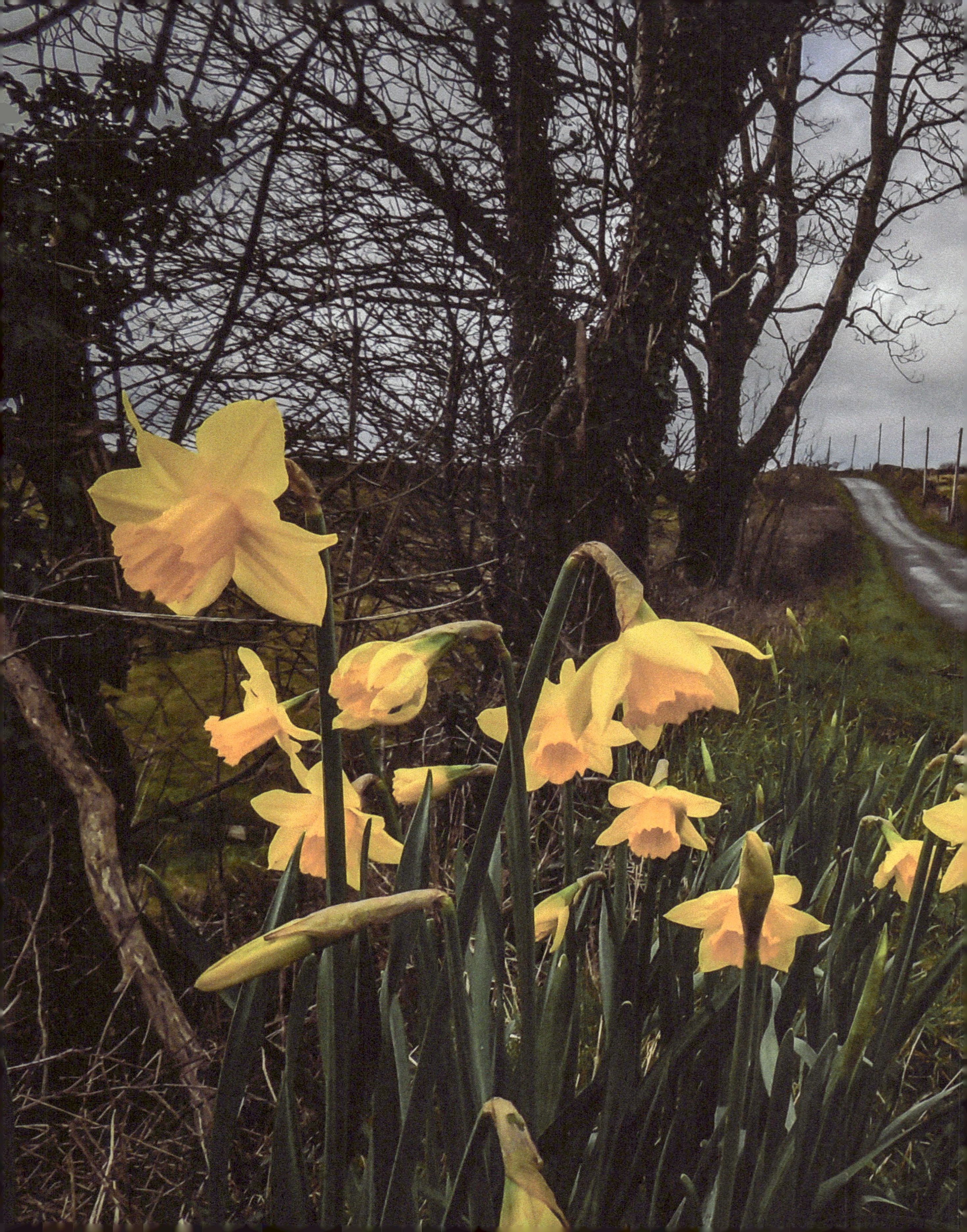

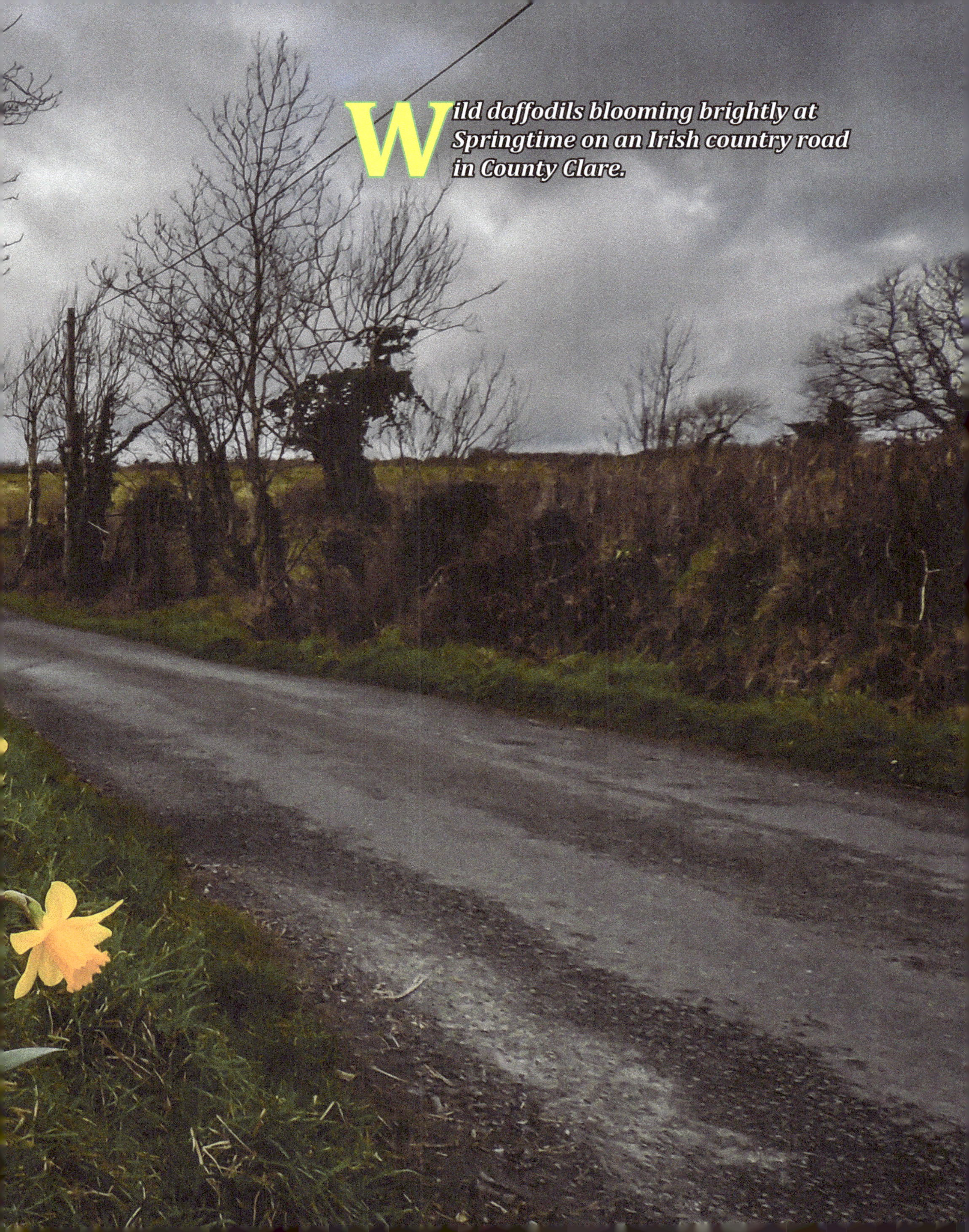

Wild daffodils blooming brightly at Springtime on an Irish country road in County Clare.

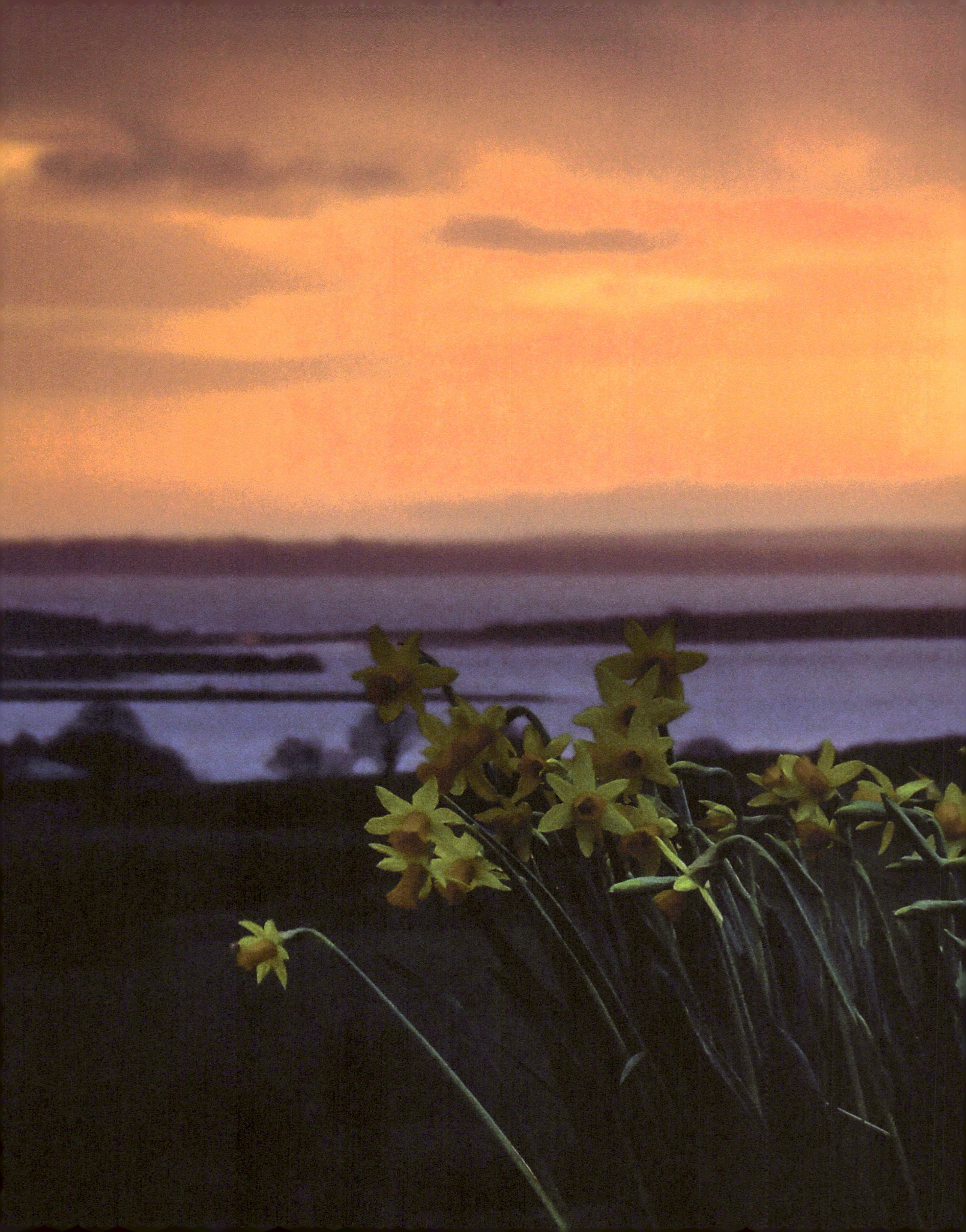

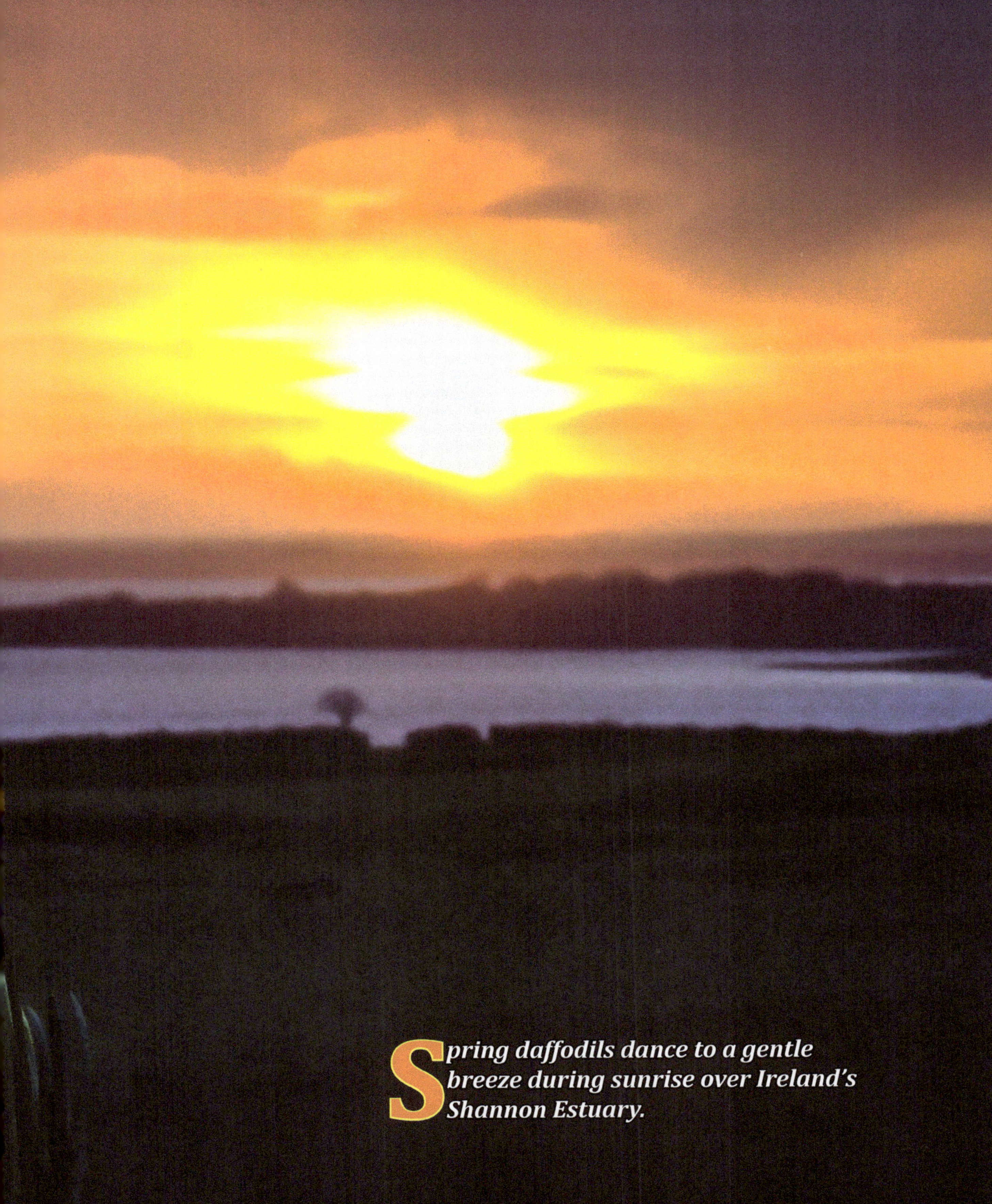

Spring daffodils dance to a gentle breeze during sunrise over Ireland's Shannon Estuary.

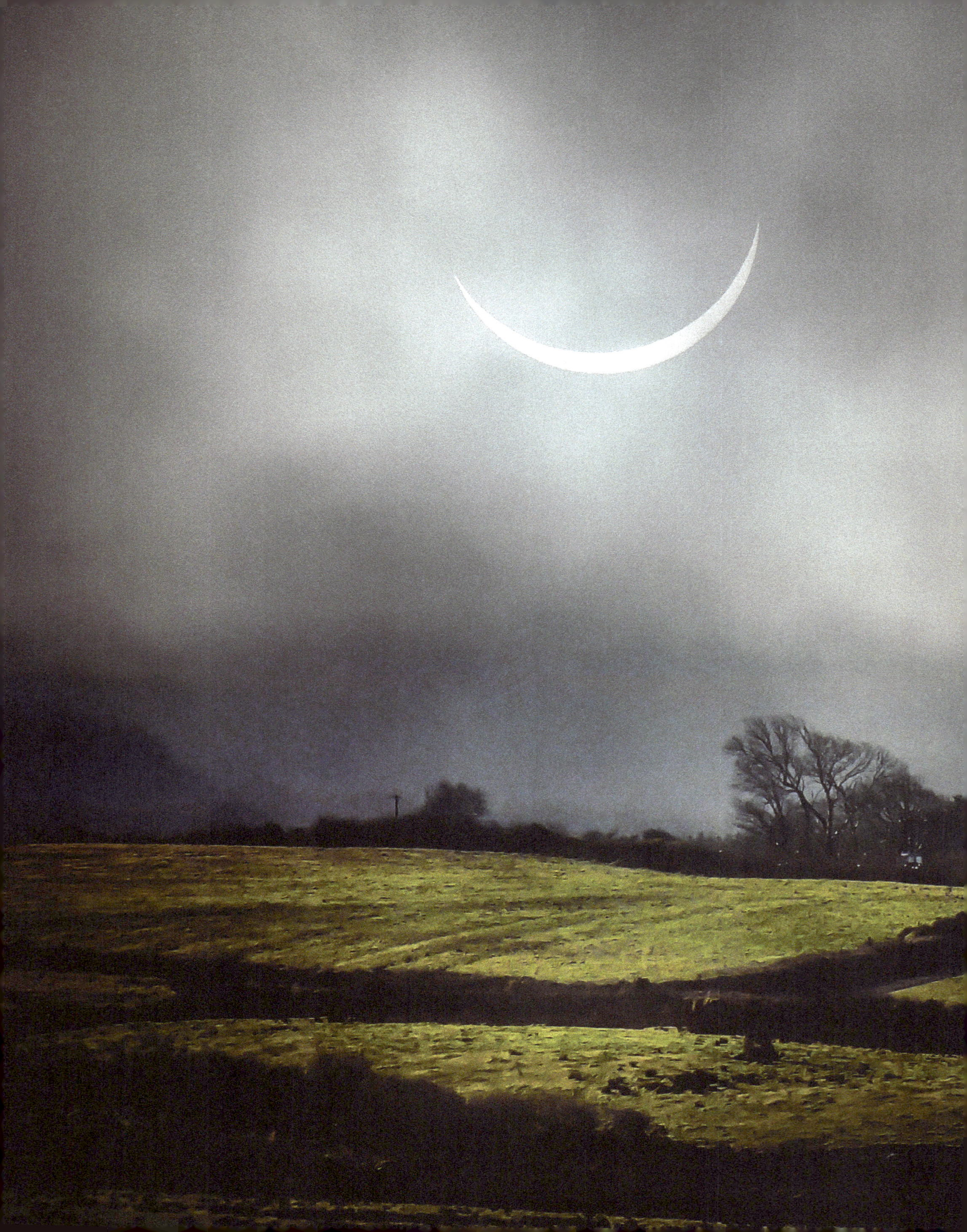

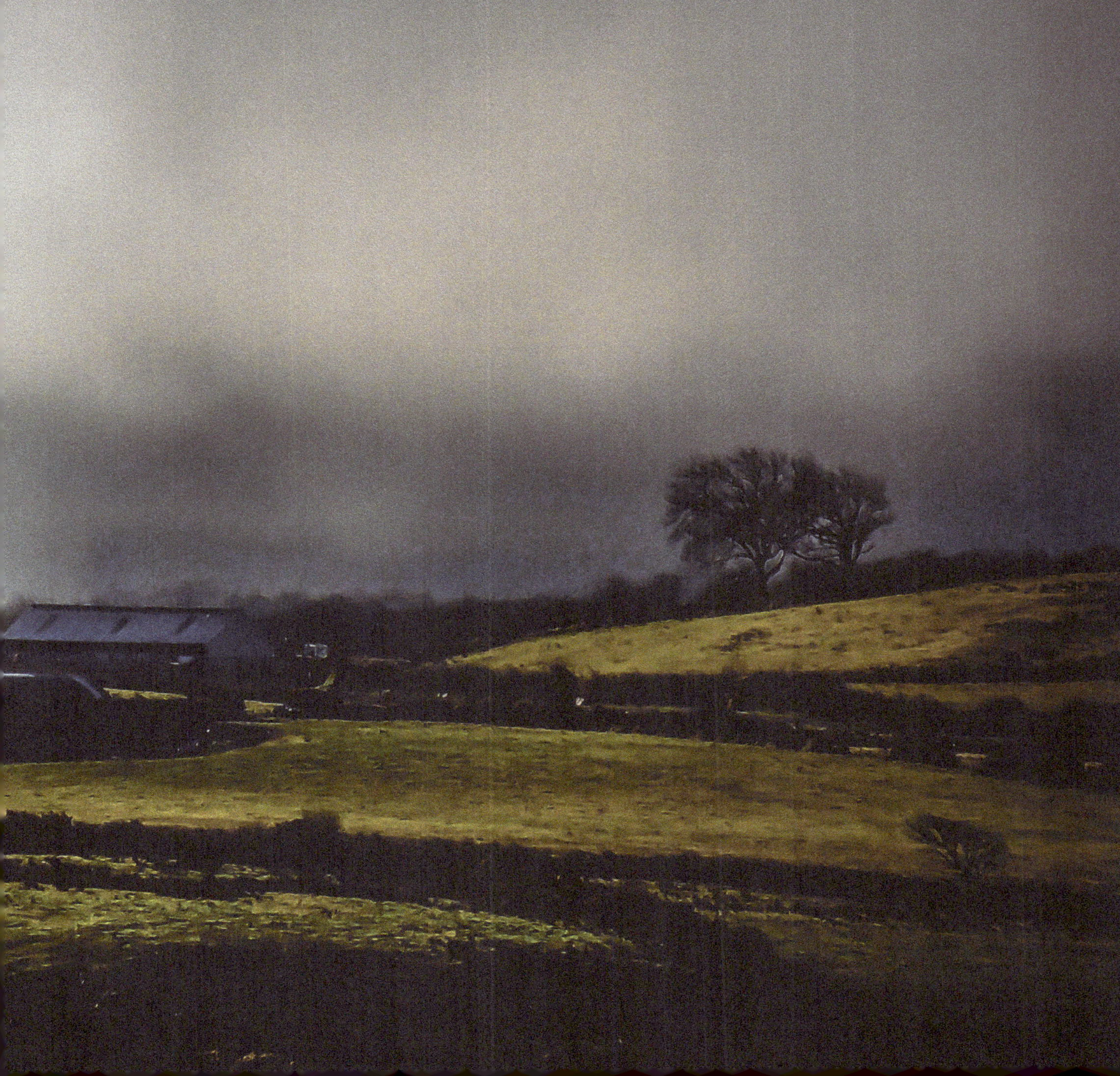

The near-total solar eclipse of 2015's Spring Equinox casts an eerie glow on this farm in the County Clare countryside between Lissycasey and Ballynacally.

The last partial solar eclipse was seen in Ireland in 1999, and the next total eclipse won't occur until September 2090, though a partial eclipse will be visible in Irish skies again in 2026.

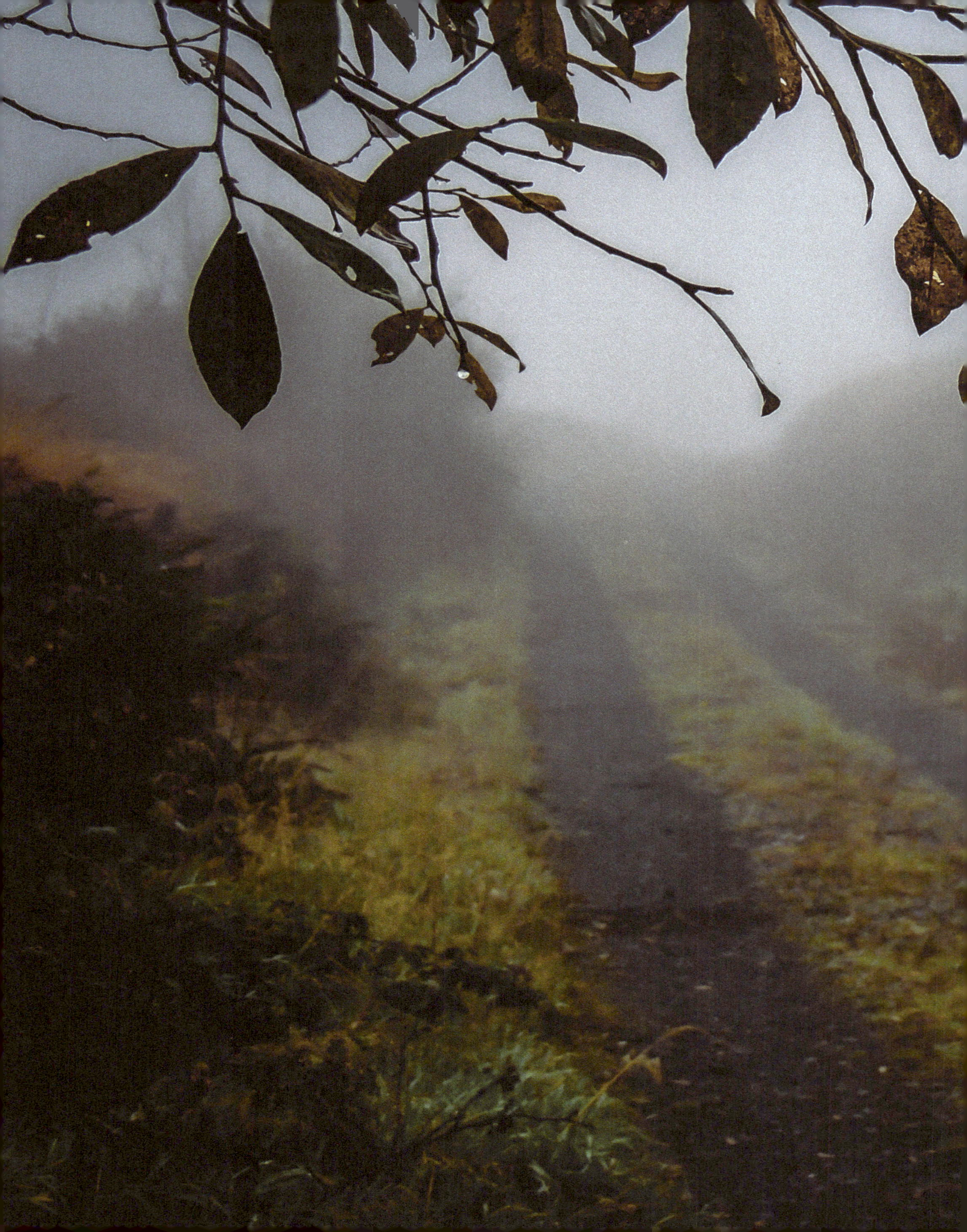

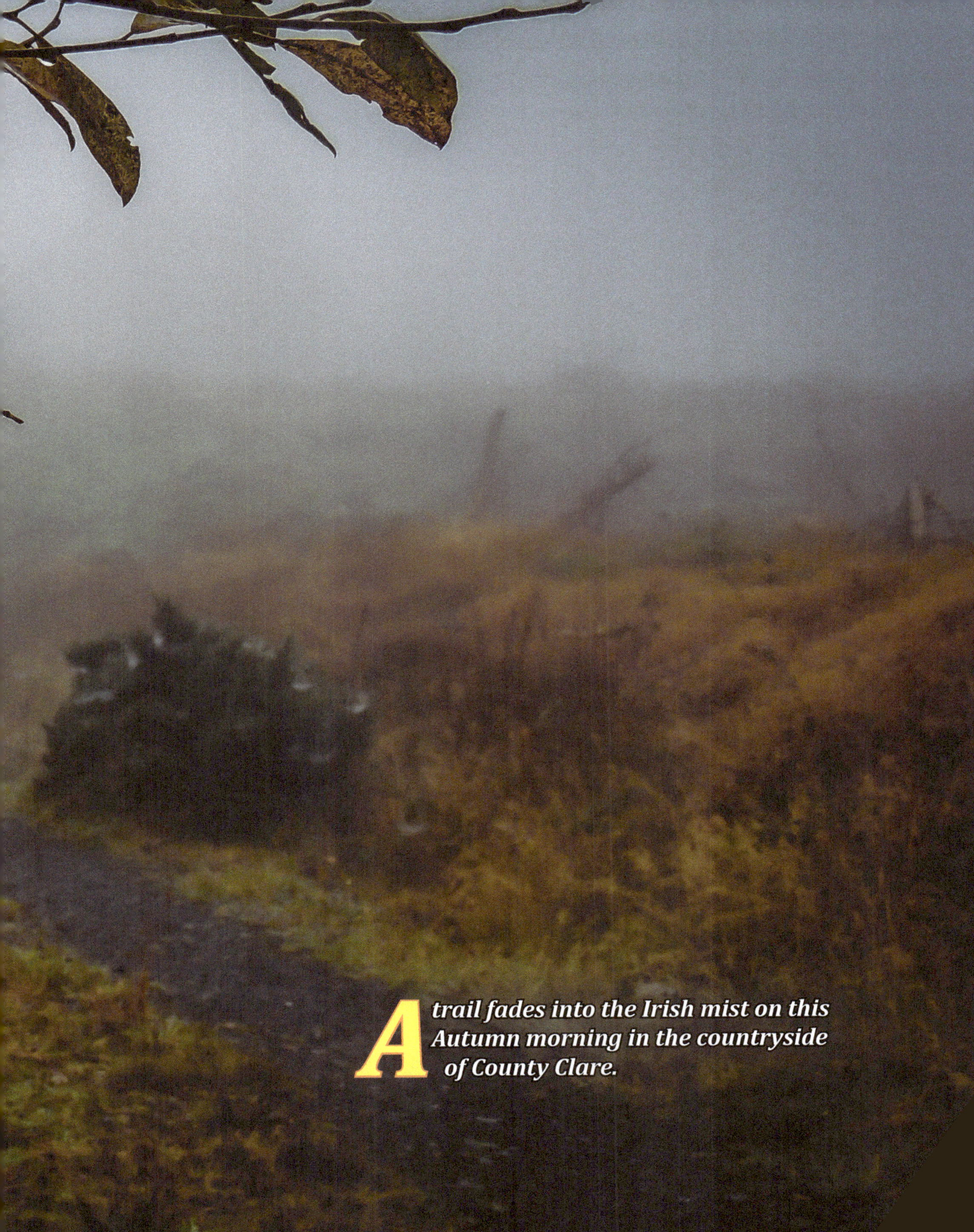

A trail fades into the Irish mist on this Autumn morning in the countryside of County Clare.

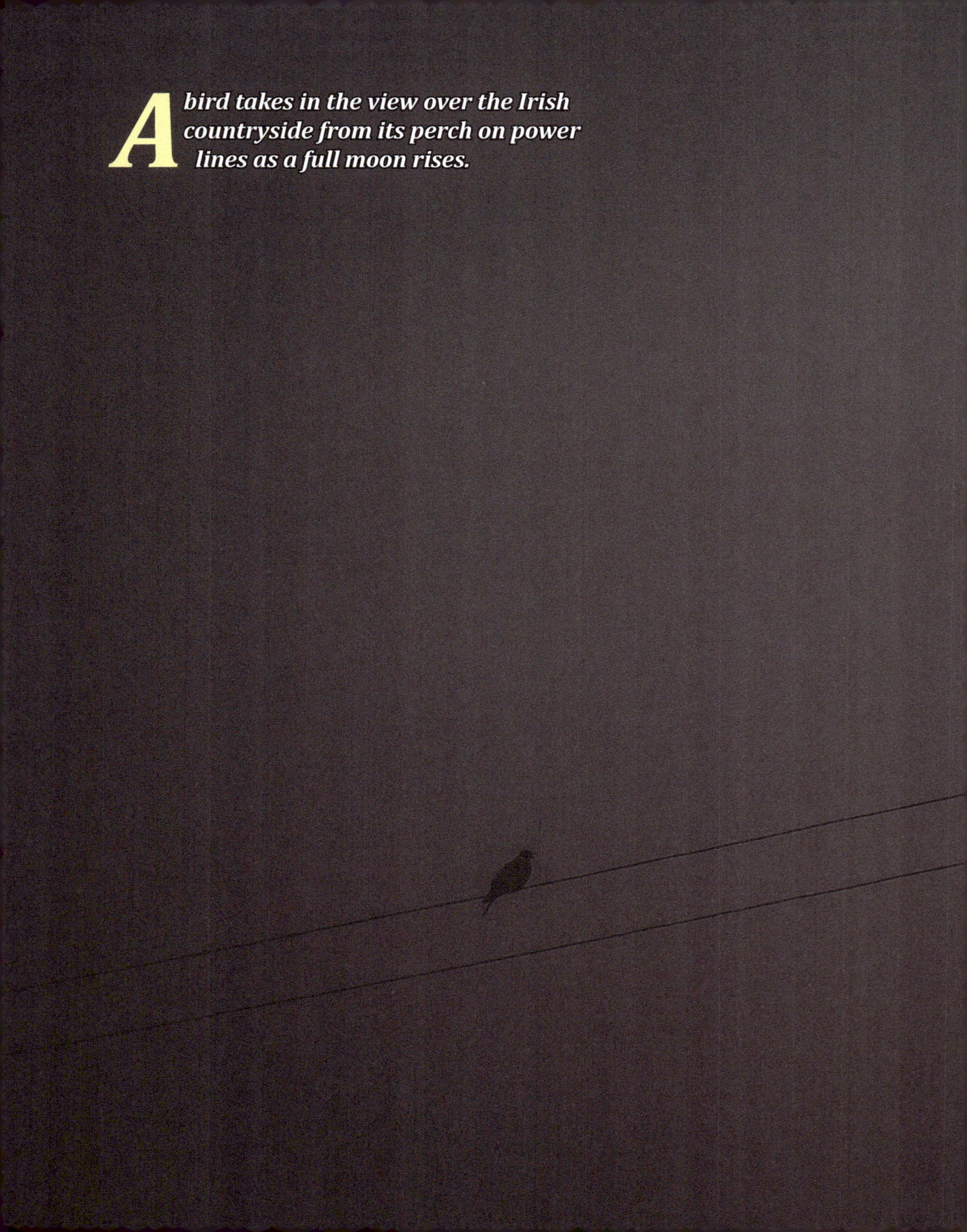

A bird takes in the view over the Irish countryside from its perch on power lines as a full moon rises.

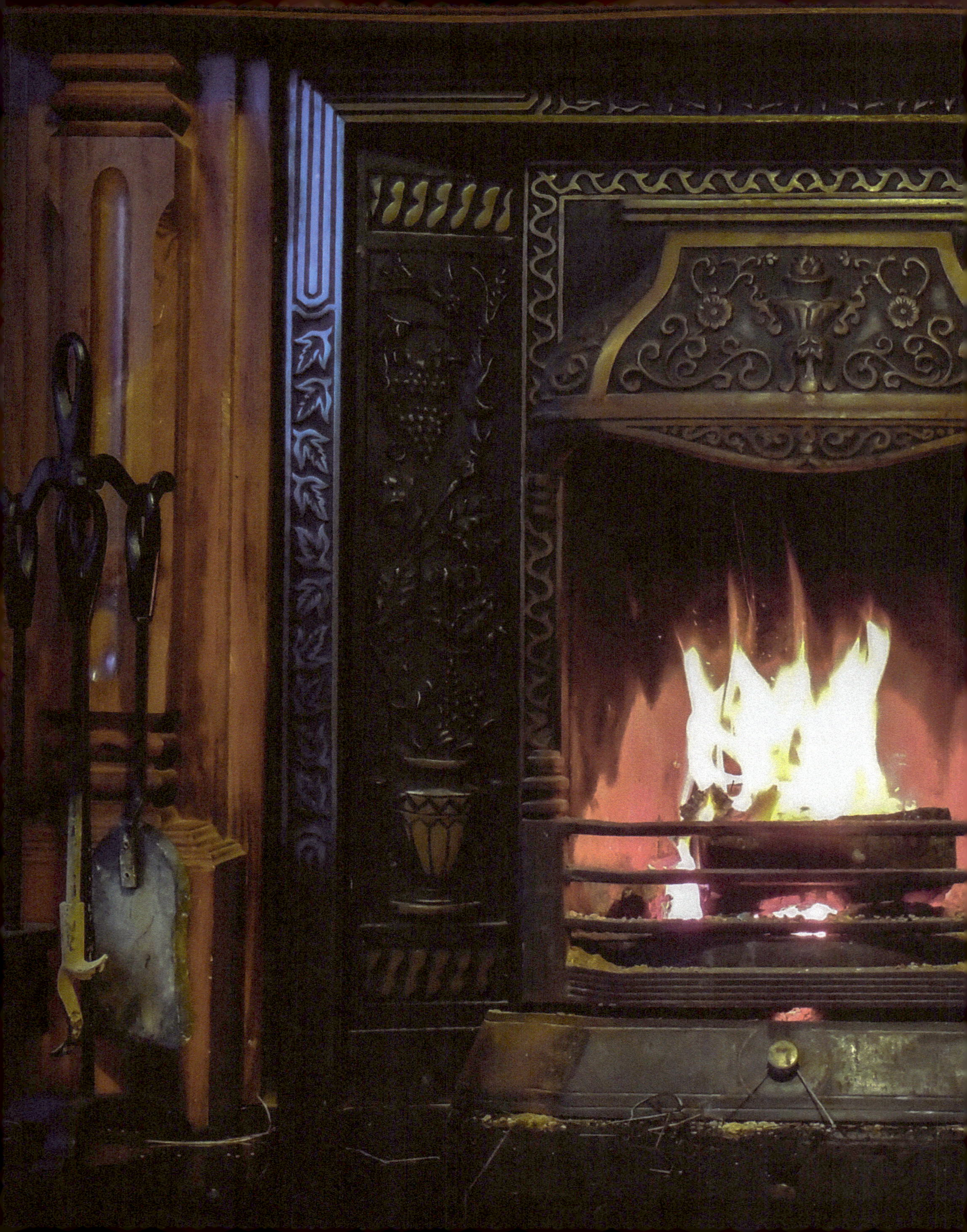

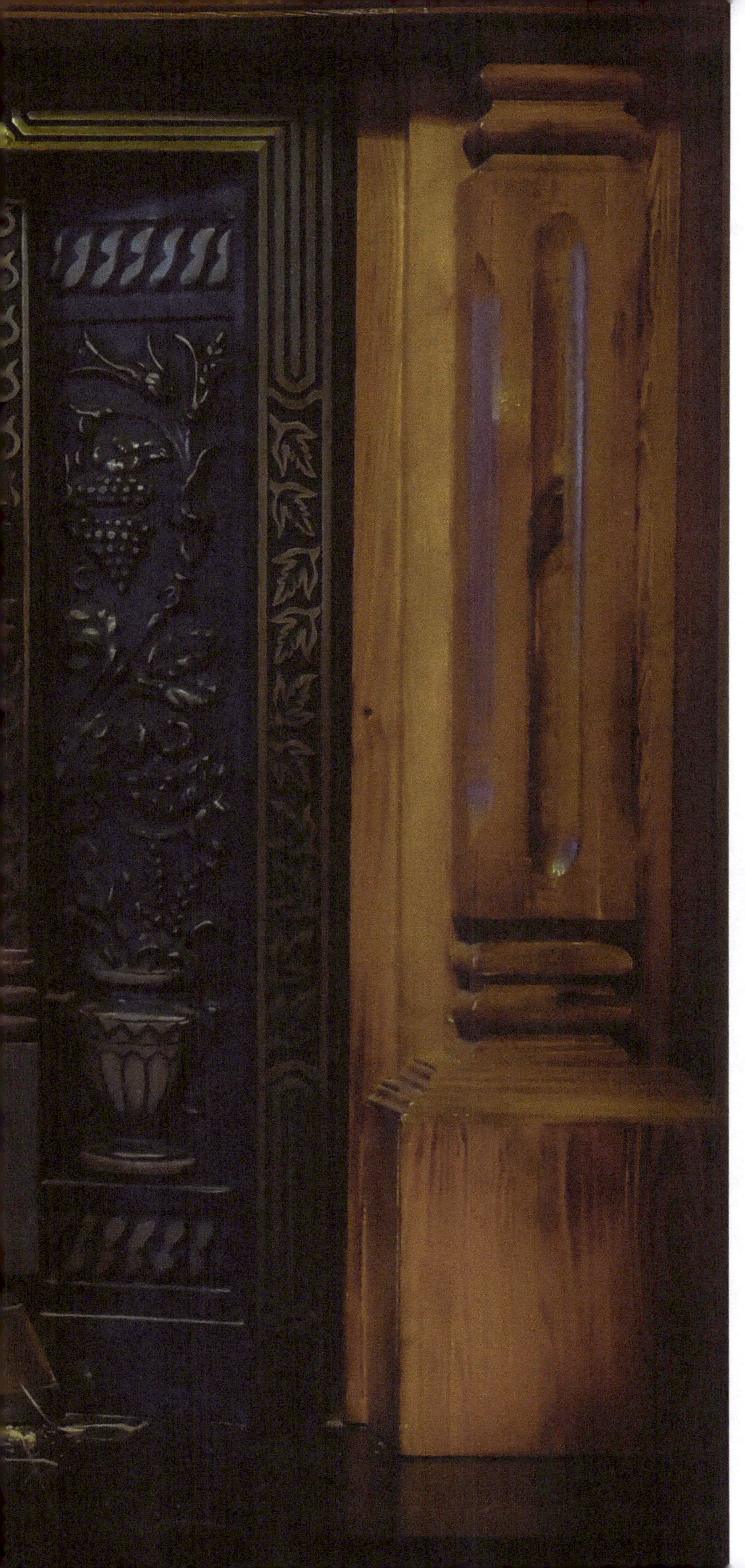

I mages of the dancing flames and the aroma of burning turf have been a hallmark of Irish homes for many centuries.

The fuel — turf or peat moss — took thousands of years to form out of organic material deposited in bogs, so no matter the changes in architectural styles, fireplace decorations or other developments in "modern life," the traditional turf fire still offers a connection to the spirit and soul of Ireland.

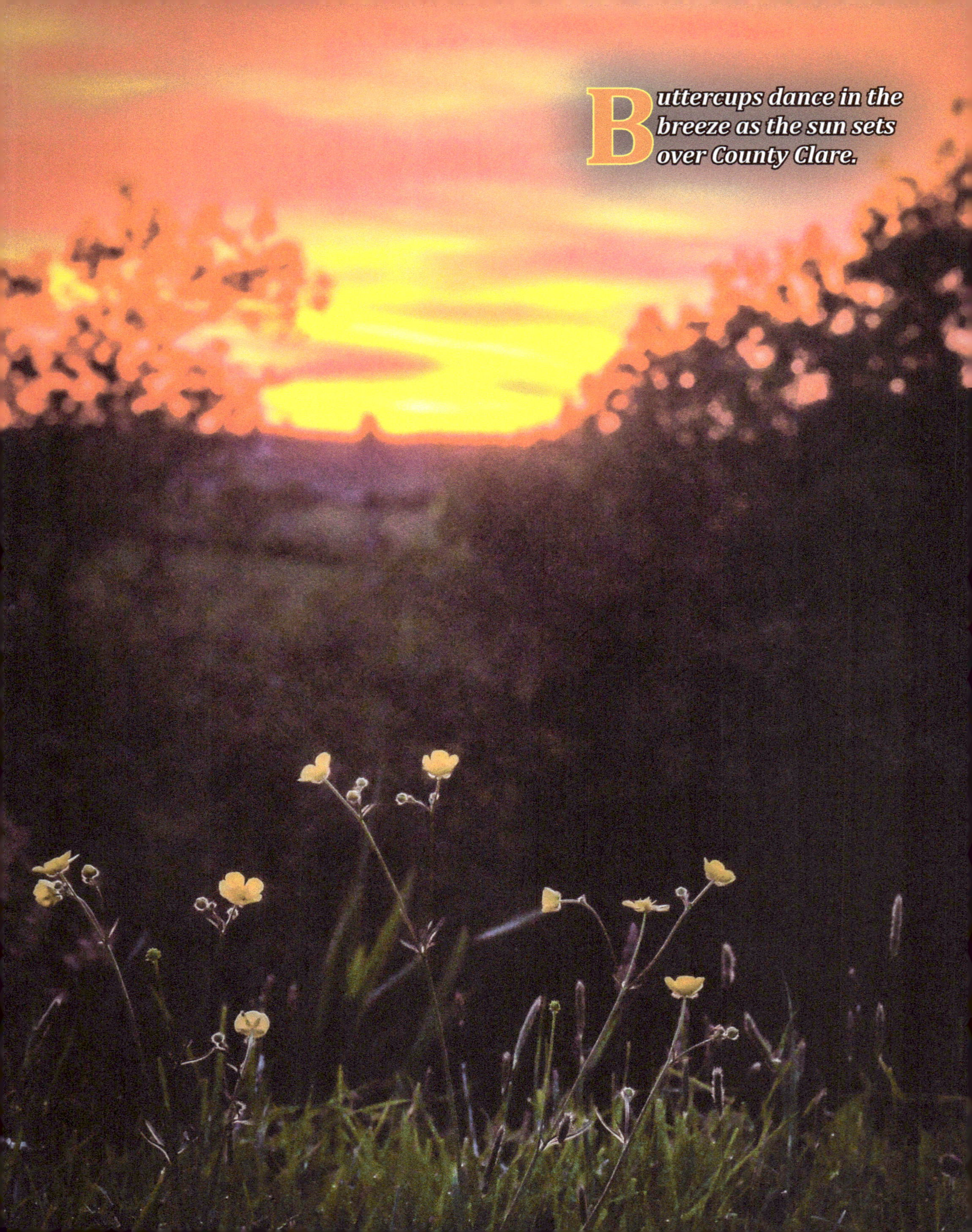

Buttercups dance in the breeze as the sun sets over County Clare.

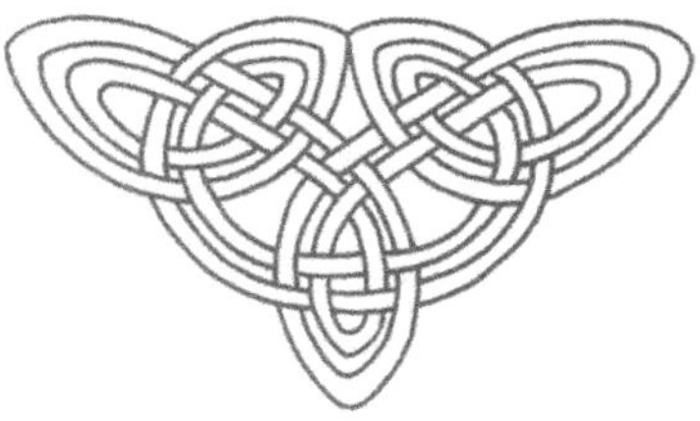

Acknowledgements

Creating this book has been a monumental project, sorting through thousands of images, editing the final choices and putting them together in a format to share with you.

My family continues to encourage and support me in these adventures. Thank you so much Alberto Truett, Francis and Helen Murphy, John and Maureen Ginnane and Anthony Murphy.

I am truly grateful for my many thousands of social media fans who have helped choose the images that have gone into this book. Your likes, comments and shares have provided great inspiration and encouragement. I love you all.

We really do get by with a little help from our friends...

Go raibh mile maith agat!

Thank you.

Other Books by James A. Truett

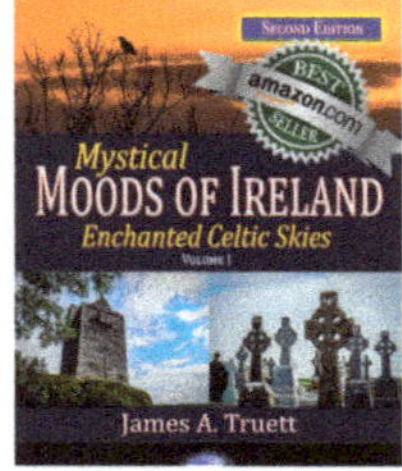

Mystical Moods of Ireland - Vol. I:
Enchanted Celtic Skies

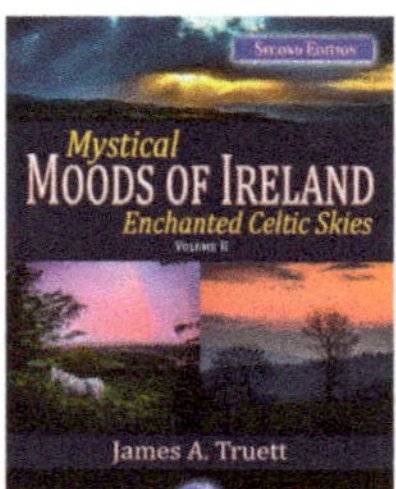

Mystical Moods of Ireland - Vol. II:
Enchanted Celtic Skies

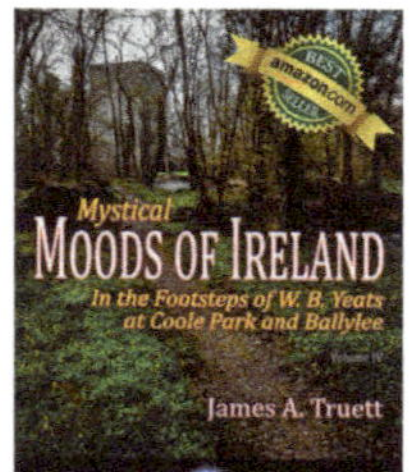

Mystical Moods of Ireland - Vol. IV:
In the Footsteps of W. B. Yeats at Coole Park and Ballylee

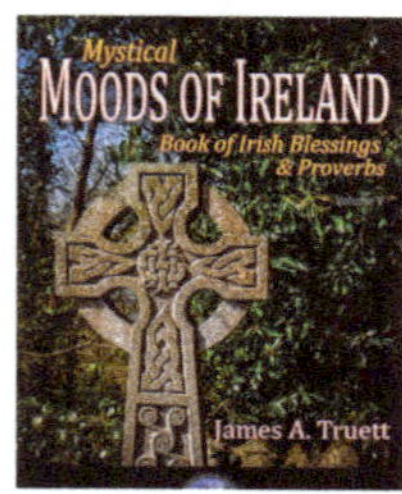

Mystical Moods of Ireland - Vol. V:
Book of Irish Blessings & Proverbs

Available through Amazon.Com and major booksellers:
www.JamesTruettBooks.Com

Follow James A. Truett's adventures
and get free previews of his books here:
www.JamesATruett.Com/subscribe

About James A. Truett

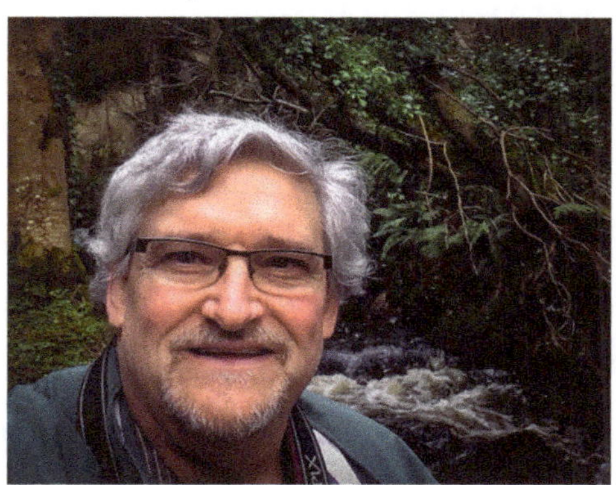

Growing up in Alaska, near the quaint hamlet of Ester, near Fairbanks, James A. Truett developed an appreciation for nature as a child, exploring the majestic wilderness of his home state both on the ground and in the air.

He began his career as a journalist and photographer for the local newspaper at the age of 14, picked up his private pilot's license at the age of 17, and by the age of 19, he had moved to Seattle and joined The Associated Press, eventually becoming one of the youngest journalists in the world to be published in every major newspaper in the world.

Over the years, he developed an avid interest in sailing and traveled extensively by boat, auto and air in the U.S., Canada, Mexico, Central America, Ireland and the UK.

After tracing his ancestral roots back to Ireland and falling in love with the beauty of the Irish countryside, he settled in County Clare from where he manages his portfolio of art, photography and publishing projects.

Connect with James A. Truett on Social Media:
www.JamesATruett.Com/social

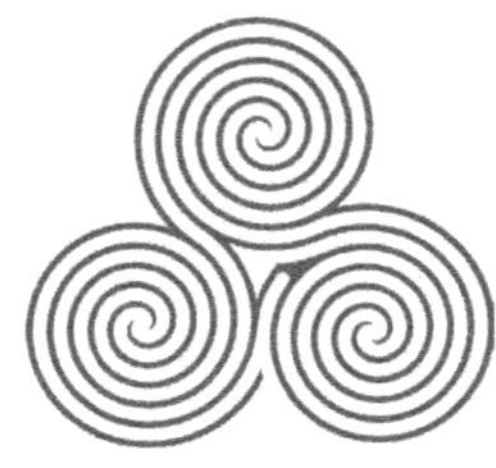

More kind words from Fans...

"James Truett's book is like a comfortable shawl that beckons to you and gives comfort and warmth and nourishment to your soul with postcard pictures of a beautiful unspoiled Ireland." **~ Aileen Stack**

"James A. Truett has documented the proof that God created Ireland to give us a glimpse of Heaven!" **~ Paula Day West**

"Magical and decadent!" **~ Pat Pearson**

"Love all the great pictures. To a place so far away, you have brought a piece of Ireland, so dear to my heart." **~ Tami Smelser**

"James A. Truett captures moments behind the lens, and then takes you on a spectacular visual journey into the wonderful wistful world that is Ireland. He also shares his wealth of wisdom as he does truly masterful work." **~ Therese Younes**

"James A. Truett, when I look at your photographs I feel as though I am there in Ireland. I have been blessed to visit your homeland. Through your posts and photos, I feel that I am given a personal tour of your beautiful, magical homeland. May you continue to be blessed with your photography and writing." **~ Debbie Snellings**

"Experiencing the beauty and history of Ireland through the talented eye and unique storytelling of James Truett is the next best thing to being there." **~ Bernadette Harvey**

"If I wanted to describe the spirit and magic of Ireland to a complete stranger, I would have no hesitation in showing them James' photos. That would make my job so much easier. Thanks James." **~ Michael Fitzpatrick**

Absolutely beautiful photographs, magical colour and there's history to read about each photograph, truly wonderful. Thank you so much James." **~ Anne Kelly**

"James' photographs and stories have rekindled my resolve to see all of the beauty of Ireland with my own eyes soon." **~ Julie Hamill**

"James A. Truett lets us join him in the magic of his beautiful Irish countryside. Stunning pictures and enjoyable information takes you there! Could dance an Irish jig!" **~ Judy Robinson**

"James captures the simple elegance and beauty of Ireland in his photography. It inspires my soul." **~ Cecilia Jean Norris**

"Wonderful view of Ireland... makes me want to visit." **~ Margaret Todd Sweeney**

"Your pictures make me feel like I'm actually there." **~ Finola McAleese**

"I visited Ireland in 1993 when my husband was there for his job. We went back in 2001 and lived there for his job for six months. Going in 2001 was the best thing in my life. I needed the peace and tranquility. Things were not good and just being there with the beauty of the land and the kindness of the people helped me immensely." **~ Margie Fleischmann**

"These pictures helped me understand why Irish immigrants thought of home when they reached the mountains of Tennessee." **~ Debbie Gifford Ellis**

"Why Ireland is made of legend, mystery, narrative and magic." **~ Lynda Bateman**

"Thank you for all the beautiful pictures of Ireland. They make me feel like I am right there with you sharing the experience!" **~ Brenda Hutchinson Williams**

"James your insight and vision of Ireland are truly brought to each picture. The stories and Irish tales take you to each place and make you feel as if you've been there. You've made my 'must see list' very exciting. Thank you for all you do." **~ Ginny Carter Davis**

"Your pictures portray what I've always thought Ireland should look like, a truly beautiful country." **~ Ruth Ruzicka**

"Being in the Irish countryside is like stepping back in time. The carriages. The sheep. The beautiful green pastures on one side, fading into the ocean on the other. I'm constantly looking over the pics I took, and any pics from Ireland. I love the feeling I get while thinking 'I stood there!'"
~ Amy Murphy

"Sit back relax and enjoy the beauty that is Ireland through the eyes of James A Truett!"
~ Yvonne Brown

"A view, a glimpse, a memory of the Ireland I left. Recollections of the beauty, the lush countryside, the sparkling green, the people." **~ Kathleen Meyer**

"I love the images and the scenes of Ireland as they are magical places to visit. It is a breath of fresh air, and Ireland is a gem -- The Emerald Isle." **~ Catherine Callery**

"Thank you, James, for giving me beautiful images of my ancestor's homeland, and the places I dream of seeing." **~ Cheryl Phillips**

"Aesthetically pleasing are the Irish territories of the rising and setting sun illuminating the land. James A. Truett shares all his captured beauty for all to awe over." **~ Brenda Woolam**

"I've seen your pictures, so pretty." **~ Kimberly Smotherman**

"When I look at your pictures, it reminds me of where I grew up. We have a amazing countryside -- all the beautiful greenery and the wonderful seaside where I used to swim as a young girl. I love Ireland, my homeland, and all the family and friends in Carrickfergus." **~ Angela Meredith**

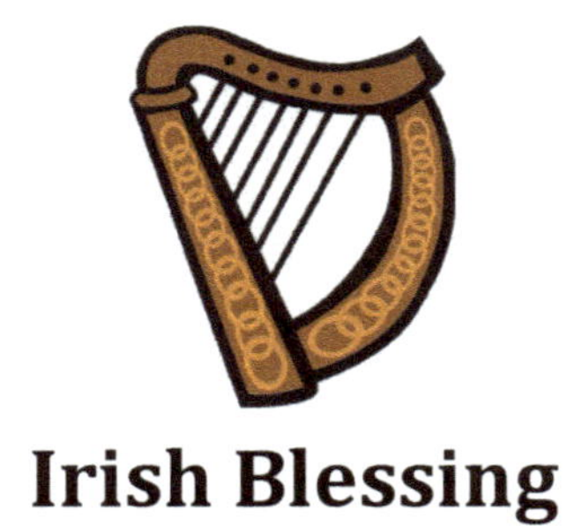

Irish Blessing

"May choruses of Spring birds fill your ears,
Sunrises and Sunsets paint masterpieces for your eyes,
Opulent Autumn colors provide comfort for your soul,
and the magic of Ireland enrich your years."

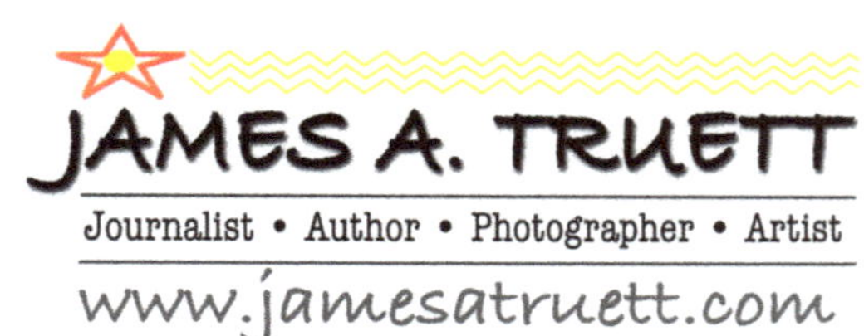